Praise for *Shrouds of Glory:*

"Groom brings to his task the idiosyncratic sensibility of a fiction writer. Thus he is able, within the conventions of history writing, to infuse his storytelling with energy, surprise, freshness and power. . . . Reminiscent of Evan S. Connell's masterpiece *Son of the Morning Star* . . . In the way it leaves the reader breathless with amazement and awe, the violent fifty-page center of Groom's book calls to mind the massacres that open and close Sam Peckinpah's 1969 movie *The Wild Bunch.* . . . In *Shrouds of Glory,* Groom has done true justice to those who fought there, in all their human complexity."

— *Chicago Tribune*

"Mr. Groom follows in the footsteps of Shelby Foote. . . . Mr. Groom has, in fact, produced a fine synthesis of one of the most important, if overshadowed, military campaigns in American history." — Greg Pierce, *The Washington Times*

"[Groom] puts his novelist's eye to searching out the telling detail and the colorful anecdote. The pages turn." — Stephen W. Sears, *People*

"[Groom] sharpens the drama of the conflict. . . . He peoples his history with vivid characters. . . . [*Shrouds of Glory*] explains why no child growing up in the South at a certain time could have resisted playing with his ancestor's rusty sword."

— Ben Brown, *USA Today*

"A thoroughly researched military history free of the usual vices of thoroughly researched military histories. The pace is quick. The descriptions are vivid and accurate. . . . Groom's ability to make these remorselessly grim events readable is an accomplishment. His contribution to the literature of the Civil War, by bringing out the neglected counterstrategy to the march to the sea, is important."

— Doug Thompson, *Arkansas Democrat Gazette*

"A well-written narrative . . . Groom's accounts of the slaughter of Hood's men at Franklin and their overrunning at Nashville by the Union forces of George Thomas convey the horror of Civil War battlefields without sacrificing narrative clarity. An excellent introduction to a complex campaign." — *Publishers Weekly*

"A vivid history . . . Highly readable and intensely evocative, a fine addition to the growing body of literature about the western war, once largely a forgotten footnote to the 'real' action in the East." — *Kirkus Reviews*

Also by Winston Groom

Shrouds of Glory ★

From Atlanta to Nashville:
The Last Great Campaign
of the Civil War

Winston Groom

Grove Press
New York

Printed in the United States of America
Published simultaneously in Canada

FIRST GROVE PRESS EDITION

Library of Congress Cataloging-in-Publication Data

Groom, Winston, 1944–
    Shrouds of glory: Atlanta to Nashville: the last great campaign of the Civil War / Winston Groom.
    ISBN 0-8021-4061-0 (pbk.)
    1. Atlanta Campaign, 1864. 2. Nashville (Tenn.), Battle of, 1864. 3. Georgia—History—Civil War, 1861–1865. 4. Tennessee—History—Civil War, 1861–1865. I. Title.
    E476.7.G76   1995   973'36—dc20   94-37242

DESIGN BY LAURA HAMMOND HOUGH

Grove Press
841 Broadway
New York, NY 10003

04 05 06 07 08   10 9 8 7 6 5 4 3 2 1

To my great-grandfather, Fremont Sterling Thrower

56th Alabama Cavalry, Confederate States Army

"I buried death in the shroud of glory."

—Jean-Paul Sartre

Organization of the Infantry, Confederate Army of Tennessee
Before the Battle of Franklin

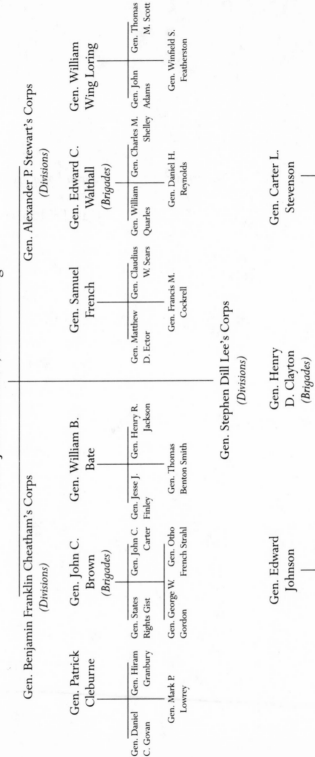

Organization of the Infantry, U.S. Army of the Tennessee

Before the Battle of Franklin

Gen. George H. Thomas

Gen. David S. Stanley
(FOURTH ARMY CORPS)

(Divisions)

Gen. Nathan Kimball

(Brigades)

Col. Isaac M. Kirby — Gen. William Grose

Gen. Walter C. Whitaker

Gen. Thomas J. Wood

Col. Abel D. Streight — Gen. Samuel Beatty

Col. P. Sidney Post

Gen. George D. Wagner

Col. Emerson Opdycke — Col. Joseph Conrad

Col. John Q. Lane

Gen. Andrew J. Smith
(SIXTEENTH ARMY CORPS)

(Divisions)

Gen. John McArthur

(Brigades)

Col. William L. McMillen — Col. Sylvester G. Hill

Col. Lucius F. Hubbard

Col. David Moore

Col. Thomas J. Kinney — Col. Edward H. Wolfe

Col. James I. Gilbert — Col. Jonathan B. Moore

Gen. James B. Steedman
(DISTRICT OF THE ETOWAH)

(Divisions)

Gen. James B. Steedman

(Brigades)

Gen. John H. King — Col. Caleb H. Carlton

Gen. John M. Schofield
(TWENTY-THIRD ARMY CORPS)

(Divisions)

Gen. Thomas H. Ruger

(Brigades)

Gen. Joseph A. Cooper — Col. Silas A. Strickland

Col. Orlando H. Moore

Gen. Jacob D. Cox

Gen. James W. Reilly — Col. Israel N. Stiles

Col. John Casement

Gen. Lovell H. Rousseau
(DISTRICT OF TENNESSEE)

(Divisions)

Gen. Lovell H. Rousseau

(Brigades)

Col. William P. Lyon — Col. Edwin C. Mason

Gen. John F. Miller

Post Forces, Nashville

Contents ★

Preface ★

Several years ago, while rummaging through the attic of my parents' home, I came across an old metal strongbox. Inside it was a sheaf of ancient papers, letters and documents, and as I sifted through them beneath the dim overhead light, the clues to a mystery were revealed to me.

My great-grandfather was Fremont Sterling Thrower, who was born in Mobile, Alabama, in 1845 and lived on until 1925. My father knew him well as a boy. He had become a judge and walked with a cane, the result of a leg wound received during the Civil War. As a child I played with his rusty cavalry sword, which today hangs on my wall. What we understood was that at the age of seventeen he had left Springhill College and joined the Confederate army, but the details of his service were clouded in time, and it was not until I found the box of papers that I knew for sure what his role in that conflict had been.

The most revealing document was his application for a State of Alabama pension for former Confederate soldiers, which had at last been approved by the federal government. My great-grandfather had enlisted as a private in what later became the 56th Alabama Cavalry regiment and had fought Union general William Tecumseh Sherman's army for nearly three years as it slowly ground down the Confederate forces in the western theater.

The Confederate Cavalry commander was "Fighting Joe" Wheeler, and under him, my relative and his friends battled all through the arduous Atlanta campaign in the army of General John Bell Hood. Just before Hood entered Tennessee in his disastrous attempt to pull off an impossible mission, Great-grandfather Thrower and his outfit were assigned to "follow and harass" Sherman, who had decided to march to Savannah and "the sea."

At Savannah he was shot in the knee, but he remained with the army until the final surrender.

Among the contents of the box was a faded handwritten letter that reads:

> To Whom it may concern:
>
> This is to certify that I was a member of Co. B, 56th Ala. Regt. and also associated daily with Mr. Fremont Thrower, who has recently deceased, left behind him an unblemished character and record as a gallant Confederate soldier throughout the War from 1862 to 1865, being faithful to duty at all times under the trying ordeal under which we were subjected. My old comrade never flickered in the balance, but promptly came to the front at every call & gallantly withstood the shot and shells of the enemy—almost daily, we were subjected to.
>
> It affords me much pleasure to state of the gallantry exhibited by my comrade in arms—and of the bravery & heroism displayed by the Confederate soldiers who composed the "little band of brothers" of the Southland, who fought the world, from 1861 to 1865.
>
> > Respectfully,
> > J. B. Marshall, 1917 4th Ave, B'ham.
> > The only survivor of Co. B, 56th Ala. Regt.
> > 19th Feby, 1925.

All this got me to thinking. Here was a man born a hundred years before me, who had not only fought in that long-ago conflict but lived on to touch my own father, who, in turn, touched me. More than a quarter century ago I became interested in Civil War history and have made a study of it ever since, but for the first time the notion came to me to write about it.

I have been principally a novelist for many years, and books like *Forrest Gump* are certainly a far cry from historical accounts. Though my great-grandfather did not accompany Hood's army into Tennessee, the documents show he did serve with it throughout the Atlanta campaign and on up to the Tennessee border, which is the concern of the first third of this book. But this story, of course, is not about him. It is about the last big Confederate campaign of the Civil War—the trek of the Army of Tennessee from Atlanta to Nashville—which has been reported in various accounts over the years, but which seemed to me to call for a new telling.

I hope that with the novelist's perspective I have been able to shed some new light on this subject. I have not employed the academic historian's device of footnotes, for which I respectfully beg forgiveness, but, like a number of Civil War writers far more eminent than myself, I feel footnotes are sometimes intrusive. Let me hasten to add, however, that I have been scrupulous in researching everything presented as fact in this book and at no time let the temptation to write "the better story" overcome my duty to recorded historical material.

In this regard, I owe a great debt to a number of people and institutions that have made the writing of this book possible. Foremost among them is the State of Alabama interlibrary loan system. This remarkable service allowed me to order scores of books, microfilms, documents, and other research material from all over America through my local library, thus saving many weeks or months of travel time. In the same interest, the library I used most was that in the city of Foley, Alabama, and to all those persons, staff and volunteers, who over the years gave me kind and uncomplaining assistance in obtaining research materials, I owe a profound debt of gratitude.

As well, the Tennessee State Library and Archives, the Universities of South Carolina, Alabama, North Carolina State, and others provided splendid and cheerful help. To Dr. Kit Carter of the University of Alabama history department go my special thanks, for reading the manuscript and rendering invaluable suggestions and criticisms. Mrs. James Jones of Sagaponak, New York, was lovely enough to lend me her late husband's early edition of the entire Official Records. Additional thanks go to Edwin Morgan, who gave good, sound reading assistance, Kenneth Whitespunner, who lent valuable old books, and especially my fine friend "Skip" Jones, who suffered through my complaints with a new computer system, then organized the whole project for me. Finally, to Anne-Clinton Groom, my lovely wife and chief executive officer of this enterprise, who was present at the creation and tirelessly engineered the details of research and development.

And, of course, I owe more than I can say to the people at Atlantic Monthly Press, not only for agreeing to publish this book, but for their tireless efforts to do it right. Colin Dickerman, my editor, is a man of great patience, tact, and intellect and shaped the project from the start. The copy editor, Jill Mason, saved me from myself more than once and is possibly the best line copy editor I have ever known. Diane Cook did a great job locating photographs and maps. And finally, Morgan Entrekin, publisher, editor, and longtime friend, has been there since the start.

To all of these, I thank you again.

Point Clear, Alabama
November 11, 1994

1

A Midsummer's Change ★

In the midnight mists on a red clay hill in northwest Georgia on May 11, 1864, a bizarre, almost Druid-like ceremony took place. There, in a candlelit tent, a man was baptized. It was unusual for a number of reasons, not the least of which was the fact that at that moment in the hills and valleys around them, more than one hundred fifty thousand armed men slept fitfully, awaiting the dawn that would open the final and perhaps bitterest campaign of the American Civil War.

The man doing the baptizing was Leonidas Polk, the fifty-eight-year-old Episcopal bishop of the state of Louisiana, who also served his Lord as an infantry corps commander in the Army of Tennessee, the main Confederate battle force in the western theater of the war. The candidate for confirmation into the church was also a lieutenant general, John Bell Hood, a gigantic young Kentuckian who, at thirty-three, was among the second generation of Confederate leaders to bear the weight of the national madness that had already cost more than half a million dead and nearly wrecked the fabric of American society. Using a horse water bucket and a tin washpan, Bishop-General Polk began to administer the solemn rites to his fellow general. When it proved awkward for Hood to kneel because of the horrible mutilations inflicted on him at Gettysburg, where his arm was mangled, and at Chickamauga, where just ten months earlier his leg was amputated at the hip, Bishop-General Polk gently suggested to the youthful and still handsome general that he remain in his chair. But struggling for his crutches, Hood declared that if he could not kneel, he could at least stand and, with the blue battle-light still flashing in his eyes, got to his feet to be received into the church.

Why Hood wished to be baptized at this odd juncture is not recorded. It might have been the wave of revivalism that had recently swept the Confederate winter quarters in those cold hills near the Tennessee border. Or it could have had something to do with Hood's volatile love affair with a beautiful young socialite from South Carolina and the embarrassment of being unable to take communion with her in her church. Then again, it may have been some premonition or omen Hood had seen or felt, warning him of his destiny and telling him to get right with his God. In any event, within two months, grave changes were in store for the participants in this midnight baptismal rite. General Polk would be dead, blown nearly in half by a Union cannonball, and Hood, the young Christian soldier, would be poised to march the Army of Tennessee and, indeed, the Southern Confederacy itself, into the battles of Atlanta and Nashville and on into oblivion.

In spite of a disheartening string of military reversals during 1863, the Confederacy was not yet washed up, as some supposed. To be sure, its losses at Gettysburg and Vicksburg and Robert E. Lee's bitter and bloody Forty Days retreat through Virginia to the Richmond-Petersburg salient were crippling. And now, with William Tecumseh Sherman's Union army bracing to rattle the gates of Atlanta, a darkness was spreading across the South that foretold of "miserable anxiety."

But in the North, many did not see it that way at all. In fact, many Northerners actually feared they were losing the war and wished to be rid of it.

In those grim days of spring and summer, a maelstrom of public and political discontent swirled over much of the United States. There were threats of a renewal of the vicious draft riots of the previous summer that left hundreds dead in New York. The price of gold had soared to an incredible $250 an ounce, reflecting an ominous lack of public confidence in the U.S. government. From the Midwest wafted unsettling rumors of something called the Order of American Knights, alleged to be a pro-Southern quarter-million-man clandestine group promising to overthrow the government. Many were so weary of the war and the mounting casualty lists and a wallowing economy it seemed nearly plausible that the South could succeed in freeing itself from the Union politically where it had so far failed militarily. Horace Greeley, the sanguinary editor of the New York *Tribune,* wrote that nine-tenths of all Americans were "anxious for peace—peace on almost any terms— and utterly sick of human slaughter and devastation." Predicting that President Abraham Lincoln would be defeated in the elections that fall, Greeley railed, "We must have another ticket to save us from utter overthrow." Not that the newspaperman wished to capitulate the Union and give up—in fact, he was calling for a sterner leader than Lincoln—but his articles summed up much of the mood of the North.

Lincoln himself was dodging fire not only from the opposition Democrats but also from prominent members of his own Republican party. At a cabinet meeting August 23, 1864, Lincoln wrote forlornly: "This morning, as for some days past, it seems exceedingly probable that this administration will not be re-elected. Then it will be my duty to so cooperate with the President-elect as to save the Union between the election and the inauguration, as he will have secured his election on such ground that he cannot possibly save it afterward." The despondent president had each cabinet member sign the back of the note as a witness, and he put it away for future use, if necessary.

For their part, the Democrats nominated as president former general in chief George B. ("Little Mac") McClellan, who had been fired by Lincoln not once but twice for getting whipped by Robert E. Lee. McClellan had expressed himself as being against the abolition of slavery and was considered to be a man who would treat with the South for peace. In fact, Lincoln had drafted a confidential document, in his "own peculiar style," so he said, proposing that a "peace commission" be appointed to see if the Confederates would agree to a restoration of the Union, with or without slavery—and this *after* issuing his Emancipation

Proclamation. Though nothing came of the peace commission, its very concept surely indicated the depths of the government's despair over the course of the war.

Naturally, all this—at least what could be known of it—was being followed with great zeal in the Confederate capital in Richmond, Virginia. The leaders of that beleaguered cause probably read into it more than was there—after all, much of the Confederate intelligence respecting the Northern mood came from reading northern newspapers. But practically everybody south of the Mason-Dixon Line realized that a Confederate victory, an important one, was necessary somewhere soon if Lincoln and the war-stubborn Republicans were to be swept out of office. The man ultimately chosen to give them that victory was none other than the newly confirmed Episcopalian, John Bell Hood.

By the early spring of 1864 the military situation between the two warring powers had boiled down to a bloody stalemate. In the eastern theater—principally in Virginia—Ulysses S. Grant, latest of five generals in chief of the Union forces, had, by a series of crablike turning movements, forced Confederate general Robert E. Lee and his Army of Northern Virginia from its entrenchments near Fredericksburg—some fifty miles from the capital at Washington—and into a defensive perimeter around Richmond and Petersburg. But those Forty Days, as the battles would come to be known, were costly for Grant in the extreme—not so much for the fifty-four thousand casualties he sustained; with a one-hundred-fifty-thousand-man army he could afford that—but rather because of the mounting horror and dissatisfaction in the North when the casualty lists began coming in. Most earlier Civil War battles had been fought as one- or two-day affairs—Bull Run, Gettysburg, Antietam, Fredericksburg, Chancellorsville, and so on—fangslashing dog fights in which the stronger dog quickly established himself and the loser ran off to fight another day. But Grant's spring offensive introduced a new kind of war, a grinding nightmare of armed embrace in which the victorious dog never turns loose of his victim, but pursues him relentlessly, attacking whenever he can.

But Lee's Army of Northern Virginia was not finished yet. His forces were still intact, and Lee, even in retreat, was a cunning commander who picked and chose his battlefields shrewdly, making Grant pay for every inch of his new strategy. Cold Harbor, for example, cost Grant seven thousand men in a charge that lasted less than an hour. The new commander in chief of the U.S. armies was earning a reputation in certain quarters on both sides as a "butcher" or "murderer" rather than a general. Grant "had such a low idea of the contest," bawled one editor, "that he proposed to decide it by a mere competition in the sacrifice of human life." Deserved or undeserved as such sobriquets might have been, the fact was that the North was becoming war wearier by the day, prompting even such stalwart Unionists as Charles Francis Adams, Jr., son of the U.S. ambassador to England, to complain that while he felt confidence in the federal government's ultimate ability to crush the Confederacy, "For all I can see, we must go floundering on indefinitely through torrents of blood and unfathomable bankruptcy."

Anyway, that was back east. On the other major battlefield of the war, the western theater, things were looking somewhat rosier for the Union cause. Unlike the eastern theater, where fighting was confined mainly to Virginia, the western theater was a huge expanse of territory bounded on the west by the Mississippi River all the way from New Orleans nearly to St. Louis and stretching eastward to the Atlantic states— more than three hundred thousand square miles, much of it wilderness or farmland, badly connected by roads or rail tracks. Union strategy in this vast department was to strangle the Confederacy by blockading its southern ports and force the capture of the Mississippi, and at the same time to chew up Southern armies state by state. By midsummer, 1863, the Mississippi River had been retaken, and federal armies had pushed Confederate forces out of Kentucky and most of Tennessee. But in autumn of that year, the Confederate Army of Tennessee, then under General Braxton Bragg, won its first significant victory of the war by routing the Union army at Chickamauga, in north Georgia, and advancing back into Tennessee near Chattanooga. However, by winter of 1864, the Union army had shoved the Confederates out again in the battle of Missionary Ridge, and so the two hostile armies faced each other near the Georgia-Tennessee line, waiting for spring and a new offensive. From the halls of the U.S. capitol in Washington to the drawing rooms of Richmond and Charleston, those who had studied the war knew the next moves would probably spell the end of the conflict, one way or the other. And so did many in the two opposing forces, including the newly baptized general, John Bell Hood.

By this stage of the war, both Northern and Southern armies had become highly modernized in technology and refined in tactics and strategy. Both relied heavily on the telegraph, steamboats, and railroads for communication and transportation, although by mid-1864 the Confederacy had been depleted of many of those valuable tools. Still, the South's practice of destroying Union-used rails, boats, and wires had evened things up to some extent.

At a first glance, the federal armies would appear to be much superior to the ragtag Confederates. Northern manufactures had been churning out mountains of supplies ever since the war began—everything from uniforms to weapons to such accoutrements as saddlebags, frying pans, haversacks, shoes and boots, razors, wagons, ambulances, medical supplies, and field glasses—all the things that keep an army on the move. The Confederacy, on the other hand, had fewer and fewer of such manufactures as the war progressed, less and less of necessary raw materials, and, owing to the Union blockade of its ports, even scantier ways to purchase them from abroad, now that its vast wealth of cotton lay rotting on its docks.

But until just before the end of the war, the Southerners made do. In its victories in the early years, the Confederates—especially the cavalry—captured vast stores of federal equipment, which they turned to their own use. In the east, Lee's army somehow managed to keep many of its soldiers in "Confederate gray" uniforms, but in the west, where the clothing fashion was more relaxed, most enlisted troops dressed in "butternut homespun," rough-weaved clothing dyed a sort of brownish yellow. Many men with captured Union blue overcoats boiled them in bleach and then again in a butternut or grayish dye. Shoes were a major problem, and the ill-shod Southerners often took the boots of dead federal soldiers after battle, as well as anything else they could use. As long as they obeyed the orders of their generals, kept their weapons well served and their battle morale high, these ragamuffins proved that uniforms do not make soldiers.

Except for manpower—in which the federals enjoyed a large advantage—the armies were about evenly matched. Confederate esprit tended to offset federal superiority in numbers and manufacturing. To cope with any disparities, the Confederates evolved a strategy of trying to strike with enough force to surprise, isolate, and destroy crucial segments of the Union armies and then exploit the ensuing confusion and panic into victory. Stonewall Jackson wrote the book on this technique. Northern armies, on the other hand, had come to rely on their overwhelming numbers to wreck the Confederates' logistics system, then simply grind their armies down by attrition.

By 1864, it had increasingly become the practice of both armies to fight from behind entrenchments. After the first year or so of the war, troops concluded that entrenchments were rarely taken by assault, and that the attackers as opposed to the defenders usually suffered horrible casualties. Fredericksburg was a classic example of this; the assaulting federal army suffered nearly eleven thousand casualties, compared to less than half that for the defending Confederates. In Pickett's charge at Gettysburg, the reverse was true, with the Confederates being slaughtered. Still, the Confederate practice was almost always to assume the offensive, and the South bled itself nearly dry on this policy.

Most Confederate leaders still relied on the Napoleonic strategy of massed forces, rapid movements, and attacking the enemy. This offensive policy worked well enough in the first half of the war, for a number of reasons. First, the Southern soldier was more apt to be willing to face the greater danger of assault because he was fighting for his family's very home and hearth, repelling what he considered to be an invasion of his sovereign country. He was also likely to be more experienced in shooting, horsemanship, and other arts of war. Furthermore, he believed his cause was *just*—that his people had the right to form their own government and be let alone by the North. Union soldiers often had vaguer motives to drive them and frequently disagreed among themselves on the merits of those motives—restoration of the Union, abolition of slavery, for example.

In fact, in what were then considered western states of the Union—Ohio, Illinois, Indiana, Michigan, and Minnesota—there was a large body of public opinion very much opposed to the war, and it carried over to the sons who were fighting it. These westerners resented the powerful influence of the New England states—which they charged had started the war in the first place with their strident anti-slavery rhetoric. These westerners were further disenchanted by the hardships the war had placed upon their lives—in particular, the inability to use the Mississippi River to transport their crops and the concomitant price gouging by the Northern railways, most of which were owned by northeasterners—principally New Englanders. These feelings became so intense that by 1864 there was serious talk of a "western Confederacy" seceding from the Union, which would have fragmented the United States, instead of just splitting it. In any case, all these factors were very important in the individual soldiers' lives, because, other things being even—or relatively even—in an infantry attack, where every second could be deadly, morale was always a critical element.

Identifications of Union and Confederate armies can be confusing, and were so at the time. Union armies were generally named after bodies of water—rivers mostly—thus, Army of the Ohio, Army of the Potomac, Army of the Cumberland, and Army of the Tennessee. Confederates named their armies after geographic terrain: Army of Northern Virginia, Army of Tennessee, for example. In these armies, the tactics of assault were formalized. Most times, a line of skirmishers was sent forward to "feel" the enemy positions and quickly retire to the main line when they encountered a large force. The main attack was carried out by a line of divisions abreast, the brigades of which were marched two deep toward a focal point in the enemy line. Regiments and companies in the brigades were also marched two deep, with "file closers"—lieutenants and sergeants—in the rear to prevent straggling. Rarely was an entire army thrown into the attack at one time; it was simply too unwieldy to control. A corps, consisting of perhaps fifteen to twenty thousand men in a line of battle about a half mile to a mile wide, was about the largest force that could be managed in a single assault.

Thus countless hours were spent on drill parade. The importance of drill—unlike in modern armies, where it is more a traditional formality than a useful practice—was therefore paramount. When the troops weren't fighting or tending to other duties, they were drilling—

obliques, half-steps, step-and-a-halfs, right turns, close-files, by the right and left flanks, and so on, all of it as intricately orchestrated as a French minuet. This was because on those large battlefields where thousands of men were marched shoulder to shoulder to mass their fire at an enemy, all were expected to arrive at a precise spot at a precise time and in a particular order to produce the desired effect, and the slightest variation in terrain—a hidden gully, a bramble thicket, or even a fallen tree—could throw the whole plan out of whack. The drilling and automatic obedience to an officer's marching command were of great significance.

The firepower of an assault could be stunning. Both armies were equipped with the standard infantry weapon of the day, a .50 plus– caliber Springfield, Enfield, or similar percussion-cap rifle that could fire a conical lead slug a thousand yards at a rate of about two shots a minute. Thus, in the full fury of an assault, assuming that one corps had attacked another, it would not be inconceivable that during any given minute sixty thousand deadly projectiles were ripping through the air toward flesh and bone. The size and weight of the bullet were sufficient to disable most men no matter where it hit them, even the hand or foot.

Not only that, but attacks were accompanied and defended against by artillery fire, which the troops feared even more than rifle bullets because its effects were so ghastly. The standard artillery weapon of both armies was the smooth-bore twelve-pound Napoleon, but both sides had a variety of other guns, rifled Parrots that could throw a projectile up to a mile and a half, modern Whitworths that could crack a shell more than two miles with devastating accuracy, and an assortment of others. An assaulting column could soon expect to come under the fire of these mutilating weapons, which, like the rifle, could fire at a rate of about two rounds a minute. At that speed, the artillery of one corps— usually between eighty and one hundred guns—could hurl nearly two hundred shots a minute toward the assaulting column. The muzzle velocity of these guns was slow compared with twentieth-century weaponry; soldiers could often actually see the rounds arcing toward them like deadly black grapefruits. One veteran of the Atlanta campaign recalled a companion who, seeing one of the seemingly slow cannonballs bouncing over the ground near him, stuck his foot out as if to stop it, and in a split second the foot was ripped completely off his leg. In the Stones River battle, General Rosecrans was horrified when his chief of staff, riding beside him, had his head taken off by a cannon shot. Worse for attacking troops was the "canister" that defenders blew at them when they neared the lines of defense. This consisted of a load of iron balls the size of large marbles that turned the cannon into an enormous shotgun, mowing down whole ranks of men in one sweep. Sometimes the artillerymen even loaded the cannon with pieces of chain and other scrap metal.

If, however, the assaulting column got through these formidable obstacles, the defending troops would likely break and run. An assault carried an impetus of its own, with an unequivocal "shock value," not unlike the tank attack of a modern armored unit. But few assaults launched by either side against a well-entrenched enemy ever succeeded in advancing much inside the lethal one-hundred- to four-hundred-yard killing ground where the full intensity of artillery canister and rifle fire could be brought to bear. When an assault did succeed, however, the result was often disastrous for the defenders; the line was pierced, or caved in, and defeat was in the air.

All through the winter of 1863 and most of the spring of 1864 the Confederate Army of Tennessee braced itself in the northwest Georgia mountains just south of Chattanooga, preparing for the attack it knew would come when the Union commander, General William Tecumseh Sherman, had fortified himself to his liking. For getting his army kicked out of Tennessee, General Braxton Bragg was replaced as Confederate commander by Joseph E. Johnston, a general quite popular with the soldiers, who had once commanded the Army of Northern Virginia before Lee. On the 4th of February, after recuperating from the loss of his leg, John Bell Hood joined Johnston and was promoted to lieutenant general and given command of an army corps.

Sherman, in coordination with Grant in Virginia, began his main offensive in north Georgia against Johnston May 12, the morning after

Hood's baptism, by engineering a huge attack against both Confederate flanks. It had taken the Union armies three years to drive the Confederates out of the upper South and retake the crucial Mississippi, but much of the Deep South, including Georgia and South Carolina, had scarcely been touched by the fighting. Now Sherman was preparing to give those states a taste of his theory of warfare, which, in both concept and execution exceeded even Grant's harsh methodology. "All that has gone on before is mere skirmishing," he told his wife in a letter on the eve of battle.

Like Grant, who was moving on Richmond, Sherman had a strategic goal: the city of Atlanta, the Deep South's most important center for arsenals, foundries, warehousing, war goods manufacturing, food stores supply, and railroad shipping. Also like Grant, Sherman would rely on the turning movement as his basic tactical weapon. Given that both Sherman and Grant outnumbered their Confederate opponents by roughly two to one, the turning movement was an obvious and practical device to gain their objective. Instead of the hell-for-leather frontal assaults that had proven so costly in the early years of the war, the turning movement—in Sherman's case relying on numerical superiority of forces—simply called for holding the enemy in place with one powerful body while another part of the army sidled around a flank, got in his rear, and rendered his position untenable.

Use of the turning movement was not a gimmick new or exclusive to Civil War armies—Alfred von Schlieffen, the renowned nineteenth-century German military strategist, avowed, "Flank attack is the essence of the whole history of war"—but most certainly it was elevated, enhanced, and refined to an art by both Union and Confederate generals. From the outset, commanders on both sides based the bulk of their military strategy on their reading of the Napoleonic Wars in Europe half a century earlier and—to a greater or lesser extent—on their personal experiences in the war with Mexico nearly a quarter century before. Studies at West Point in those days were sure to have included such classic turning movements as Napoleon employed in his Italian and Austrian campaigns, as well as those of victorious U.S. generals Winfield Scott at Cerro Gordo and Zachary Taylor at Monterey during the Mexican conflict. In the Civil War, the turning movement had become the major set piece in the overall grand strategy of the Union armies. In the eastern theater—in Virginia—five Union generals had tried it, and all had failed, mostly because a wiley Robert E. Lee had anticipated their maneuvers and countered them with flanking movements of his own. In the west, the federal strategy had been more successful, with the Confederates being flanked all the way out of Kentucky and through Tennessee to Vicksburg, and now Sherman was poised for another go at it. At the tactical level, modern advancements in the ranges of both heavy and light armaments—coupled with the vastly increased rate of firepower during the Civil War—practically mandated the turning movement rather than a straightforward charge, and Sherman was among those generals who thoroughly grasped this vital development.

At any rate, by the time Sherman was ready to make his move in the spring of 1864 he had amassed some one hundred twenty thousand men, as well as mountains of supplies and rail cars to carry them. Now the temperamental Ohioan was fully prepared to do as Grant had ordered him: "Move against Johnston's army, break it up, and get into the interior of the enemy's country as far as you can, inflicting all the damage you can against their war resources."

Confederate commander Joe Johnston, however, a trim fifty-seven-year-old West Pointer, wasn't prepared to take this lying down. He had a plan of his own, though, unfortunately, it did not jibe with what the authorities in Richmond had in mind. Studious and cautious—some would say a "textbook general"—Johnston had divined a scenario he believed would cope with the numerical odds against him: stay flexible, fortify every position, and let Sherman come on. Make him attack, make him pay, retreat if necessary but always be on the lookout for a mistake. Surely, Sherman must make one—and then he could be whipped. Richmond, on the other hand, with an eye on the political storm gathering in the North, still wished to see Johnston go on the offensive and aggressively push Sherman back into Tennessee—if possible, all the way up to Nashville and beyond—and this difference of opinion soon gave way to bitter and acrimonious communications between the Confederate commander and his overlords in Virginia.

*   *   *

The Union Army of the Tennessee amassed by Sherman was, like the Confederate's Army of Tennessee, an amalgam of various smaller armies that over the years of fighting—and as Confederate territory shrunk—had been consolidated into a single, powerful engine of destruction. It was composed of the armies of the Cumberland, Ohio, and Tennessee, commanded respectively by Generals George Thomas, John Schofield, and James McPherson. Each army could contain about thirty to forty thousand men, depending on the task at hand. Each was further divided into three corps of ten to twelve thousand, which in turn were comprised of three divisions of about three to four thousand infantrymen each. In addition, Sherman had at his disposal some three divisions of cavalry commanded by Generals Edward M. McCook, Kenner Garrard, and George Stoneman, as well as 254 pieces of artillery. With this one-hundred-twenty-thousand-man juggernaut he moved out in early May to smash Joe Johnston.

Initially, Johnston's Army of Tennessee contained only two corps, Hood's and that of General William J. Hardee, each totaling about twenty thousand men. As Sherman began his campaign, however, Johnston was reinforced by Bishop Polk and his twenty-thousand-man corps from Mississippi, bringing his total infantry to sixty thousand, more or less. His cavalry consisted of five thousand sabers under the command of Major General Joseph Wheeler, and with the addition of Polk's artillery, Johnston boasted 188 guns—to take on an army twice that size.

In the old days, Confederates might have said the two sides were about evenly matched, but the old days were long gone. This Union army was vastly improved by three years of fighting from Shiloh to Vicksburg, Stones River to Chattanooga, Chickamauga to Lookout Mountain; and now here they were in Johnston's face at Dalton, Georgia, and it was going to take a lot more than courage and savvy to keep them off his back.

*   *   *

As the crow flies, Atlanta is a hundred miles southeast from Dalton, and Johnston figured that gave him some pretty good room to maneuver. Not only that, but since armies didn't fly, to get at either Johnston or Atlanta, Sherman was going to have to traverse some of the roughest terrain ever contested during the war—myriad mountains, hills, valleys, gaps, forests, swamps, gullies, passes, rivers, and ravines, each presenting Johnston with a formidable opportunity for defense. At the outset, Johnston had his army drawn up along several miles of stone and clay called Rocky Face Ridge, facing west, with a passage known ominously as Buzzard's Roost dividing it in two. It was not a position a prudent man would attack head-on, and William Tecumseh Sherman was a prudent man. He had learned his lesson the hard way a year before, at Chickasaw Bluffs above Vicksburg, when he had embarrassingly failed to carry such a position, and he wasn't about to repeat the mistake now.

First, Sherman sent Thomas's Army of the Cumberland at Johnston's center to hold him while Schofield's Army of the Ohio attacked due south into the Confederate right flank. McPherson, meanwhile, had maneuvered his Army of the Tennessee way around the Confederate left flank to the southeast and was aiming at the railroad linking Dalton with Atlanta. Trouble was, when McPherson got there, he found the cat was out of the bag. Outflanked, and with their only escape route about to be cut, the Confederate army had withdrawn southward without a fight to the small railway town of Resaca, where they had set up another defense. This time Johnston stood firm while Sherman attacked him to no avail, and then he launched a counterattack of his own, led by Hood. The federals were driven back, but darkness set in, and by morning it was apparent that Sherman was executing another flanking movement. After desultory fighting all day, Johnston decided to abandon Resaca and retreat southward again. Thus, he conformed to the pattern that he had in mind, more or less, of fortifying and causing Sherman to pay for his ground, all the while waiting for him to make his mistake. Sherman wasn't making mistakes, however, and Johnston was letting his enemy shove him that much closer to Atlanta.

Johnston cunningly laid a few traps for Sherman along the way, moving Hood and Hardee around in hopes of catching one of the three federal armies alone and where it could be cut off. But none of that worked, and Johnston continued his retreats until he had lost nearly two-thirds of the ground between Dalton and Atlanta. Though no major battle had yet been fought, attrition was taking its toll, mostly on the Union army, which so far was losing men two to one against the Confederates. In a dispatch to Washington, Sherman reported that his loss at Resaca was 3,375 wounded. William Murray of the 20th Tennessee, who was there, remarked later that Sherman "did not say how many he had killed, but there are 1,790 Yankees buried there and 170 Confederates." In another telegram shortly afterward, Sherman sourly told Washington, "Johnston retires slowly, leaving nothing and hitting hard if crowded."

Hood, meanwhile, in whatever spare time there was, had been sending private reports on the progress of the campaign to Jefferson Davis and Braxton Bragg, who, after being replaced by Johnston, had been elevated to chief military advisor to the Richmond authorities. Davis, Bragg, and Secretary of War James A. Seddon composed a sort of triumverate for running the war from Richmond. Mostly they had let Robert E. Lee alone to do what he thought best, but in the western theater there had been nearly as many lost battles and changes in high command as the federals had experienced in the Army of the Potomac. Hood had gotten on excellent personal terms with Davis during the months he spent in Richmond recuperating from the loss of his leg, and it was later suggested that his correspondence with the Confederate president and other authorities was in the nature of an intrigue against Johnston, with whose defensive policies Hood had begun to strongly disagree. Whatever the case, by the time Johnston reached the area of Kennesaw Mountain, about twenty-five miles northwest of Atlanta, he knew he had to make a stand. It was a little more than a month since the campaign had started; he had lost nearly five thousand men and had yet to give Sherman a serious check.

In addition, Sherman was having his own problems. In pursuing the elusive Johnston, he had saved time and distance by cutting loose from the Western & Atlantic Railroad that ran from Atlanta through Dalton and north to Chattanooga and Nashville and beyond, from whence came the material to supply his army. He still had one flank astride the tracks, but further maneuvering in a southeastern sidle to turn Johnston's left would leave him without a means of resupply by rail, and three weeks of rainy weather had rendered the roads impassable. For several weeks Sherman tested and feinted and demonstrated without success trying to dislodge the Confederates, but they would not budge from their strong position. About the only thing of substance he accomplished was the killing of General Polk, who was struck by a cannonball in the presence of Generals Hardee and Johnston while they were reconnoitering the enemy from a hill. So this time Sherman swallowed the bait and attacked, perceiving that not only the Confederates but, he said, "Our own officers had settled down into a conviction that I would not assault fortified lines. All looked for me to outflank." But any army, he declared, "must be prepared to execute any plan which promises success." Thus convinced, he ordered an assault on the Confederate center at Kennesaw Mountain on June 27.

The attack was a miserable failure, reaffirming the opinions of veteran soldiers that assaulting troops who were behind fortifications was suicidal. Three thousand of Sherman's men were lost, and several generals were killed while inflicting "comparatively little loss on the enemy," according to Sherman, who sought to put a better face on it by reporting that at least it was "demonstrated to General Johnston that I would assault, and that boldly."

Johnston, on the other hand, was finally able to report a victory to the Confederate high command in Richmond. Telegraphing on the day of the Kennesaw battle that Sherman had been repulsed with great losses, Johnston now undertook to provide his superiors with an explanation of why he had retreated to the very outskirts of Atlanta without giving Sherman a major offensive battle. Citing "long cold wet weather," "sickness," and "the superior forces of the enemy," Johnston wrote that he had "intended to take advantage of the first good position to give battle" but had so far not found one.

Understandably, the Richmond authorities were upset. Two days after receiving Johnston's telegram, Braxton Bragg fumed to Jefferson Davis, "No doubt [Johnston] is outnumbered by the enemy, as we all are everywhere, but the disparity is much less than it has ever been between those two armies.'' As they worried and waited and wondered whether Johnston was going to defend Atlanta at all, or simply let himself get outflanked by Sherman all the way down to the Gulf of Mexico, Bragg and Davis must have remembered Hood's secretive letters to them, in which he outlined his own strategy for dealing with Sherman: ''We should march to the front as soon as possible . . . so as not to allow the enemy to concentrate and advance upon us.'' In another of those private letters, Hood wrote, ''I . . . am sorry to inform you that I have done all in my power to induce General Johnston to accept the proposition you made to move forward. He will not consent.'' Possibly it was about this time that Davis began to mull over a change in command for the Army of Tennessee.

In any event, the undaunted Sherman immediately began his maneuvering again and was able to wire Washington that ''the effect was instantaneous. The next morning Kennesaw was abandoned,'' and Sherman maneuvered on, minus nearly sixteen thousand casualties since his campaign had opened six weeks before, compared to Johnston's losses of nine thousand. This episode went to prove by example the theory of attritive warfare embraced by Sherman and Grant: that the North could afford to lose more men than the South because it *had* more men, and sooner or later the Confederacy was going to run out of replacements. Such a reduction of military science to its most brutal basics foretold by fifty years the awesome slaughter that would visit European battlefields in the century to come.

For the next several weeks Johnston fought what seemed to be little more than a delaying action all the way to the Chattahoochee River, the final big defensive terrain feature before Atlanta, then he drew himself up for another fight. But Sherman flanked him again, this time turning his right with an upriver sweep by McPherson's army. Johnston retreated once more, toward Peachtree Creek, and resumed calling on the Richmond authorities for reinforcements—mainly for the cavalry divisions of Generals Nathan Bedford Forrest and John Hunt Morgan, then operating in other states, which he wished to send to Sherman's rear up in Tennessee to cut off Union supplies and communications. All this was about enough for Jefferson Davis, whose relationship with Johnston had been fitful and unpleasant since the two were at West Point, not to mention early in the war when Johnston quarreled with him over the seniority of his promotion. Frightened that Atlanta would be surrendered without a fight, Johnston's friend Georgia Senator Benjamin Hill telegraphed Johnston after testing the mood of the Richmond government, "You must do the work with your present force. For God's sake do it."

But Johnston did not do it. On July 11 he wired Richmond his recommendation that the Union prisoners at Andersonville be evacuated, clearly a sign to the Confederate authorities that Atlanta was about to be forsaken. General Bragg was immediately sent down to meet with Johnston and assess the situation. On the 15th of July Bragg reported back gloomily, "I cannot learn that he has any more plan for the future than he has had in the past." Two nights later the following wire from the adjutant general was received at Johnston's headquarters:

> Lieutenant General J. B. Hood has been commissioned to the temporary Rank of General under the late law of Congress. I am directed by the Secretary of War to inform you that as you have failed to arrest the advance of the enemy to the vicinity of Atlanta, far in the interior of Georgia, and express no confidence that you can defeat or repel him, you are hereby relieved from the command of the Army of the Department of Tennessee, which you will immediately turn over to General Hood.

And so the army's fate was sealed, for better or worse, as it now had as its leader a "fighting general" to contend with the seemingly irresistible maneuvering of Sherman.

The decision to replace Johnston with Hood was not made without considerable handwringing in Richmond. Davis and the rest of the government obviously wished for the Army of Tennessee to attack Sherman, but Johnston simply would not do it—or at least he had not done it—and time was running out. Everybody knew Hood's reputation as a fighter; he was a proud alumnus of the Robert E. Lee–Stonewall Jackson "get 'em on open ground and hit 'em with all you've got" school of military thought. He had proved that from the beginning during the Peninsular campaign in 1862 and at Second Manassas and of course at Gettysburg and Chickamauga. But there was more than just lingering doubt about Hood's ability to command an entire army. Less than a year before, the biggest command he had held was a division, and he had led a corps for only a few months. Now he was to be responsible for one of the two great armies that held the key to survival for the Confederacy.

In recommending Hood to Davis during his panicky visit to Atlanta, Bragg had candidly stated that the young Kentuckian was not "a man of genius, or a great general." But under the present emergency, Bragg went on to say, Hood was "far better" than anybody else available. A few days earlier and on his own hook, Davis had wired Lee about the proposed change. Lee, who had his hands full with Grant around Richmond, telegraphed back, "Hood is a bold fighter. I am doubtful as to other qualities necessary." Soon afterward Lee followed up with a letter to the president in which he described Hood as "a good commander, very industrious on the battlefield, careless off" and went on to say, "I have had no opportunity to judge his action when the whole responsibility rested upon him. I have a high opinion of his gallantry, earnestness and zeal." It was almost as though Hood got the job through default—the best of a bad lot.

Nor was the ascension of General Hood greeted with boundless enthusiasm by the Army of Tennessee. In fact, it was viewed in most quarters with shock—in some cases, bitter disappointment and even tears. Sam Watkins, a twenty-five-year-old private in a Tennessee regiment, who had been with the army since the beginning of the war, decried Hood's appointment as "the most terrible and disastrous blow that the South ever received." He went on to say, "I saw thousands of grown men cry like babies." An entire squad of pickets, Watkins recalled, threw down their guns upon hearing the news and marched off, "the last we ever saw of them." W. D. Murray, of the 20th Tennessee Regiment, complained that the replacement of Johnston "threw a damper over [the] army from which it never recovered." Murray described how "great stalwart, sun-burnt soldiers by the thousands would be seen falling out of line, squatting down by a tree or in a fence corner, weeping like children.''

Exaggerated as some of this might have been, the news was not met with much welcome in the officer corps, either. Lieutenant General William Hardee, who had graduated from West Point fifteen years before Hood and was a year his senior in rank, asked to be relieved, miffed at being passed over for the promotion. One division commander remarked that Hood had '' 'gone up like a rocket.' It is to be hoped that he will not come down like the stick.'' Another told Hood face to face that he regretted Johnston's removal, although he promised him cooperation. Others expressed similar sentiments—not an encouraging start for the new commander of the Army of Tennessee.

Hood himself recalled his reaction to the news of his promotion— or, as he described it, ''the embarrassing circumstances under which I assumed command of the Army of Tennessee'': ''About 11 o'clock, on the night of the 17th, I received a telegram from the War Office, directing me to assume command of the Army. This totally unexpected order so astounded me, and overwhelmed me with the sense of the responsibility thereto attached, that I remained in deep thought throughout the night.''

Near sunrise next morning the sleepless Hood set out for Johnston's headquarters and was met by General A. P. Stewart, who had been promoted to command of the late Bishop Polk's corps. Stewart, likewise disturbed by the news, suggested to Hood that they ''unite in an effort to prevail on General Johnston to withhold the order, and retain command of the Army until the impending battles have been fought.'' Hood readily assented to this plan, possibly because in spite of whatever earlier ambition he might have harbored to command the army, he surely recognized the immediate danger it was in now and did not wish to preside over its defeat. In any case, Johnston, saying in effect that ''orders is orders,'' would have none of it. By this time General Hardee had arrived on the scene, and, Hood, Hardee, and Stewart fired off a telegram to Jefferson Davis asking that the command change be suspended until the battle of Atlanta was fought. Davis declined, citing Johnston's policies as ''disastrous'' and concluding that he could not suspend the order ''without making the case worse than it was.''

So that was that—or almost. Hood went in to see Johnston one last time and urged him, "for the good of the country, to pocket the correspondence, and fight for Atlanta, as Sherman was at the very gates of the city." He pleaded that he "did not even know the position of the two remaining Corps of the Army," and he begged Johnston, he said later, to at least "remain with me and give me the benefit of his counsel whilst I determined the issue." Hood then described Johnston's reaction to this request: "With tears of emotion gathering in his eyes, he finally made the promise that, after riding into Atlanta, he would return that same evening." However, as Hood sourly put it, "He not only failed to comply with his promise, but, without a word of explanation or apology, left that evening for Macon, Georgia."

There was one final flurry of reaction to the news of the change of command in the Army of Tennessee, and that came at Union army headquarters on the other side of Peachtree Creek, where some officers remembered Hood's impulsive habits at the card table during the old army days on the frontier. It was generally agreed that the new Confederate commander, though brave and audacious, was "reckless." General John Schofield, Hood's old roommate at West Point, warned Sherman, "He'll hit you like hell, now, before you know it." Schofield proceeded to describe the new Confederate commander as "bold even to rashness and courageous in the extreme" and, when he wrote later, may even have provided the further intelligence that Hood was "not well up in mathematics" while at the military academy. (Hood had graduated forty-fourth out of fifty-two cadets.)

The tall, red-haired Sherman took all this in and then wrote to his wife, "I confess I was pleased at the change."

2

★ I Will Go On While I Can

At West Point they called him "Sam" Hood, and while he was not a particularly good student, he was at least "a jolly good fellow," according to his old classmate John M. Schofield, who had to tutor him through mathematics. Fifteen years later, as the fighting around Atlanta became ever more desperate, Schofield considered that he might have "made a mistake" in helping his new adversary through those studies.

John Bell Hood was not born into Southern aristocracy as it was practiced in the Virginias and Carolinas—and even in Kentucky—but he was certainly close enough to its fringes to become aware of aristocratic values and customs. His father was a physician whose family had been in America since the late 1600s and had moved from Virginia to Kentucky shortly after the Revolutionary War. By the late 1850s the Hood family had acquired more than six hundred acres of fertile farmland and several dozen slaves, but by the time John Bell turned eighteen he had rejected life as a farmer or doctor to become a soldier. In 1849 his maternal uncle, Richard French, an influential lawyer and congressman, secured for his tall, handsome nephew an appointment to the United States Military Academy.

West Point in those days was a difficult, almost draconian place with incessant hazing, meager food, a demanding curriculum, and exhaustive military drilling. Hood struggled through all that in the bottom third of his class and without incident until, in his senior year, he was caught absent without leave, busted to cadet private, and given nearly enough demerits to get him kicked out of the academy. The man who disciplined Hood was the superintendent of West Point, Colonel Robert E. Lee, but there nevertheless developed a close attachment between the two men that would continue through the war.

After graduating forty-fourth of the fifty-two in his class, Hood was commissioned as an infantry lieutenant and sent sailing around to California—just as Sherman had been seven years earlier—where he landed in San Francisco in the middle of the gold rush. He was rudely awakened to frontier economics when he and a fellow officer hailed a carriage to take them from the dock to their hotel. The price, the driver told them, was twenty dollars in gold. "This aspect of affairs," Hood recalled, "—our pay being only about sixty dollars a month—compelled us to hold a consultation with our brother officers and to adopt the only alternative: to proceed on foot to whatever quarters we desired to occupy." Soon posted to a fort farther north, Hood began to understand that California's horribly inflated economy—he called it "this country of gold and extravagance"—was driving him to rack and ruin, and along with his fellow officers he began hunting expeditions in the plentiful countryside to supply their officers' mess. There was enough game left over to sell at market. To improve matters further, Hood and another lieutenant, George Crook, later to win much fame as an Indian fighter, got some land and sowed a large crop of wheat. Just before its harvest, though, Hood was transferred to the soon-to-be-famed Second United States Cavalry in Missouri. Back in San Francisco to await his ship, he stopped in at a bank, where he met, for the first time, its president, William Tecumseh Sherman, whom he later remembered as possessing "a piercing eye and nervous impulsive temperament."

At Jefferson Barracks, near St. Louis, Hood reported to his new commanding officer, Colonel Albert Sidney Johnston, later to be the first commanding general of the Army of Tennessee. The deputy commander was Colonel Robert E. Lee, and one of the majors was another Virginian, George H. "Pap" Thomas. Of the officers in this star-

crossed regiment, seventeen would go on to become Civil War generals. In the autumn of 1855, Hood and the Second Cavalry marched
southward to the Texas frontier, but not before Hood received a draft of
a thousand dollars in gold from his old pal Crook, his share of the wheat
crop sale.

Texas winters were bitterly cold and the summers were stiflingly
hot as Hood and the regiment policed the frontier for marauding Indians. His only serious encounter occurred in 1857 when his troop of two
dozen soldiers was patrolling a barren stretch of desert near the Mexican
border. Two weeks and 150 miles out of camp, they stumbled on a band
of about fifty Indians and promptly rode into a trap. Unsure whether the
Indians were friendly or hostile, Hood was somewhat relieved when
they began waving a white flag. He cautiously approached them with
seventeen of his cavalrymen. Suddenly, the Indians threw down their
flag and began firing on the soldiers, a moment later igniting a huge
brush pile they had constructed. Simultaneously, warriors rose up from
the sparse shrubbery, while others charged down a slope. "The warriors were all painted, stripped to the waist, with either horns or
wreaths of feathers on their heads," Hood said later. "They bore shields
for defence, and were armed with rifles, bows and arrows." The fighting was fast and furious, often hand to hand. Hood's men fired until they
had emptied their guns and then found that, "Owing to the restiveness
of the horses, we could not reload while mounted." The cavalrymen
withdrew about fifty yards to assess their situation. Two men had been
killed, and four, including Hood, were wounded. At nightfall the Indians gathered their wounded and dead and moved off, and Hood wisely
did likewise.

For this brief but savage action, Hood received a commendation
for gallantry from the department commander and not long afterward
was promoted to first lieutenant, a rank he retained until the end of his
service in the United States Army. In the autumn of 1860, after nearly
ten years of military duty, Hood requested and received a leave of absence from the army, but just as he was headed back east, orders overtook him directing him to report to West Point as cavalry instructor. It
was a plum of an assignment for any young officer, but Hood turned it

down. As he recounted the story, the adjutant general of the army "turned quickly in his chair, saying, 'Lieutenant, you surprise me; this is a post and position sought by almost every soldier.'" Hood later explained, "I feared war would soon be declared between the States, in which event I preferred to be in a position to act with entire freedom." Thus ended the active career of Sam Hood with the United States Army, and, his prediction having come to pass, he resigned his commission in April 1861 and tendered his services to the Confederate states.

Aside from the desert Indian fight, one other incident of interest occurred during Hood's service in Texas. While riding over the countryside one day with his colonel, Robert E. Lee, Hood became the recipient of some fatherly advice that he later put to use. "While enjoying the scenery and balmy air as we passed over the high and undulating prairies of that beautiful region, the conversation turned to matrimony" Hood later recalled. Thinking that his young protégé "might form an attachment for some of the country lasses," Hood remembered that Lee counseled him, "Never marry unless you can do so into a family which will enable your children to be proud of both sides of the house." This aristocratic pronouncement made such a deep impression on the dashing lieutenant from Kentucky that he repeated it in his memoirs many years afterward. Within a few years, however, he was to put the advice to practice in a fiery romance with a young Confederate beauty that set Richmond society agog.

In the spring of 1861, when the United States was still breaking apart, Hood went back home to Kentucky and met with the former vice president, John Breckinridge, hoping to offer his services to his native state. But, "after long debate and considerable delay," he became convinced that Kentucky would not secede, and he boarded a train for Montgomery, Alabama, then the Confederate capital, where he was appointed first lieutenant in the untested Confederate army. Sent to Richmond, he reported to his new commanding officer, none other than his old mentor, Robert E. Lee, and was immediately dispatched to Yorktown, Virginia, to join Colonel John Magruder, who was expecting an attack from the federal troops believed to be assembling at Fort Monroe. Years later, Hood recalled the anxiety of that first day in the field: "As no tent or quarters had been assigned me, I sent for my trunk and sat upon it in the sand a greater portion of the night, gazing intently every few minutes in the direction of Fortress Monroe, in the expectation momentarily of beholding the enemy. The following morning, it was ascertained that the Federals were not within thirty miles of this line. . . .''

Magruder put Hood in charge of all the cavalry companies around Yorktown and immediately promoted him to captain and then to major. This unusual leapfrog in rank was brought about so as to give young Hood seniority over the other officers commanding companies. Soon the companies were organized into the Fourth Texas Cavalry Regiment, and Hood was again promoted, this time to colonel in command. All through the winter of 1861 Hood drilled and instructed and honed his troops. At the beginning of spring 1862, to his own astonishment, he was promoted once more, to brigadier general, and given command of a brigade of Texans. On the 7th of May, the Union army, under General George McClellan, was advancing up the Yorktown Peninsula through Williamsburg toward Richmond, and Hood was ordered to drive it back. In its first serious action, the Texas brigade encountered federal troops near Eltham's Landing and handily routed them with what Hood called "a happy introduction to the enemy." Three weeks later, Hood and his brigade distinguished themselves at the battle of Seven Pines, or Fair Oaks, and a month later—under the direction of General Stonewall Jackson—they were embroiled in the confused Seven Days battles in the swamps and marshes outside Richmond. At the battle of Gaines Mill, the Texans swept the field and sent the federals tumbling back through White Oak Swamp and on to Malvern Hill, where the Confederate army suffered its first defeat of the campaign. But McClellan, convinced that the Confederates were about to bag his entire army, continued to retreat, and soon the threat to Richmond was ended. Hood emerged from the campaign with a shining reputation as a bold and able combat officer and was promoted to division commander.

At this point, Hood and his men were detached to the command of General James Longstreet and headed north toward what would be the celebrated Second Battle of Manassas, or Bull Run. There, Jackson's corps swiftly and stealthily maneuvered around the army of General

John Pope, while Longstreet, with Hood's division in a prominent position, proceeded to savagely grind up the Union forces as they unsuccessfully tried to dislodge Jackson. Pope was thoroughly defeated, and his army went reeling back to Washington in disarray. Hood called it "the most beautiful battle scene I have ever beheld." Again, he had acquitted himself brilliantly and had become a rising star among Confederate officers.

With little pause for rest, Lee now moved his army up into Maryland, but Hood was not at the head of his column—he had been put under arrest. On the final day at Second Manassas, his men had captured some federal ambulances, and Hood pressed them into service. General N. G. ("Shanks") Evans, who was senior to Hood, declared that the vehicles should go to his men, and when Hood refused to turn them over, Evans had him arrested. Hood explained, "I would cheerfully have obeyed directions to deliver them to General Lee's Quarter Master for the use of the Army, [but] I did not consider it just that I should be required to yield them to another brigade of the division, which was in no manner entitled to them." In any case, he was on his way back to Culpeper, Virginia, to await court-martial when Lee was notified of the affair and sent instructions that he be brought along on the Maryland expedition, arrested or not. As the army moved toward Antietam, the Texans began to shout, "Give us Hood," and Lee, who heard this, sent for Hood and said to him, "General, here I am just upon the eve of entering into battle, and with one of my best officers under arrest." He told Hood that if he would apologize about the ambulances, he would release him, but Hood refused, again citing the justness of his position. Lee shook his head and then informed his stubborn young protégé that he was "suspending" his arrest until after the impending battle had been fought, and Hood cheerfully galloped to the head of his column.

What followed was one of the bloodiest and most fateful battles of the war. As Lee for the first time moved north to threaten Philadelphia, Baltimore, and Washington, McClellan—back in command of the Union army after Pope's disaster at Manassas—moved quickly to intercept him. Finally, on September 16, 1862, following two days of spiteful little conflicts in the surrounding mountains, Lee moved his forty thousand men out in the open to take on McClellan's eighty-seven-thousand man army.

In the late afternoon, Hood's division took position in an open field in front of the Dunker Church a little more than a mile from the town of Sharpsburg and about the same distance west of Antietam Creek. About sunset, he was attacked by almost an entire corps commanded by General Joseph Hooker. The fighting lasted late into the night, and Hood's men held their ground. By this time, Hood later recalled, his men were on the verge of starvation—they "had had no meat for several days and little or no bread; the men had been forced to subsist principally on green corn and green apples." When the firing died down, Hood sought out Lee and asked if his men could be relieved from the line for the rest of the night to cook up some rations. Lee told him he knew of no troops he could spare, but suggested that Hood apply to Jackson, who had come up on his left, for relief. Hood found the venerable Stonewall asleep under a tree, awakened him, and "made known the half-starved condition of [his] troops." Jackson immediately dispatched several brigades to replace Hood's and the Texans gratefully marched off to the rear to fry up some dough. "He exacted of me, however," Hood said later, "a promise that I would come to the support of these forces the moment I was called upon."

By this time it was near dawn, and as the sky turned from gray to pink, the full fury of a federal attack broke upon the line Hood's men had recently occupied. Most of Hood's division had not even had time to prepare their food when a messenger dashed up requesting that Hood move immediately into battle. His still hungry soldiers "were again obliged to march to the front, leaving their uncooked rations in camp."

The brigades that had replaced Hood had suffered a violent and bloody assault through a forty-acre field of standing corn in which, as General Hooker himself described it, so much hot lead was flying that "every stalk in the northern and greater part of the field was cut as closely as could have been done by a knife." Slowly the overwhelming federals pushed the Confederates back until they were forced into the woods and fled. Hooker was preparing for a final, victorious push when Hood's starving and angry Texans arrived on the scene. No more than twenty-four hundred strong, they faced a full two corps massing in their front. As the heavy blue columns began moving toward them, Hood's men emerged from the woods and attacked them head-on, pouring volley after volley into the Union ranks until men began to drop "like a scythe running through our line."

Slowly and fiercely, the Texans drove Hooker's men back across the corn field, stumbling and slipping through the mangled and dismembered remains of blue- and gray-clad alike. Hood himself described how "men were mowed down in heaps to the right and left" and said, "Never before was I so continuously troubled with fear that my horse would further injure some wounded fellow soldier, lying helpless upon the ground."

In the thick of the battle, an officer of Jackson's staff arrived to appraise the situation, and Hood's message to him in reply became as famous in the Confederate army as Admiral Farragut's "Damn the torpedoes" pronouncement was to become for the Union. "Tell General Jackson," Hood said bleakly, "that unless I get reinforcements I must be forced back. But I am going on while I can."

The reinforcements never came, and Hood, his exhausted men now out of ammunition and facing a galling fire from several new batteries of Union artillery, ordered a withdrawal to the little white Dunker Church, its outside walls now peppered and blasted away by shot and shell. Presently, the division of General Lafayette McLaws arrived, just as the federals were making a final assault. McLaws's troops pitched into the unsuspecting blue line and drove it back with fearful slaughter, as Hood's men marched to the rear to resupply their ammunition. When they returned to take up position in the woods behind the church, the day's fighting was mostly over on this northern part of the field, though the battle raged nearly out of control southward and in the center. Hood and his men bivouacked for the night, and at dawn, as the sky began to glow over the rigid corpses of thousands of slain men in the corn field, Stonewall Jackson rode up to Hood, who had already arrived at the scene to survey the situation.

"Hood, have they gone?" Jackson asked.

Looking east and north toward the vast Union camps through the morning mists, Hood replied that "they" had not gone. Jackson said acidly, "I hoped they had," and rode away to look after his used-up command. Without mentioning anything about it to Hood, who was not even in his corps but was still serving under Longstreet, Jackson wrote a letter to the adjutant general in Richmond, recommending Hood's promotion to major general and calling him "one of the most promising officers of the army."

All that day the Confederate army remained at Antietam, facing down the enemy and burying the dead. That night they pulled up stakes and headed southward, crossing the Potomac and marching into the autumnal beauty of the Shenandoah Valley. "Where is your division?" someone asked Hood after the battle. "Dead on the field," he replied, and he was sadly correct; nearly two-thirds of the Texas brigade were casualties. During the campaign, more than thirteen thousand Confederates had fallen and nearly fifteen thousand federals.

The action on the Confederate left during the battle of Antietam had saved the day for Lee and the Army of Northern Virginia. Hood, McLaws, and General Alexander Lawton, who had taken Hood's place when he went back to cook rations, had staved off three successive attacks from more than thirty thousand Union troops—nearly five-to-one odds.

Hood also regained a measure of personal relief after the battle. Expecting to be placed back under arrest for the ambulance-appropriation incident, he was released of those charges by Lee. "In lieu of being summoned to a court-martial," Hood said, "I was shortly afterwards promoted to the rank of major general."

Lee rested the Army of Northern Virginia in the Shenandoah Valley most of the autumn, its rich granaries and larders and calm pastoral beauty providing a wonderful restorative for the battered soldiers. Hood's men, along with the others, received a supply of clothing and shoes. But soon it was time to move on. McClellan had again been replaced as Union commander, this time by General Ambrose Burnside, who promptly began to march his army toward Fredericksburg, about halfway between Richmond and Washington.

Lee reached Fredericksburg first, and, while he originally considered trying to frustrate Burnside's designs by maneuver, he took a look at his position in the town and decided to stay and receive the federal assault. With one hundred twenty-five thousand men and more than three hundred pieces of artillery, Burnside held a decided advantage in manpower and firepower over Lee's seventy-eight thousand soldiers and 275 guns, but with the Rappahannock River at its front and rising heights in the rear, Fredericksburg was a veritable fortress for Lee's army. For example, Colonel Porter Alexander, in charge of a battalion of Longstreet's artillery, remarked to his commander, "General, we cover that ground now so well that we comb it as with a fine-tooth comb. A chicken would not live on that field when we open up on it." And the irascible Mississippian William Barksdale, commanding his brigade from within the town itself, told a messenger, "Tell General Lee that if he wants a bridge of dead Yankees, I can furnish him one."

With these grim declarations in mind, Lee and his soldiers watched the huge federal buildup across the river. By December 11, 1862, Burnside had constructed enough pontoon bridges to carry his men across, which they did the following morning, his troops burning and looting the town. Lee's army was drawn up on the heights behind the city; Longstreet's corps, with Hood's division in its center, was on the left, and Jackson's corps defended the right flank. To get at them, the federals had to march straight up the long sloping heights into the face of all the rifle and cannon fire the Confederate army could bring to bear. That morning, Hood recalled, he was riding toward Lee's headquarters, when he was joined by a solemn Stonewall Jackson. In a peculiarly out-of-character lapse, Hood said, "[Jackson] asked me if I expected to live to see the end of the war. I replied that I did not know, but that I was inclined to think I would survive; at the same time I considered it mostly likely that I would be badly shattered before the termination of the struggle." Hood then asked Jackson the same question, and "without hesitation he answered that he did not expect to live through to the close of the contest. Moreover, that he could not say that he desired to do so." With this strange conversation ringing in his ears, Hood rode off to prepare his men for the attack.

Burnside's Union troops were slaughtered, of course. During the late morning and long afternoon of December 13, the blue-clad soldiers were mowed down in ranks in a series of charges up and down the Confederate line. It was here that Lee, watching the battle with Longstreet, uttered his famous remark: "It is well that war is so terrible. We should grow too fond of it." Hood's division performed its duties, receiving and repulsing the federal attack by its old adversary from Antietam, "Fighting Joe" Hooker, and the next day the Union army withdrew across the river, leaving 12,600 casualties to the Confederate's 4,200.

A lull enveloped the Virginia theater of war for nearly five months during the winter of 1862–63, and during that time a momentous event also enveloped John Bell Hood—he fell in love.

She was Sally "Buck" Preston, eighteen-year-old daughter of an aristocratic South Carolina family, who was staying in Richmond that winter at the home of family friends, Colonel and Mrs. John C. Chesnut. Chesnut was then an aide to Jefferson Davis; his wife, Mary Boykin Chesnut, was a fashionable hostess about town. Hood's chief surgeon, John Darby, was engaged to Buck Preston's sister, Mary, and, evidently thinking that his commanding officer might like to meet his fiancée's younger sister, in mid-March the good doctor brought Hood to the Chesnuts' for tea.

Hood's reputation had preceded him, and he clearly impressed Mrs. Chesnut, who wrote in her diary: "When he came, with his sad Quixote face, the face of an old crusader who believed in his cause, his cross, his crown—we were not prepared for that type exactly as a beau ideal of wild Texans. Tall—thin—shy, blue eyes and light hair, tawny beard and a vast amount of it covering the lower part of his face—an appearance of awkward strength. Someone said that great reserve of manner he carried only into ladies' society."

Also present at this tea was Lieutenant Charles Venable, formerly a mathematics teacher at South Carolina College, who said that while he had often heard of the "light of battle" shining in a man's eyes, he had seen it only once, and that was when he brought Hood orders from Lee. When he found Hood in the heat of the battle, Venable told Mrs. Chesnut, "The man was transfigured. The fierce light of his eyes—I can never forget."

These flowing tributes notwithstanding, Buck Preston refused, for some reason, to appear when Hood visited the Chesnuts, and it was several days before he finally met her. His division was being marched through the streets of Richmond in a freezing snowstorm on the way back to the Rappahannock when Hood spotted his surgeon, the Chesnuts, and the Preston sisters watching from the sidewalk.

"Hood and his staff came galloping up, dismounted, and joined us," Mary Chesnut wrote. Buck's sister, Mary, gave him a bouquet, and Hood took out a bible from his pocket and pressed one of the flowers in it. As the marching troops joked and kidded their commanding general for keeping the company of the women, Buck "stood somewhat apart, rather as a spectator of this scene" until Dr. Darby introduced her to Hood.

After he had remounted his horse, Mrs. Chesnut remembered, Hood looked down at Buck, slowly turning the animal as he eyed her carefully, then leaned down and said something to Dr. Darby, who smiled. After Hood had ridden off, Buck went up to Darby and asked eagerly, "What was that he said to you? About me?"

"Only a horse compliment," Darby replied. "He is a Kentuckian, you know. He says you stand on your feet like a thoroughbred."

All through the cold spring Hood pursued Buck Preston whenever he could get down to Richmond. She was a true beauty, and she was smart, but she was also young and coquettish and a born flirt. Caught up in the midst of war, where it seemed like the handsome scions of every important family of the South were trooping weekly through Richmond—all for her taking—she was simply overwhelmed. And now came perhaps the handsomest and most famous and eligible bachelor of them all, thirty-two-year-old Major General John Bell Hood, as deadly earnest about courting Buck Preston as he was about killing Yankees.

Trouble was, Buck couldn't make up her mind. As Mrs. Chesnut observed, "Buck, the very sweetest woman I ever knew, had a knack of being 'fallen in love with' at sight and never being 'fallen out of love with.' But then," she added ominously, "there seemed a spell upon her

lovers—so many were killed or died of the effects of their wounds,"
and she went on to enumerate five of Buck's fallen swains. One young
visitor to the Chesnuts was teased about whether he was courting Buck.
"I would rather face a Yankee battery," he said, declaring that whoever
fell in love with her, "You will see his name next in the list of killed and
wounded." The statement turned out to be prophetic.

The next fateful battle in the east found Hood away from the army. Lee
had sent Longstreet's corps south of Richmond to scrounge up food and
forage when yet another Union commander—this time "Fighting Joe"
Hooker—was appointed by the Lincoln administration. Hooker quickly
attempted to get around Lee's flank near the village of Chancellorsville,
but the effort came to naught when Lee—with only half his army present—intercepted and routed him using the now legendary Jackson to
sneak around and attack him from the flank. Here though, the Confederates were deprived of their ablest field commander when Jackson was
accidentally shot down in the dark by his own men. Hood, who had
tried to model himself in Jackson's style, was deeply distressed at the
news of the death and wrote so to Lee, who responded with a long letter
that pierced the core of the Confederacy's military dilemma in 1863 and
on to the end of the war: "I agree with you also in believing that our
Army would be invincible if it could be properly organized and officered. There never were such men in an Army before. They will go any-
where and do anything if properly led. But there is the difficulty—
proper commanders—where can they be obtained?"

The pain and worry in Lee's tone was inescapable. It wasn't the
loss of Jackson alone; every battle seemed to take a heavy toll on experienced, high-caliber officers both in Lee's army and in the Confederate
forces in the west. Colonels commanding regiments were shot down
before they could make brigadier, brigadiers were lost before they got
division command, and so on. Of the 425 men who reached the grade of
general in the Confederate army, 77 were killed in battle and a far larger
number wounded. By comparison, of the 583 individuals who served as
generals in the Union army, only 47 were killed—18 percent and 8 per-

cent, respectively. Two years into the war, the success of the Confederacy was largely due to the leadership of its officer corps, which was taught, à la Napoleon, to lead *par exemple,* thus exposing them to great dangers in combat. The simple fact was that the Confederacy was running out of good officer material, and Lee—and, presumably, Hood—knew it and deplored it.

In any event, huddled in winter quarters during the cold months of 1862–63, Hood—when he was not in Richmond courting Buck—was preparing for the big spring and summer campaign, which would take them north through Maryland and on up to the sleepy town of Gettysburg, Pennsylvania.

Hood recorded that his division during this time was in "splendid condition." Lee was in search of a big victory, badly needed, one that he hoped would cut the war short. His opponent this time was General George Meade, who replaced the hapless "Fighting Joe" Hooker after his debacle at Chancellorsville. All through June the Army of Northern Virginia advanced through the Valley of the Shenandoah, then crossed the Potomac, and was making its way toward Harrisburg, Pennsylvania, when it was intercepted, almost by accident, at Gettysburg on the 1st of July, 1863. A division had detoured into the town to visit a shoe factory they heard was there and found, instead, part of the federal army.

Most of Lee's army, including Hood's division, did not arrive on the field until late in the night or the following morning. Hood recorded that he got there about daybreak. The previous day's battle had seen the Union infantry shoved back by the Confederates through the town and up onto a rocky north-south eminence ominously called Cemetery Ridge, where they entrenched and braced for an attack. Lee's forces were spread out opposite in what has been called a "fish hook," with the shank at the southern end and the barb twisting around the town of Gettysburg to the north. Hood's division occupied the end of the Confederate line—the eye of the fish hook—on the extreme left flank of the federal forces. That flank was anchored by a black rock-faced mountain, several hundred feet high, known as Little Round Top.

Lee was determined to attack Meade there and then, despite Longstreet's plea to wait for the division of General George Pickett to arrive on the field. "I do not like to go into battle with one boot off," Longstreet remarked to Hood, but Lee had already told Hood, "The enemy is here and if we do not whip him, he will whip us." And so the fate was sealed.

The plan that day was that General Richard S. Ewell, who had replaced Jackson as Second Corps commander, would open a demonstration to the north near the barb of the fish hook. The newly formed Third Corps, under General A. P. Hill, would hold the center but not attack. The big show fell on Longstreet's First Corps, which was to move in line opposite the federals at the southern end of the hook, then attack *en echelon,* obliquely from south to north—by brigades and divisions—sweeping up the Emmitsburg Road, which ran alongside Cemetery Ridge, in front of the federals and driving them back on themselves. It was a very complicated scheme of battle, for it required supreme coordination to maneuver twenty thousand men in twelve brigades to a timed objective—gathering strength as they came along like an avalanche—and of course the forty thousand federals in that part of the line would not just be sitting there watching them. Longstreet, unhappy with the arrangement and said to be in a sulk, moved his corps ponderously all that morning and most of the afternoon, placing Hood's division, and that of Lafayette McLaws, in their jump-off positions.

Hood occupied the southernmost flank of the Confederate line. Just before he reached position astride the Emmitsburg Road, he sent scouts to find out just how far the federal left flank to his front extended. He was astonished to learn that it extended no farther than Round Top, and that by simply marching around to the southeast behind Round Top he could "assault the enemy in flank and rear" and also overwhelm all the Union wagon trains, which were parked there. It seemed to Hood an imminently more sensible design than the one Lee had concocted— namely attacking north along the Emmitsburg Road, where his men would be exposed to fire not only from their front, but from their flank and rear as well as they passed across the federal front.

Hood dispatched a messenger to Longstreet to offer this suggestion. Longstreet said No. "General Lee's orders are to attack up the Emmitsburg Pike," he told the messenger, who galloped off to deliver it to Hood, who, meantime, had opened up with his artillery batteries on the federals opposite him. Hood then sent a second request to Longstreet, asking that the attack be suspended and that he be allowed to move around the federal flank. He told Longstreet that he "feared nothing could be accomplished by an attack." Again Longstreet sent the reply, "General Lee's orders are to attack up the Emmitsburg Road." In urgent frustration, Hood sent Longstreet a third request to call off the attack and suggested that the corps commander come up and look for himself. But the answer from Longstreet came back as before, "General Lee's orders are to attack up the Emmitsburg Road." Hood had just digested this bad news when a colonel on Longstreet's staff galloped up and personally repeated the instructions. Hood threw up his hands and gave the order to attack. As his brigades were moving out, Longstreet himself appeared on the scene, whereupon Hood reiterated to him his fears that the attack as planned was doomed. Again he asked to be allowed to turn the flank at Round Top, and again, for a final time, the answer was No. "We must obey the orders of General Lee," Longstreet declared, and so Hood went riding off into the smoke and dust of battle after his troops.

Hood's attack did not explicitly follow the plan that Lee had ordered, anyway; most of the division, rather than moving obliquely up the road, wound up attacking easterly to get at the Union infantry occupying an unholy spot of rock and boulders known as the Devil's Den. Hood himself had ridden on northward to a peach orchard, where, about twenty minutes into the fight, as he recollected it, he was shot down by a shell fragment that shattered his left arm; he was carried off on a stretcher. The rest, of course, is history. Longstreet's three-hour assault that day shoved the federals back, but it was confused and poorly executed and failed to rout them. Next morning, having tested the Union right the first day and its left the second, Lee decided he would now try to break its center. To this end he summoned General George Pickett and ordered him to lead an attack of some twelve thousand men on July 3, which resulted in the disaster of Pickett's Charge and the Confederate defeat at Gettysburg.

Hood rode the two hundred miles back to the Shenandoah Valley

in an ambulance with wounded General Wade Hampton. It was an ex-
cruciating journey. The doctors had managed to save his arm, but
barely, and it would be withered and worthless to him from then on.
Hampton, Hood recalled, "was so badly wounded he was unable to sit
up, whereas I could not sit down." The price the Confederacy paid at
Gettysburg was dear indeed: seventeen of the fifty-two generals present
were casualties, five killed and the others wounded or captured, including the indomitable Barksdale who had offered Lee "a bridge of dead
Yankees" back at Fredericksburg. Eighteen colonels were killed or captured, and in excess of twenty-five thousand Confederate troops had
become casualties. Union casualties were almost as high, except for the
generals. Colonel Arthur Fremantle, a British officer of the famous
Coldstream Guards who had been sent to observe the Confederate army
and who was present at Gettysburg, said to his companions, "Don't you
see your system feeds upon itself? You cannot fill the places of these
men. Your troops do wonders, but every time at a cost you cannot afford." Fremantle summed up by praising the spirit of Lee's army at
Gettysburg. "But," he added, "they will never do it again." In this
prediction he was sadly mistaken.

Hood's wound was tended at Staunton and then at Charlottesville,
and, finally, in August he was moved to Richmond, where undoubtedly
he resumed his courtship of Buck Preston and also was reported to have
criticized Lee's action at Gettysburg. At about that time it had been decided to hurry most of Longstreet's corps by rail out west near the Ten-
nessee-Georgia border to counter the threat posed to General Braxton
Bragg's Army of Tennessee by the federal general William S. Rosecrans,
who was massing large numbers of Union troops near Chattanooga for a
push on Atlanta. In the second week of September, Hood's veteran division moved through Richmond to board the train in its circuitous passage into northern Georgia, and Hood, "but partially recovered,"
could not restrain himself from "[placing his] horse upon the train and
following in their wake."

Rosecrans had nearly made a fatal mistake in dividing his army into
three wings and marching them southeast out of Chattanooga around
the ends and through the gaps of the Lookout Mountain massif that

stretched nearly forty miles across the triangle that connected the Ten-
nessee-Alabama-Georgia border. What it meant was that each of Rosecrans's wings was nearly twenty miles from the next—more than a
day's march away—and thus none would be able to come to the support
of the others. When Bragg learned of this obvious tactical blunder, he
gleefully determined to lay a trap for one of the divided wings and crush
it with two-to-one odds. The wing he first selected belonged to General
George Thomas, coming down in the center of the federal formation
through a gap smack in the middle of Lookout Mountain. Next, Bragg
schemed to turn on one of the other two Union wings and administer
the same treatment. Perhaps never in the war so far had the Confederates had such an opportunity—the virtual destruction of a Union
army—with numerical odds for once favorable to themselves.

But it was not to be. Indecisiveness, confusion, and, above all,
delays by Southern divisional commanders alerted Thomas to the peril,
and before the trap could be sprung, the federal general withdrew his
corps to a strong position in the rugged mountainous country where the
Confederates could not immediately get at him. A similar attempt to
ambush the northernmost Union column also failed, for the same reasons, and by September 17, 1863, the three federal wings had converged in the foothills of the mountains near a blackwater creek in
northern Georgia called Chickamauga, which in the Cherokee tongue
meant "river of death." With their backs to the river of death and the
entire federal army of sixty-five thousand in front of them, Bragg's
Army of Tennessee nevertheless enjoyed the knowledge that its own
forces totaled about the same number as the enemy's—a rare occasion.
Fighting began to break out down the line the following day.

Meantime, Hood arrived on the battlefield. According to his memoirs, he mounted his big roan, called Jeff Davis, in the boxcar and, with
his mangled arm in a sling, "had [his] horse to leap from the train," and
joined his division already in action. Bragg gave Hood command of the
forces in the Confederate center—nearly a full corps. Night ended that
day's fight, and by sunup next morning, Bragg was ready to begin the
assault he believed would grind up Rosecrans. Again, it was not to be—
not that day at least. The same sort of confusion and poor intelligence

that had marred the plan to trap Thomas now infected the Army of Tennessee at Chickamauga. Believing that he had located a flank of Rosecrans's army, Bragg ordered an attack, only to find that it was not the flank at all, and his troops were in danger of annihilation. He withdrew from that situation, but basically the fight had gotten out of his control—it was simply soldiers versus soldiers in a melee of murdering in the tangled Chickamauga thickets. Night closed on the field without much of anything being accomplished on either side.

Next morning, September 20—a Sunday—Bragg ordered a big dawn attack by the right wing of his army, commanded by Bishop Polk, but the sun was four hours high in the sky before the movement got underway. As soon as Polk's five divisions were thrown into the fight, Bragg ordered his left wing into the fray. These men, under the overall command of Longstreet but led on the field by Hood, smashed into the federal center and splintered it. In the midst of this, about noon, Hood dashed to the head of the smoke-hazy battlefield to realign one of his divisions that had gotten at angles with the federals in their front. This done, he watched with grim satisfaction as his men rushed forward to roll over the Union breastworks, killing and scattering foe and capturing prisoners. While he watched, a bullet shattered the thigh of his right leg, and, reeling in shock, he fell—"strange to say, since I was commanding five divisions—into the arms of some of the troops of my old brigade, which I had directed so long a period, and upon so many fields of battle."

Thus ended Hood's part in the battle of Chickamauga, but he got much if not most of the credit for its success. "Go ahead, and keep ahead of everything," were his final instructions to his staff as stretcher bearers arrived to carry him off the field. In the hospital, surgeons were not sure his life could be saved, let alone his mutilated leg; they amputated at upper thigh, leaving a stump of only a few inches. Newspaper reports quickly circulated that Hood was dead. Friends of the fallen general began to grieve—including Robert E. Lee—but a few days later dispatches were received that he was alive and recuperating at the home of one of his divisional colonels in the Armuchee Valley about fifteen miles from the battlefield.

Meanwhile, Bragg's Confederates had driven Rosecrans from the field and won the most important victory in the history of the Army of Tennessee. Unfortunately, Bragg failed to capitalize on it by thoroughly destroying Rosecrans's army, a failure due in no small measure to the stubborn action of Union general "Pap" Thomas, Hood's old West Point instructor and formerly his superior officer in the Second Cavalry, who refused to retreat in confusion like everybody else and held up the Confederates enough to earn himself the nickname, "The Rock of Chickamauga." It would not be long before Hood would face Thomas again, this time in a dead earnest death-lock at Nashville.

3

★ Crazy Like a Fox

Just a couple of years earlier they were calling "Cump" Sherman crazy. In fact, in the autumn of 1861 the War Department had relieved him of his duties as head of the military department of the Cumberland at Louisville, Kentucky, and sent him home on sick leave for what in those days would have been called a nervous breakdown. Naturally, the newspapers had a field day, declaring that Sherman was "insane" and "stark mad." Mostly, his crime was that he had told the truth, but with his distracting personal habits of fidgeting and nervousness, the truth got blown out of proportion. What Sherman had done wrong, among other things, was to inform the secretary of war that it was going to take two hundred thousand Union soldiers to beat the Confederacy *just* in the Mississippi Valley. In 1861, who would have dreamed of such a thing? And so he was branded a nervous Nellie and a nut. But he hadn't been far from wrong; in fact, he was something of a visionary.

Before the outbreak of hostilities, Sherman was the superintendent of the Louisiana State Military Academy. On Christmas Eve, 1860, he was having dinner with one of his professors, David F. Boyd, a Virginian who taught languages. There was a knock at the door, and someone handed Sherman the mail, including a copy of the local newspaper announcing that South Carolina had just seceded from the Union. As Sherman read the passage containing the formal withdrawal language, he broke down and "cried like a little child," as Boyd recalled it, but as soon as he composed himself, he delivered a prophetic oratory to his astonished dinner guest: "You people of the South don't know what you are doing. This country will be drenched in blood, and God only knows how it will end!" Sherman went on to compare the resources of the North with those of the South, as well as the determination of the United States not to allow the Union to be broken, finally predicting to Boyd, "You are bound to fail. . . . If your people will but stop and think, they must see that in the end you will surely fail."

Nearly four years later, here was Sherman at the threshold of Atlanta: the right man in the right place at the right time, and with the very means to bring his prophecy true—namely, the Army of the Tennessee, one of the two most destructive military forces ever assembled on the planet (the other was with Grant, up around Richmond). Nobody was calling Cump Sherman crazy now.

William Tecumseh Sherman was born in Ohio in 1820, son of a state supreme court justice and prominent lawyer, but upon his father's death the family "became very poor," as Sherman remembered. He was happy to get an appointment to West Point in 1836, where, in 1840, he graduated sixth in his class. The tall, lanky, red-headed second lieutenant, barely twenty, was immediately shipped off to Florida to fight Seminole Indians who were refusing to join the "trail of tears" to the Oklahoma Indian Territory. Finishing his tour without killing any Indians, Sherman was relieved from Florida and, in an ironic but not unusual military fashion, was posted during the next several years to half a dozen Southern garrisons, which took him through practically every inch of the vast battleground over which he would lead the Army of the Tennessee twenty years down the road. As Sherman himself put it many years later, "The knowledge thus acquired was of infinite use to me. . . ."

In the summer of 1846 Sherman sailed around Cape Horn to California, stopping over in Rio de Janeiro, where he went to the opera;

Valparaiso, Chile, which did not impress him; and finally on to Monterey, the capital of what was then called Upper California. When Sherman arrived, the state was in a curious flux involving the Mexican War, the discovery of gold, and a local insurrection stemming from a dispute between Colonel John C. ("Pathfinder") Frémont and General Stephen Kearny. Typically, Sherman found himself embroiled in all these events. In 1850 he returned east long enough to marry Ellen Ewing, daughter of the secretary of the interior, in a fancy wedding attended by the president of the United States and practically every other political luminary of the day. In 1853 Sherman resigned from the army and began operating a bank, first in San Francisco and later in New York. Both failed, and he went to work for his brother-in-law's Kansas law firm as a bill collector. But that didn't work out either, and by 1859 he was so hard-pressed for money that he took the position of superintendent at the new Louisiana military academy, with fifty-six students and an annual salary of $3,500. Two years later, Civil War would change his fortunes forever.

Outside of Atlanta in July 1864, John Bell Hood did not wait long to validate General Schofield's prediction that he would hit Sherman "like hell," and he proposed to do it in such a way as to demonstrate his disdain for fighting behind breastworks. When Hood assumed command of the Army of Tennessee, it disgusted him that entrenching had become habit. Under Joe Johnston, every time the Confederates halted, they got out their spades and axes and constructed pits, trenches, and other earthworks, usually protected in front by an abatis of felled trees with sharpened stakes pointing toward the enemy. A proponent of the offensive, Hood deplored this practice because he thought it impaired the morale and fighting spirit of the men. "A soldier cannot fight for a period of one or two months constantly behind breastworks, with the training that he is equal to four or five of the enemy by reason of the security of his position, and then be expected to engage in pitched battle and prove as intrepid and impetuous as his brother, who had been taught to rely solely on his own valor."

He stated his case in a nutshell: He knew the Union army always dug entrenchments when they halted, but to attack those fortifications he would ideally have wished to lead men who had never served behind them.

Often recalling his experiences in the hallowed Army of Northern Virginia, where, he declared, breastworks were frowned on under Robert E. Lee, Hood probably would have been surprised to learn that in his absence from that army during the long recuperation from his amputation and his subsequent transfer to the Army of Tennessee, Lee's men had begun digging breastworks just like everybody else. In any case, from the moment he took command of the Army of Tennessee, Hood determined that his army was going to have to go on the offensive if it ever hoped to defeat the bluecoats and their overwhelming numbers, and he was resolute that his men must learn to get out from behind their breastworks and go on the attack, even if it killed them.

On July 20, 1864, little more than two days after taking command, Hood hurled two-thirds of his army at the right of Pap Thomas's fifty thousand spread-out federals, who were anchoring Sherman's right flank north of Atlanta, down by Peachtree Creek. The idea was to catch the bluecoats in motion up against the creek and destroy them before they could get back across. But something went wrong. First, the attack was delayed several hours for some unknown reason, and, when it was finally launched, Thomas was not exactly where he was supposed to be. By nightfall, the Confederates were back in their previous positions at a cost of five thousand men. Hood had gained nothing. This was the first of four attacks, or "sorties," that Hood would order to decide the battle of Atlanta; it was called the battle of Peachtree Creek.

Sherman, noting that Hood's attack "illustrated the future tactics of the enemy and put [us] on our guard," quickly closed up his lines, thus depriving the Confederates of similar opportunities in the future. Next day, Hood pulled his army back to a new, shorter line closer to the city and ordered Hardee's corps on a nightmare twelve-mile march south and then east, under cover of darkness, to come up on the Union left flank and launch a surprise dawn attack the following morning. It was a plan worthy of a Lee or a Stonewall Jackson, and, in fact, Hood, who had learned much under the tutelage of those two military novas,

practically copied the strategy from Jackson's famous sneak around
Hooker at Chancellorsville. But this assault also was delayed, and it was
not until noon that Hood heard the ferocious sounds of battle as the Confederates struck General James B. McPherson's Army of the Tennessee.

McPherson, commander of one of Sherman's three armies, himself
had been conferring with Sherman back at an old house he was using for
headquarters when the fighting broke out. He immediately excused
himself and galloped back toward his position. Only a few minutes later,
Sherman recalled, "One of McPherson's staff, with his horse covered
with sweat, dashed up to the porch and reported that General McPherson—
Hood's friend and West Point classmate—was either 'killed or a prisoner.'"
Within the hour the former proved true, and the body of the handsome
and popular young commander was brought back to Sherman's headquarters and laid out on a door someone had taken off its hinges. Riding
accidentally into a Confederate position in some woods, McPherson had
been ordered to surrender, but he cavalierly tipped his hat and dashed
away at a gallop, only to be shot down.

All that sweltering July 22 afternoon—in what is usually called the
battle of Atlanta—the Southerners hurled themselves at Sherman's
men, in some cases overrunning their positions and capturing prisoners,
flags, artillery, and the like. At midpoint Hood threw his old corps,
temporarily under command of General Benjamin Franklin Cheatham,
into the fight. Tennessee Private Sam Watkins remembered that the
roar of battle "sounded like unbottled thunder." Watkins's regiment
was one of the few that actually took some federal breastworks, but
soon the Union artillery was opened up on them. Watkins had taken refuge in a federal trench when he said, "A cannon ball came tearing down
the works, cutting a soldier's head off, spattering his brains all over my
face. . . ." The attack nearly accomplished Hood's designs, but nearly
was not good enough. By dark the result was about the same as it had
been two days earlier—nothing much accomplished except the loss of
nearly eight thousand men and possibly revenge for the killing of Bishop
Polk a month earlier, although Hood remarked of McPherson's death,
"No soldier fell in the enemy's ranks, whose loss caused me equal
regret."

From the 22nd to the 27th of July things were fairly quiet on all fronts, except for the incessant skirmishing and sniping between the lines. But then Hood detected that Sherman was moving large bodies of infantry around by his right flank; it was the very plan Sherman had been discussing with McPherson the day he was killed. So Hood conformed to the Union movements by making shifts to the left, quickly realizing that Sherman's objective was to sever the last of four rail lines connecting Atlanta with the rest of the Confederacy.

Following McPherson's death, the Army of the Tennessee had passed into the hands of General O. O. Howard, a one-armed, thirty-two-year-old West Point graduate, and it was this army Sherman had sent sidling around counterclockwise to get at the Macon Railroad. To frustrate that attempt, Hood dispatched again his old corps, now under the command of the newly arrived thirty-year-old General Stephen Dill Lee, who had superseded Cheatham. Lee's orders were to get into position to block Howard's advance and wait for A. P. Stewart's corps to come up that night and smash into the unsuspecting federal flank first thing in the morning. Like the maneuvering of July 22, Hood's was a daring, even brilliant plan, but when Lee found Howard near a meeting house called Ezra Church, instead of setting up to block him as he'd been told, Lee pitched into him, and a savage battle commenced. One private, noting the stretcher bearers shuttling back and forth, remarked, "Their litters . . . were as bloody as if hogs had been stuck on them." Before the afternoon was over, Stewart's corps had been sucked into the fray, and, again, the result of half a dozen brave charges and equally brave repulses was not much more than a body count, this time about twenty-five hundred Confederates, compared with seven hundred federals. The battle of Ezra Church marked the end of Hood's third sortie.

Nearly exhausted, Hood and his army retired to their entrenchments around the city to await developments. He had attacked Sherman north, east, and west and failed to break him. Even attack-minded Jefferson Davis, appalled at the nearly fifteen thousand casualties since Hood had taken command, wired the Confederate general, "The loss consequent upon attacking the enemy in his entrenchments requires you to avoid that if practicable." For the next few weeks things quieted down again, or would have, except that Sherman had sent away to Chattanooga for some huge siege guns, and these he set to shelling Atlanta's business and residential districts, terrorizing and, in many cases, killing and maiming the citizens. He seemed to delight in this activity, reporting to Washington, "We can pick out almost any house in town," and urging the newcomer Howard, "Let us destroy Atlanta, and make it a desolation." But eventually Sherman tired of the inactivity and idleness that affected everyone but the artillerymen. He had sent his cavalry on several missions to destroy the railroads, and they had failed miserably each time—in one case an entire brigade was captured, and its commander General George Stoneman thrown into a Confederate prison camp. Sherman continued to be galled as fat Confederate supply trains chugged into the Atlanta depot every morning; finally, he determined to re-employ his infantry and "proceed to the execution of my original plan."

Meantime, Hood began to realize that in his present posture he was just waiting for the other shoe to drop. After the grand successes of Wheeler's cavalry against Sherman's, he concluded that the Union horse troopers no longer posed a threat to him and so decided to send Wheeler's five thousand troops to the north to break up Sherman's railroads and communications and force him to retreat for lack of supplies. For nearly a month Wheeler's men operated behind Sherman's lines from Atlanta nearly to Nashville, smashing track, exploding bridges, stealing cows, raiding supply cars, knocking down telegraph poles, and generally creating a lot of havoc. But Sherman's repairmen stayed on the job, and about as quickly as Wheeler destroyed something, the federals patched it up again. As Sherman watched his own bulging rail cars arrive intermittently from Tennessee, he concluded that Wheeler's cavalry—and, for that matter, any cavalry, including his own—"could not or would not work hard enough to disable a railroad properly."

As the month of August opened hot and sultry, Sherman wired the War Department, "We keep hammering away all the time, and there is no peace, inside or outside of Atlanta," adding that he was "too impatient for a siege." He took his time, however, preparing "the execution of his original plan." By the 26th he was ready, and the astonished

Confederates next morning reported that "the Yankees were gone." There was great rejoicing in Atlanta, and, according to Sherman himself, "Several trains of cars (with ladies) came up from Macon to assist in the celebration of their grand Victory." The people of Atlanta could scarcely believe it as they emerged that morning from their dark basements and bomb-proof dugouts into the steamy sunlight to hear the pealing of church bells. It was the first quiet day in weeks, after a bombardment that had reduced much of the city to rubble. Some residents and soldiers timidly wandered out to the old federal lines and began picking up souvenirs—discarded cookwear, furniture, clothing, and other things Sherman's men had left behind. In Atlanta itself, there was jubilation; bands played in the streets, and people began congratulating each other on their deliverance.

Sherman had "gone," but not far. Strangely, it took Hood two days to figure that out. Sherman had ordered Thomas's Army of the Cumberland and Howard's Army of the Tennessee to fall back from their positions and, pivoting on Schofield's Army of the Ohio, begin a great "left wheel" the following day, aimed directly at the Macon Railroad, south of town. This irresistible force pounced on a section of the line on the 29th and thoroughly wrecked it. As Sherman's three armies continued their deliberate hook around the Confederate left flank, Hood ordered Hardee to rush his corps down to Jonesboro, with Lee's corps following, and attack at first light on the 31st. But again, as in two of the other three sorties, tardiness ruined the plan. Somewhere between, "I told him to do it," and, "I ordered it done," Hardee didn't get off his attack until 2 P.M., which meant, Hood bitterly recalled, "The Federals had been allowed time, by the delay, to strongly entrench." Moreover, in exercise of a mentality later exhibited by French generals in the First World War, Hood complained that Hardee's assault "must have been rather feeble," since his casualties were comparatively small in relation to the forces engaged. In any case, Sherman now had control of the Macon Railroad, and Hood knew Atlanta was doomed. What remained was to try to save his army.

The night of September 2, Sherman, at the head of his column near Jonesboro, said he "was so restless and impatient" that he could not sleep and round about midnight was startled by a series of stupendous explosions that lit the sky and trembled the earth from the direction of Atlanta, twenty miles away. At first he worried that the Confederate's main force was overrunning General Henry W. Slocum's corps, which he had left behind and directed to "feel forward to Atlanta." But next morning he learned to his delight that Hood had evacuated Atlanta and had ordered eighty-one rail cars of high explosives torched off to keep them from falling into Union hands. The jubilant Sherman wired Washington, "Atlanta is ours, and fairly won."

Fairly won it might have been, but not without its price. In the hundred days since the campaign had begun, the butcher's bill paid by Sherman was 31,687 men; by the Confederates 34,979—nearly 20,000 in the month and a half that Hood had held command.

As best he could, Hood began gathering his battered army near Jonesboro, either to make a last stand, or in the event of a miracle, to find some way to defeat Sherman if he attacked him. Sherman had no intention of attacking him, however. Instead, he ordered his three armies to march away from Hood's front and go back to Atlanta for some well-deserved rest. In any other circumstances that would have infuriated Washington—since Sherman's principal task had been to destroy the Army of Tennessee—except that the news of the capture of Atlanta was greeted with such a sigh of relief by Republicans that nobody was about to complain.

It has been written that Lincoln's election in 1860 was "an appeal to arms," and thus the presidential election of 1864 was "to determine whether the appeal should be sustained or denied." Two days before Sherman captured Atlanta the Democrats nominated George McClellan on a peace platform, and practically nobody would have bet a plug nickel on Lincoln's chances of being reelected. Now, in an ironic twist—ironic because Sherman loathed politics and disagreed with Lincoln's abolishing slavery—the conqueror of Vicksburg and Atlanta had done more to change the face of American politics that year than any man alive.

It wasn't long before Sherman began concentrating on his proposition to make Atlanta "a desolation." Upon entering the city on September 7, he was greeted by a committee, including the mayor, who pleaded for protection of the citizens and their property, but Sherman had already decided otherwise. "I . . . at once set about a measure already ordered, of which I had thought much and long, viz., to remove the entire civil population." And he didn't care what anybody thought about it; as early as September 4, he had declared, "If the people raise a howl against my barbarity and cruelty, I will answer that war is war, and not popularity seeking. If they want peace, they and their relatives must stop the war."

Sherman forthwith sent a letter to Hood, communicating his plan and suggesting that the two sides call a truce to facilitate the expulsion of the people of Atlanta. Frustrated and enraged, Hood replied, "I don't consider that I have any alternative in this matter . . . the unprecedented measure you propose transcends, in studied and ingenious cruelty, all acts ever before brought to my attention in the dark history of war. In the name of God and humanity, I protest, believing that you will find that you are expelling from their homes and firesides, the wives and children of a brave people."

This response seems to have touched off something in Sherman— apparently he had much to get off his chest—and thus commenced one of the most extraordinary correspondences of the war. Sherman fired off his reply to Hood next day. Blaming Hood for the destruction of Atlanta for making his lines too close to the city, Sherman told him it was "a kindness to these families of Atlanta to remove them now, at once, from scenes that woman and children should not be exposed to." He went on to accuse General Johnston of expelling Southerners from their homes when his army approached, and justified his action on that ground. And then he let loose his spleen:

> In the name of common sense, I ask you not to appeal to a just God in such a sacrilegious manner. You who, in the midst of peace and prosperity, have plunged a nation into war—dark and cruel war—who dared and badgered us to battle, insulted our flag, seized our arsenals and forts that were left in the honorable custody of peaceful ordnance-sergeants, seized and made "prisoners of war" the

very garrisons sent to protect your people against negroes and Indians, long before any overt act was committed by the (to you) hated Lincoln Government; tried to force Kentucky and Missouri into rebellion, in spite of themselves; falsified the vote of Louisiana, turned loose your privateers to plunder unarmed ships, expelled Union families by the thousands, burned their houses, and declared, by an act of your Congress, the confiscation of all debts due Northern men for goods had and received. Talk thus to the Marines, but not to me, who have seen these things.

Having said all that, Sherman challenged, "If we must be enemies, let us be men, and fight it out as we propose to do, and not deal in such hypocritical appeals to God and humanity."

For a moment, it might have seemed to Hood that Sherman was putting the blame on him personally for the entire war, as well as calling him a sacrilegious hypocrite. He never recorded his reaction to Sherman's letter, but it must have been considerable because it took him two days to write back. His reply speaks for itself: "I see nothing in your communication which induces me to modify the language of condemnation with which I characterized your order. It but strengthens me in the opinion that it stands preeminent in the dark history of war for studied and ingenious cruelty." Hood bitterly defended Johnston, saying that he "depopulated not villages, nor town, or cities, either friendly or hostile . . . [but] offered and extended friendly aid to his unfortunate fellow-citizens who desired to flee from your fraternal embrace." He went on to say, "I made no complaint of your firing into Atlanta in any way you thought proper. I make none now, but there are a hundred-thousand witnesses that you fired into the habitations of women and children for weeks." Then he undertook to rebut Sherman point for point:

You charge my country with "daring and badgering you to battle." The truth is, we sent commissioners to you, respectfully offering a peaceful separation, before the first gun was fired on either side. You say we insulted your flag. The truth is, we fired upon it, and those who fought under it, when you came to our doors upon the mission of subjugation. You say we seized upon your forts and arsenals, and made prisoners of the garrisons sent to protect us against negroes and Indians. The truth is, we, by force of arms, drove out insolent intruders and took possession of our own forts and arsenals, to resist your claims of dominion over masters, slaves, and Indians, all of whom are to this day, with a unanimity unexampled in the history of the world, warring against your attempts to become their masters.

And he continued, like a lawyer making the summation of his career:

You say we falsified the vote of Louisiana. The truth is, Louisiana not only separated herself from your government by a unanimous vote of her people, but has vindicated the act upon every battle-field from Gettysburg to the Sabine. . . . You say that we turned loose pirates to plunder your unarmed ships. The truth is, when you robbed us of our part of the navy, we built and bought a few vessels, hoisted the flag of our country, and swept the seas, in defiance of your navy. . . . You say we have expelled Union families by the thousands. The truth is, not a single family has been expelled from the Confederate States that I am aware of. . . .

And so on and so on. Hood was really on his soapbox; it was almost as if, in his frustration at losing the battle to Sherman, Hood felt compelled to whip him on paper—the pen over the sword:

You order into exile the whole population of a city, drive men, women, and children from their homes at the point of a bayonet . . . and add insult to the injury heaped upon the defenseless by assuming that you have done them a kindness . . . and, because I characterize what you call a kindness as being real cruelty, you presume to sit in judgement between me and my God. . . . You came into our country with your army, avowedly for the purpose of subjugating free white men, women and children, and not only intend to rule over them, but you make negroes your allies, and desire to place over us an inferior race, which we have raised from barbarism to its present position, which is the highest ever attained by that race, in any country, in all time.

Hood closed with a flourish: "You say, let us fight it out like men. To this I reply—for myself, and I believe for all the true men, ay, and women and children in my country—we will fight you to the death! Better die a thousand deaths than to submit to live under you and your negro allies!"

Sherman digested all this and penned a curt reply: "We have no 'negro allies' in this army; not a single negro soldier left Chattanooga with this army, or is with it now. There are a few guarding Chattanooga, which General Steedman sent at one time to drive Wheeler out of Dalton." Calling further correspondence "profitless and out of place," Sherman couldn't resist accusing Hood of starting the whole controversy in the first place "by characterizing an official order of mine in unfair and improper terms."

What this remarkable exchange between two army commanders had to say about the war at this point—four long "dark and cruel" years into it—would prove extremely telling in the months to come. Hood was whipped, his army was whipped, and Atlanta was lost, or "fairly won," according to Sherman; yet there was no hint of any middle ground. All between them was defiance and finger pointing over who had started the war and why—the old arguments and recriminations. In any case, whipped or not, Hood still had enough fight left in him to tell off his conqueror, and—as time would tell—he wasn't kidding about the pledge he laid down to "fight you to the death."

4

This Army Is Going to Do ★ Something Wrong

"On that day, peace waved those little white wings and fled to the ends of the morning."

So wailed the Richmond *Examiner* about the fall of Atlanta. For all the rejoicing up North, the Confederacy spent its energy in despair; prices had soared—butter was $2 and $3 a pound, pantaloons were selling for $40, flour was $50 a barrel. Lee, like Hood, was besieged before one of the last crucial cities of the South. There were unsettling rumors in Richmond that Governor Brown of Georgia was about to make a separate peace with Sherman to save his state. The Confederacy was on the verge of unraveling, but Jefferson Davis did not see it that way. On September 21, three weeks after Atlanta was lost, he boarded a train bound for the new end-of-the-line at Jonesboro to see personally about Hood and his Army of Tennessee.

Meantime, Hood was not exactly inert. Immediately after the expiration of the truce with Sherman to secure the ejection of Atlanta's civilians, he began to move his army westward. By September 21 he had established a new base at Palmetto, Georgia, about twenty miles due west from Jonesboro. From there his plan was to move north with the whole army, instead of trusting the job to cavalry alone, and cut off Sherman's supply lines to Chattanooga and Nashville. There was good logic to this. First, he realized that it would be futile to again attack the army that had just beaten him. That issue had been settled. Second, if he could wreck Sherman's supply lines, in a matter of days the Union army would be starving in Atlanta, and the federal commander would have no choice but to either go after Hood or march off someplace else, probably to the south, to find food and supplies—in which case Hood planned to fall upon his exposed rear and grind him up. At least that was the plan when Jefferson Davis arrived at Palmetto at 3:30 on a wet and stormy Sunday afternoon, September 25, 1864.

According to Sherman's intelligence reports—for he had got hold of newspaper accounts of Davis's stopover appearance at Macon—the Confederate president was "perfectly upset" by the fall of Atlanta.

Sherman crowed that Davis had told the crowds "that now the tables would be turned; that General Forrest was already on our roads in Middle Tennessee; that Hood's army would soon be there. He asserted that the Yankee army would have to retreat or starve, and that the retreat would prove more disastrous than was that of Napoleon from Moscow. . . . He made no concealment of these vainglorious boasts, and thus gave us the key to his future designs. To be forewarned was to be forearmed, and I think we took full advantage of the occasion." When Sherman reported all this to Grant, the taciturn commander in chief at first didn't believe that Jefferson Davis was that far down south, but after Sherman wired him a printed copy of Davis's Macon speech, Grant mused over "who would furnish the snow for this Moscow retreat?"

In any case, Sherman already knew from his own army's solemn telegraphic reports from up north that Forrest was "on our roads in Middle Tennessee," and he soon dispatched General Thomas to Nashville, along with two divisions, to "meet the danger." Also, he requested that Washington send to Nashville all available troops in the western theater, which Grant agreed to in a wire on September 27.

What Hood was up to was another matter. "I could not get spies to penetrate his camps," Sherman complained. (In the mountain regions of Tennessee and north Georgia there were usually a few Union sympathizers whom federal commanders could employ as spies, but on the flat plains around Atlanta, a hotbed of the Confederacy, Union sympathizers were fewer and farther between.) It wasn't long, however, before Sherman found out anyway.

When Jefferson Davis stepped off the train that rainy sabbath, Tennesseans from Frank Cheatham's division were there to meet him. The ramrod-stiff president stepped out on the station platform and told them, "Be of good cheer, for within a short while your faces will be turned homeward and your feet pressing the soil of Tennessee." Whatever military plan Davis had in mind just then, it seemed a pretty wide extension of Hood's proposal merely to operate in Sherman's rear. But in any case, Davis had other matters to attend to first:

High on the list was what to do about General Hardee, who had asked to be relieved when Hood was promoted. Now it was Hood who wanted him gone. In three of Hood's four battles for Atlanta, Hardee had been in command; in all three he had been tardy in executing his attacks, and Hood privately blamed him for the defeats. If Hood was to stay, Hardee himself wanted out, he told the Confederate president. Davis promptly relieved him and sent him to South Carolina; Frank Cheatham was given permanent command of Hardee's corps. Next, Davis told Hood he intended to bring in General Pierre Gustave Toutant Beauregard, former commander of the Army of Tennessee, to take charge of a new "Military Division of the West, containing everything from Georgia to the Mississippi River. Nominally, Beauregard was to be Hood's superior, but as it worked out, he became not much more than a sort of glorified military advisor.

That settled, Davis turned to the paramount question at hand, which, as one veteran later put it, was, "What in hell would we do next?" The president was in accord with Hood that Sherman's supply lines must be cut, forcing him out of Atlanta one way or another. Later, Davis said he told Hood the most important thing was to force Sherman into a battle and annihilate him, whether Sherman followed him up north or started out in some other direction. To accomplish that, Hood said Davis promised him some fifteen to twenty thousand troops from General Kirby Smith's command across the Mississippi. That said, Davis boarded the train for other points and other speeches, including a well-attended one at Augusta, where he again pledged, "We must march into Tennessee . . . and push . . . the enemy back to the banks of the Ohio.'' Exactly what was agreed by Davis and Hood in their secret meetings is not known—Davis's constant emphasis on taking the army back to Tennessee did not exactly square with what he said later about annihilating Sherman's army—but it would become the subject of dire recriminations in the years ahead. And *dire* was also the word for the Confederate situation at this point, dire all the way around but for one amusing episode recalled by Captain Samuel Foster of General Hiram Granbury's Texas brigade in Patrick Cleburne's division.

It seemed that after Davis and Hood finished making their momentous decisions, the Army of Tennessee was lined up for a review, and some of the president's political entourage, their podium lighted by pine torches, were making speeches, including former Texas governor F. R. Lubbock, who, as Foster recorded in his diary, ''naturally supposing that the Texas soldiers would be glad to see him, thought he would take this occasion to introduce himself and we would give him a grand cheer.'' By mistake, Foster said, ''He stopped in front of an Irish Regiment just on our right before he got to us. Thinking he had found us, rode square up about the center, pulled off his hat and says, 'I'm Governor Lubbock of Texas,' and just when he expected to hear a big cheer, an Irishman says, 'an who the bloody Hell is govener Lubbock,' with that peculiar Irish brogue, that made the governor wilt. He turned his horse and galloped on to catch up with the President and party and passed by us without even looking at us.'' Humorous as this scene might have been, the grand review of the army did not come across as entirely satisfactory, and especially not for Hood in the presence of all the political luminaries of the Confederacy who had arrived with Davis. Some brigades, Hood glumly reported afterward, were ''seemingly dissatisfied, and inclined to cry out, 'give us General Johnston.' I regretted I should have been the cause of this uncourteous reception to His Excellency; at the same time, I could recall no offence save that of having insisted that they should fight for and hold Atlanta forty-six days, whereas they had previously retreated one hundred miles within sixty days.''

Whatever Davis thought of this he kept to himself and on the 27th departed, leaving the fortunes of the Army of Tennessee and, thus, the fortunes of the Confederacy, to remain in the hands of John Bell Hood—as well as with Beauregard, who was on his way to look into things and see what could be done.

Sherman, from his decidedly different point of view, had known for some time what had to be done—or at least what he wanted to do—but he was getting resistance from his Washington bosses about doing it.

Sherman knew that neither his nor Hood's army could afford to linger around Atlanta, panting and licking its wounds in the red Georgia dirt. So before the dust had settled over the battlefield he began to conceive a plan of operations so radical and daring it defied military sense as it was then practiced. What he proposed was to cut loose from Atlanta and, with two oversized corps totaling sixty-five thousand men, march off into enemy territory some three hundred miles across Georgia, to Savannah and the Atlantic Ocean. During this adventure, he would be completely severed from his supplies and communications along the rail lines that stretched back more than a thousand miles through Nashville, St. Louis, Cincinnati, and the rest of the huge Union army support network that had been amassing in the western theater for the past four years.

Actually, Sherman had begun to conceive of a grand march even before Atlanta fell. He realized, as he wrote later, "We could not afford to remain on the defensive, simply holding Atlanta and fighting for the safety of its railroad." Initially, though, his idea was to crash down through southwest Georgia and Alabama to capture Mobile, the last port on the Gulf of Mexico still open to the Confederates. But in the midst of the bitterest Atlanta battles, Admiral David G. Farragut and his ironclad armada "damned the torpedoes" at the head of Mobile Bay and seized control of the port. So Sherman began to work on another plan, this one even more audacious: He would take his army southeastward through Macon and Augusta to Savannah, where, presumably, it could be picked up by Union transport ships and moved north to reinforce Grant for the capture of Richmond.

But as his scheme began to evolve, there were doubters—Thomas, for one. Sherman and his senior general were spending a pleasant autumn evening at a house Thomas occupied on Atlanta's Marietta Street, "which had a veranda with high pillars," when Sherman discussed with him what he had in mind. The prudent Rock of Chickamauga warned Sherman against straying so far from his lines of supply, but Sherman was determined; as he wrote Washington, "If the North can march an army right through the South, it is proof positive that the North can prevail in this contest." In the back of his mind, however, Sherman was not so much enamored of tearing up railroad tracks and ruining Confederate military bases as he was of the psychological effect of such an expedition. People all over the North, and more especially the South, and even more especially Europe (which at that stage could still conceivably enter the conflict on the Confederate side), when confronted by this "proof positive," would realize that the game was up, he reasoned.

But it was not just doubting Thomas who was against the idea. Secretary of War Edwin Stanton was violently opposed, as was the irascible General Henry Halleck, powerful military advisor to Lincoln and the War Department. At this stage, Grant was not too keen on it, either, and Grant's forceful chief of staff and alter ego John A. Rawlins was positively horrified at the idea. All these men saw dangers in addition to marching the Army of the Tennessee into the unknown; there was also the problem of Hood. How, they asked, could Sherman leave the Confederate army free to roam about at will, gobbling up hard-won Union garrisons in Tennessee or even Kentucky and possibly as far as St. Louis or Chicago? Sherman thought he had answered that question by deciding to send Thomas to Nashville and reinforce him with troops from all over the west. In any case, letters and wires raced back and forth from Atlanta to Washington, but nothing was resolved because at this point nobody knew what Hood was going to do. Except Hood.

In the weeks between his defeat at Atlanta and the arrival of Jefferson Davis for the Palmetto council of war, Hood had managed to strengthen the Army of Tennessee to a respectable 44,403 by the return of exchanged prisoners, recuperated wounded, rounded-up awols, and new recruits. On the day after Davis's departure, Hood issued orders that put the army on the move again.

At three different places along the Chattahoochee River, long columns of gray-and butternut-clad Confederates crossed to the northern bank on pontoon bridges. Captain Sam Foster, relater of the Governor Lubbock fiasco, had this to say in his diary: "Had orders last night to cook up three days rations—which kept the cooking business going all night—this army is going to do something wrong—or rather it will undertake something that will not be a success." Foster went on to defend his grave prediction by correlating Jefferson Davis's previous visits to the Army of Tennessee with its failures immediately thereafter. Twice Davis had visited, and twice they were beaten. "Now, after all that experience," Foster gloomily recorded, "he comes here just after the fall of Atlanta to concoct some other plan for our defeat. . . ."

Be that as it was, on the morning of October 1, Confederate Brigadier General William H. ("Red") Jackson, commanding the remainder of the cavalry that Wheeler had left behind when he went north to Tennessee, pounced on the railroad at Marietta, Georgia, severing Sherman's army from its supply line to Chattanooga and Nashville. Meantime, the three corps of Hood's infantry marched on, and by nightfall next day, they were fifteen miles from Palmetto, rolling north and gaining momentum, like a darkening thundercloud. As the army encamped for the night, one of Hood's preeminent division commanders, Irish-born Major General Pat Cleburne, found himself serenaded by his men. Touched, Cleburne made a speech in which he compared the Confederate cause with the plight of Ireland, warning that if their cause failed, the South would find itself "trampled and downtrodden" and closed with this flourish, "If this cause which is so dear to my heart is doomed to fail, I pray heaven may let me fall with it."

Next day, moving parallel to the Western & Atlantic Railroad, Hood struck out at the little stations along the tracks that Sherman had garrisoned with his rear-guard troops. On October 3, he instructed General A. P. Stewart to take his corps and capture the station at Big Shanty, north of Atlanta, which he did next day, destroying a dozen miles of track and taking Union prisoners, and then on to Ackworth station, where he did likewise. As they approached Allatoona Station, Hood received the information that there were large stores of federal supplies there—including about one million rations—so he sent Major General Samuel French, a forty-five-year-old New Jerseyite turned Mississippi planter, and his three-thousand-man division to destroy them. When the Confederates reached Allatoona, however, they found that it was garrisoned not by some thin rear-rank guard but by nearly a full division commanded by Brigadier John M. Corse, whom Sherman had urgently dispatched by rail up to Rome, Georgia, when he first heard Hood was on the move. Now, in as great a panic, he rushed them down the line to defend Allatoona. When French and his men appeared on the scene early in the morning of the 5th, a Wednesday, French sent Corse a note:

> Around Allatoona, October 5, 1864
>
> Commanding Officer, United States Forces, Allatoona:
> I have placed the force under my command in such positions that you are surrounded, and to avoid a needless effusion of blood I call on you to surrender your forces at once, and unconditionally.
> Five minutes will be allowed for you to decide. Should you accede to this, you will be treated in the most honorable manner as prisoners of war.
> I have the honor to be, very respectfully yours,
>
> S.G. French
> Major General commanding forces
> Confederate States

Corse digested this communication and immediately replied:

> Headquarters Fourth Division, Fifteenth Corps
> Allatoona, Georgia, 8:30 A.M., October 5th, 1864
>
> Major-General S. G. French, Confederate States, etc.
> Your communication demanding surrender of my command I acknowledge receipt of, and respectfully reply that we are prepared

for the "needless effusion of blood," whenever it is agreeable to you.

I am, very respectfully, your obedient servant,

John M. Corse
Brigadier General commanding forces
United States

Those were pretty bold words for a man outnumbered three to two, but Corse, a twenty-nine-year-old failed politician, had a lawyer's sense of the brazen. In any event, it wasn't long afterward that, as one veteran wrote, "a desperate little battle was fought."

Sherman, meanwhile, had been stewing in his own juice. Anxious as he was to get moving on his march to the sea, he had no choice, as Hood had predicted, but to follow him north and drive the Confederates away. Accordingly, he left Slocum's corps to guard Atlanta and mustered his remaining sixty thousand men to chase after Hood. With both Thomas and Schofield sent up to Tennessee to see about the defenses of that state, Major General Jacob Cox was put in temporary charge of the Army of the Ohio, and Major General D. S. Stanley was given the Army of the Cumberland. O. O. Howard remained in command of the Army of the Tennessee. Declaring that it was "absolutely necessary to keep General Hood's infantry off our main route of communication and supply," Sherman marched across the Chattahoochee and set out for Allatoona himself. A day earlier, Sherman had had his signalmen wig-wag a flag message over the heads of the enemy from the top of Kennesaw Mountain, telling Corse to proceed in a big hurry to Allatoona. When Sherman finally arrived at the top of the mountain—at almost the precise moment that Corse was throwing down his gauntlet to French—he reported "a superb view of the vast panorama to the north and west. To the southwest, about Dallas, could be seen the smoke of campfires, indicating a large force of the enemy, and the whole line of railroad from Big Shanty to Allatoona—a full fifteen miles—was marked by the fires of the burning railroad." Shortly afterward, he wrote, "We could

plainly see the smoke of battle about Allatoona, and hear the faint rever-
beration of the cannon.''

Sherman immediately ordered Cox's Twenty-third Corps to
march west and get between Hood's main force and that of French at
Allatoona and to ''burn houses or piles of brush as it progressed, to indicate the head of the column.'' Next, he sent the rest of his army straight
toward Allatoona to support Corse. That done, Sherman settled back to
watch, ''with painful suspense,'' the battle raging at Allatoona.

Flamboyant as Corse's refusal to surrender might have been, French, a
West Point graduate and Mexican War hero, insisted that he never received it or, for that matter, any other communication from the Union
commander. Instead, he said, he waited nearly twenty minutes. At 10
A.M., ''No reply having been sent me, the order was given for the assault. . . .'' French's version seems to be borne out by a Confederate
artilleryman on the scene, E. T. Eggleston, who wrote in his diary that
day, ''The enemy procrastinated giving an answer when our troops
stormed the works. . . .''

It was one of the most savage small battles of the entire war. Allatoona consisted of a mountain pass that the rail line ran through, a few
houses, the huge Union storage park at the depot, and several redoubts
manned by infantry and artillery. French's men overran these last in an
hour of ''murderous hand-to-hand conflict that left the ditches filled
with the dead,'' and Corse was forced to withdraw his remaining men
to the redoubt in the center. Meantime, having captured the vast federal
stores, French determined to burn them. When parties were sent to do
that, however, ''the matches furnished would not ignite and no fire
could be procured,'' the general wrote disgustedly in his after-action
report.

To make matters worse, a little past noon French received word
that some of his signal officers had intercepted one of Sherman's wig-
wag messages to Corse saying, ''Hold on, I am coming,'' and shortly
afterward someone brought him news that the federal infantry was moving up fast in his rear along the tracks. That was enough for the Confederate commander, who, not wishing to be trapped between Corse and

whatever was marching up behind him, ordered a withdrawal. By 3:30 P.M. he had his division reformed and moving southwest the fifteen or so miles back to Hood's army.

The ferocity of this fight is easily told in the casualty figures. French had 799 casualties, 25 percent of his command, while Corse suffered 707, a full 35 percent of those he had brought with him, including himself—he signaled Sherman next day, "I am short a cheekbone and an ear, but am able to whip all hell yet." While the part about Corse's wound was not exactly true—in fact, he had received only a scratch—Sherman thought enough of the defense of Allatoona to write him a citation. When the proud young Iowa general met his commanding officer to receive it, however, Sherman observed the ear and cheek still intact and remarked, "Well, Corse, they came damned near missing you, didn't they?"

Besides Corse's gallant defense and the hundreds of dead and wounded left on the rocky mountain ground, there was a final item of interest about the battle of Allatoona. Shortly after accounts of the battle began appearing in the press, Reverend P. P. Bliss, a world renowned evangelist of his day, composed a song based on Sherman's suddenly famous wig-wag signal, "Hold on, I am coming," which the papers had immediately embellished to "Hold the fort, for I am coming."

Bliss first sang it at a revival at the Chicago Tabernacle, and it has remained a gospel standard until today:

> *Ho! my comrades see the signal*
> *Waving in the sky,*
> *Re-inforcements now appearing*
> *Victory is nigh.*

> *Hold the fort, for I am coming*
> *Jesus signals still!*
> *Wave the answer back to heaven*
> *By thy grace we will.*

Having his own tune to march by, Hood, at 4 A.M. next morning, put his columns on the long haul again, plodding through a cold hard rain just ahead of Sherman's legions. Crossing over the old battlefields of the previous May, they passed by still fresh graveyards, the bleached bones of horses, and the wrecks of shattered wagons and "saw acres of timber killed by minnie balls."

"As we were coming along today in the piney woods," Sam Foster wrote in his diary, "we passed an old man who had been to mill. Sitting on his horse by the side of the road waiting for us to pass. This was at 1 o'clock P.M. and he said he had been there nearly all day. He said he didn't know that there were so many men in the whole world."

5

If You Want It, Come and ★ Take It

As the battle of Allatoona was getting under way, Jefferson Davis, on his way back to Richmond, stopped over in Augusta, Georgia, to meet with Beauregard, who was hurrying in the opposite direction to join the Army of Tennessee. Davis used the occasion to make a speech on a Sunday evening, in which he reiterated plans for Hood to "march into Tennessee" and "give the peace party of the North a [movement] no puny editorial can give." The calamity of losing Atlanta might have rendered the president's words a little hollow, except for one thing: all wasn't going as well as might be expected for Lincoln and the Republicans.

Certainly, much air was let out of the Democratic balloon by the capture of Atlanta—they had barely disbanded their convention when word came of it—but there were still plenty of Northern skeptics and malcontents who believed Lincoln was pursuing a war of chaos and needless bloodletting. In his acceptance speech as presidential nominee, George McClellan proclaimed he was for peace "without the effusion of another drop of blood," prompting George Templeton Strong, one of the great doomsayers of his time, to moan, "The great experiment in democracy may be destined to fail a century sooner than I expected. . . ." What McClellan actually indicated in his speech was that, while he would not require the Southerners to abolish slavery as a condition to end the war, he would require them to rejoin the Union. But that position immediately alienated the former commanding general from a huge segment of his own party who wanted peace *now,* at any price, and in newspapers and speaking stumps all over the North, McClellan was denounced as a sell-out artist and worse. Lincoln, on the other hand, still had his feet held to the fire by radicals in his own party who protested he was not doing enough to emancipate slaves and win the war, and thus both candidates became, in some measure, victims of the political schizophrenia that was sweeping the federal states. Naturally, the newspapers, ever anxious to stir up trouble, were having a field day with these controversies.

Meantime, the Confederates down in Richmond and elsewhere had all eyes and ears desperately bent toward these goings on, and every report that echoed southward through the mists of war was hashed and stewed and served up as further evidence that the Union was in confusion and peace was near at hand. But they still needed that one great victory to push them over the line, and it was hoped that John Bell Hood might give it to them.

Sherman, meanwhile, had no time for any such political speculations; he was engaged in an all-out effort to stop Hood's enterprising destruction of his railways northward. At first the red-haired commander registered pleasure at the ability of his engineers to repair the damage Hood was doing. The breakup of tracks from Big Shanty to Allatoona, for example, required some thirty-five thousand new crossties, six miles of iron, and ten thousand men to put them right, but within a week Union trains were running along them once more. Sherman liked to tell the apocryphal story of "a group of rebels, lying in the shade of a tree, one hot day, overlooking [the Union] camps about Big Shanty." One of the soldiers remarks, "The Yanks will have to git up and git now," because Wheeler's cavalry had blown up a tunnel down the road, and their rations were cut off. "Oh, hell," says another, "don't you know that old Sherman carries a *duplicate* tunnel along?"

In fact, Sherman was getting nervous and cross—as it was his habit to do—about the prospect of defending fifty to a hundred miles of track against Hood's entire army. "We will lose a thousand men each month, and will gain no result," he groused to Grant. "It will be a physical impossibility to protect the roads, now that Hood, Forrest, Wheeler, and the whole batch of devils, are turned loose without home or habitation." He went on to make yet another plea for his great excursion to the sea. "I can make this march, and make Georgia howl! We have on hand over eight thousand head of cattle and three million rations of bread, but no corn. We can find plenty of forage in the interior of the State."

The same day he wired that to Grant, Sherman wired Thomas in Nashville that he wanted to destroy the Chattanooga-Atlanta railroad *himself,* to ruin it for the Confederates and "to make for the sea-coast." "We cannot defend this long line of road," Sherman told his second in command.

The following morning, Monday, October 10, Hood's army simply vanished from Sherman's sight, disappeared into the rugged mountainous forests around Rome, Georgia. Confused by Hood's maneuvering, Sherman fired off a message to Slocum back in Atlanta to watch out, for Hood might be doubling back on him. Furthermore, he complained to Corse, now occupying his originally intended position at Rome, "I can not guess [Hood's] movements as I could those of Johnston, who was a sensible man, and only did sensible things." Then Sherman anxiously renewed appeal to Grant by wire, reiterating his desire to get moving toward the ocean.

"Answer quick," Sherman pleaded, "as I know we will not have the telegraph long." Whatever Grant's response was, Sherman never got it. As he had feared, Hood's cavalry wasted no time cutting the wires and chopping down the telegraph poles that Sherman's men had so painstakingly constructed behind them all the way from Chattanooga to Atlanta—his only link with army headquarters in the North.

While they might have vanished from Sherman's anxious eyes, the Confederate army had certainly not vanished from the face of the earth; in fact, it had marched lightning fast around to the west of Rome through a gap in the mountainous forests that led to the Chattooga River Valley, and the next day reappeared at Resaca, some fifteen miles north, where Hood demanded the surrender of the Union garrison in the manner of Sam French at Allatoona, with the exception that Hood threatened, "No prisoners will be taken." The commanding officer at Resaca was one Colonel Clark R. Weaver, who, after looking things over, responded thus:

> Headquarters Second Brigade, Third Division
> Fifteenth Corps, Resaca, Georgia, October 12th, 1864
>
> To General J. B. Hood:
> Your communication of this date just received. In reply, I have to state that I am somewhat surprized at the concluding paragraph, to the effect that, if the place is carried, no prisoners will be taken. In my opinion I can hold this post. If you want it, come and take it.
>
> I am, general, very respectfully, your most obedient servant,
> Clark R. Weaver, Commanding Officer

It seems nowhere recorded what Hood's personal reaction was to this audacious rebuke, but his response was to march his army off and leave Colonel Weaver and his people alone. In fact, Hood had other fish to fry, namely, the Union garrison at Dalton, Georgia, where the whole unpleasant business had begun six months before. It was Hood's intention to wreck Sherman's railroad all the way back from Resaca through Dalton to Tunnel Hill, which was just south of Chattanooga. His long-term intentions, however, were less clear.

A couple of days earlier, on October 9, the same Sunday that Sherman was telegraphing Grant about not being able to hold his railroads and going on his march and making Georgia howl, General Beauregard finally caught up with Hood's army at a little mountain spa called Cave Springs, near the Alabama line. The forty-six-year-old Louisianan was himself a man of grandiose plans. Having graduated second in his West Point class, Beauregard had been breveted for gallantry in the Mexican War, served as superintendent of the U.S. Military Academy, and was a former commander in chief of the Army of Tennessee. Through much of the war, Beauregard had proposed to Richmond an assortment of complex and daring schemes for the Army of Tennessee to execute, but all had been shot down by Davis and his advisors as too difficult or too risky. Now he was charged with the supervision of a kindred spirit in Hood, whose strategy at this late date was born, by necessity, of desperation.

Hood revealed to Beauregard his intention to move quickly to wreck the northern stretch of rail line all the way back up to Chattanooga, and then, he said, he meant to fall back to Jacksonville, just across the Alabama line near Gadsden, where he had already sent his excess wagons and artillery. There, it was presumed, Hood would offer Sherman battle if the federal commander came after him; if Sherman went off in some other direction, Beauregard understood that Hood would follow him and fight him wherever he could. Nothing, apparently, was discussed about Hood marching his army up to Nashville.

Meantime, Hood's troops trudged up toward Dalton, past the grim reminders of their previous visit there. Sam Watkins, the young Tennessean with the ascerbic tongue, remembered the journey this way: "We passed all those glorious battlefields . . . frequently coming across the skull of some poor fellow sitting on top of a stump, grinning a ghastly smile; also the bones of horses along the road and fences burned and destroyed, and occasionally the charred remains of a once fine dwelling house. Citizens came out and seemed glad to see us, and would divide their onions, garlic and leek with us. The soldiers were in good spirits, but it was the spirit of innocence and peace, not war and victory."

If that was the way his men felt, Hood did not see it. He was dead set on what he had come to Dalton to do, and about noon on October 13 he sent another of his threatening notes to Colonel Lewis Johnson, commander of the twelve hundred or so blue-clad soldiers inside the garrison. At first, Johnson, like Corse and Weaver before him, declined to surrender—and for reasons other than simple allegiance to duty. Most of Johnson's command consisted of the 44th Colored Troops—probably the same that Sherman had made reference to in his testy correspondence to Hood when he wrote, "We have no 'negro allies' in this army. . . . There are a few guarding Chattanooga, which General Steedman sent at one time to drive Wheeler out of Dalton." Apparently,

Sherman had assumed that the 44th Colored had been removed back to Tennessee, but he was mistaken, and now these unfortunate men were slowly and steadily being surrounded by division after division of Hood's army.

Although some zealous field commanders had organized black units early in the war, the U.S. government—amid a great deal of criticism—had officially introduced blacks into the Union army only after Lincoln's Emancipation Proclamation in the fall of 1862. At that time, the war was going badly for the North, and enlistments had dropped to a trickle. Subsequently, some one hundred eighty thousand blacks were inducted into the army—some by enlistment, others by conscription—the majority of them refugees from the Southern states. As more and more slaves fled the Southern plantations, they sought refuge in the North or in Union-occupied cities of the South, like Nashville. With no home or money, many became idle and were soon rounded up by the authorities and sent into the army. They were not particularly welcomed by the white soldiers and officers and for a time even received lower pay than whites. Furthermore, substantial numbers of the Colored Troops complained that they were put to menial tasks as laborers, teamsters, cooks, and even servants. Sometimes whole black regiments were set to work cleaning the camps of white troops. Sherman himself, who detested the notion of colored soldiers, replied when once asked if Negroes were not as good as whites to stop a bullet, "Yes, but a sandbag is better." But by the last years of the war it had been figured out that black units would fight like the white ones, and more and more they were being employed in the front lines. By the end of the war, some thirty-seven thousand U.S. Colored Troops had perished in the conflict, and a dozen had been awarded the Congressional Medal of Honor.

The Army of Tennessee had rarely encountered black enemy soldiers, but when they did, they were inclined to treat them roughly. Official Confederate policy toward the Colored Troops was ambiguous. Nathan Bedford Forrest had devised his own way of dealing with them, which, at its best, involved treating them not as prisoners of war but as runaway slaves, unless they could prove otherwise. At worst, Forrest had been accused (in a still controversial affair) of massacring five hundred colored troops at Fort Pillow near Memphis not six months before. The best the blacks could probably hope for was to be put to hard labor on some Confederate project, rather than being housed away in a prison camp like Andersonville—which, on second glance, was probably not such a bad alternative. In any event, after several hours of debate, Johnson ran out a white flag and gave up his garrison without a battle. Later, in his official report, he stated as one of his reasons that "the division of Cleburne, which was in the immediate rear of the rebel general [Hood] . . . was over anxious" to fight.

There was serious irony in this. Not nine months earlier, Patrick Ronayne Cleburne himself, in the misty mountain chill right there at Dalton, had made public one of the most controversial memoranda of the war: his proposal for freeing slaves and their families if they would join the Confederate army. It was a proposition that, while not entirely unheard of, was extraordinary coming from such a high-ranking official as a major general in the army, and it was to cause Cleburne trouble and possibly cost his life before the war was out.

What Cleburne had postulated was, on its face, simple mathematical logic. The North had many more times the manpower of the South to draw from. And even if Confederates killed federals at the rate of two to one, they would still run out of soldiers before the thing was done. Cleburne reasoned the whole business out in a lawyerly document of nearly forty thousand words and, after securing signatures of endorsement by a dozen or so fellow officers, made a formal presentation before General Joe Johnston and the entire command staff on the night of January 2 in the guarded back room of a house in the town of Dalton.

Cleburne's premise was that any slave who agreed to remain true to the Confederacy would be granted freedom. This, he argued, could be expected to produce the following results: Lincoln's Emancipation Proclamation would be nullified, and those in the North whose main purpose in continuing the war was to eliminate slavery would be left without a cause; it would give the Confederacy the enormous resources of nearly four million slaves, swelling the armies, as well as boosting other military and quasimilitary purposes; it would incline England and France—basically opposed to slavery but desperately in need of Confederate cotton to run their mills—to side with the South and send their powerful navies to break up the Union blockade.

"The President of the United States," Cleburne declared, "announced that he already has in training an army of 100,000 negroes as good as any troops, and every . . . new slice of territory he wrests from us will add to this force." He went on to argue, much as he had told his serenading soldiers a few weeks earlier when the army marched out from Palmetto, that "subjugation" by the North would be far worse for the Southerners than losing their slaves. Subjugation must be prevented at any cost, Cleburne pleaded, speaking from the height of personal experience as an Irishman.

For a moment after he had finished, the room was frozen in stunned silence, and then a commotion began as several of the dozen or so generals present began denouncing the idea as "monstrous" and "revolting," among other things. Some were supportive and still others, including Johnston himself, were noncommittal. However, Johnston later refused to submit the proposal to the War Department, claiming it was more a political question than a military one. Nevertheless, a copy soon found its way into the hands of Jefferson Davis—mailed to him by General W. H. T. Walker, perhaps vindictively since he was opposed to it. Within a short time Cleburne got his answer from Richmond. The Confederate government ordered his document and all his opinions about it suppressed on grounds that it was too controversial and would lead to dissension in the South. Moreover, his audacious suggestion, it was later speculated, probably cost him promotion to corps command, and thus he remained exposed to fire as a division commander until his end.

And so once again at Dalton—scene of his original "crime"—Cleburne, with his "over anxious" division straining to lash out at Colonel Johnson's regiment of Colored Troops, must surely have been struck with an Irishman's sense of irony at the scene. And had he lived long enough to see it—which he did not—he could only have wondered at the mockery of it all when President Davis himself, just before the end of the war, finally got around to recommending just what he had proposed.

Knowing none of this, Sam Watkins, the keen observer, remembered that he and his comrades were simply glad to be back at Dalton,
"not that we cared anything about it, but we just wanted to take a fare-
well look at the old place." He also recorded that as soon as the garrison
was surrendered, the 44th U.S. Colored Troops were marched out and
immediately put to work ripping up the railroad tracks toward Tunnel
Hill.

For the next day or so, practically everyone joined in the destruction of the railroad tracks. "It is getting to be fun for the men," Sam
Foster wrote. "They are just making a frolic of it." They had learned
their work well from federal soldiers, who produced something called
"Sherman's neckties" out of the Confederacy's steel rails by roasting
them over the ripped-up crossties until they were red hot, then bending
them double around trees or telegraph poles. The Southerners described their version of the handiwork as "Old Mrs. Lincoln's hair-
pins." As Hood rode through his divisions, he jubilantly declared that
the Union army had been "flanked out of Atlanta," and, recorded Foster, "The whole army are in high spirits . . . we begin to believe that Jeff
Davis and Hood made a ten strike when they planned this thing." By the
time they had finished, twenty-five miles of track from Tunnel Hill to
Resaca had been demolished.

By now, Hood had accomplished about all he wished in north
Georgia, and with Sherman's army breathing down his neck, he set out
on a southwestward march toward the Alabama state line. Had he intended to move on up into Tennessee at this point, the obvious route
would have been simply to keep going north past Chattanooga, where
the only federal forces before him would have been three divisions scattered mostly around the Alabama-Tennessee line, plus eight or ten
thousand raw recruits under Thomas at Nashville. But Hood seems to
have been sticking to the original plan formulated between Davis and
himself at Atlanta and reiterated to Beauregard a week earlier, which
was to draw Sherman into the open somewhere and give him a fight.
This was on his mind as the army plodded over the frosty Appalachian
foothills of northern Georgia near the old Chickamauga battlefield,
where they had won their first and only major victory of the war a year

before. Then, for two days, the 15th and 16th of October, Hood halted
his army "in a beautiful valley about nine miles south of Lafayette,"
where he lapsed into "serious thought and perplexity." At first, he recalled later, he thought he had "discovered that improvement in *morale*
of the troops which would justify [him] in delivering battle" against
what he estimated to be Sherman's sixty-five-thousand-man army
marching in his pursuit. But then he hit an unpleasant and unexpected
snag—or so he said afterward. On the eve of the supposed battle, he
took a sort of poll of his commanding officers as to whether or not their
troops were "at least hopeful of victory." Much to his annoyance and
disappointment, he said, "The opinion was unanimous that although the
Army had much improved in spirit, it was not in condition to risk battle
against the numbers reported by General Wheeler."

This revelation placed Hood in a serious and crucial dilemma. He
reasoned that if all his senior officers felt the army was not up to a fight
with Sherman, that option was out. Nor could he simply take position,
entrench, and wait for Sherman to come to him, because Sherman
would undoubtedly repair his railroad, re-arm and re-supply himself,
and arrive on the scene not only with his considerable forces, but with
those of Thomas as well—it would be Atlanta all over again. And so
while the men basked in the lovely valley of the Chattooga River, the
autumn leaves turning gold and red around them, John Bell Hood made
a fateful and momentous decision. "I conceived the plan of marching
into Tennessee with a hope to establish our line eventually in Kentucky," he said. The scheme, as it began to take shape in the general's
mind, was to destroy Schofield's army before it could link up with
Thomas's forces at Nashville, march on, and crush Thomas. Then,
resupplied from Nashville's vast federal stores, the Army of Tennessee
would continue to move north. "In this position," Hood theorized, "I
could threaten Cincinnati, and recruit the Army from Kentucky and
Tennessee."

As the plan started to flicker in Hood's imagination, it began to assume the dimensions of a grand design to win the war. Marching eastward through the Cumberland Gap, its ranks swelling with reinforcements and new recruits, the Army of Tennessee could come up

behind Grant's host then besieging Lee at Richmond. "This move, I believed, would defeat Grant and allow General Lee, in command of our combined Armies, to march upon Washington or turn upon and annihilate Sherman," Hood declared later. He had still believed, before he marched, that the twenty thousand reinforcements Davis promised him from Texas and Louisiana would join him any day.

6

★ They Must Be Killed

Cump Sherman was furious. Here it was past the middle of October, and he and his army were right back in north Georgia, where they had started from last May. Neither Grant nor Halleck nor anyone in Washington would authorize his great march to the sea, and, to make matters worse, though he had chased the Confederate army all over the countryside, he had found nothing but the destruction Hood had left in his wake.

"The lightness and celerity of his army convinced me that I could not possibly catch him on a stern-chase," Sherman grumbled, noting that Hood had now crossed the Alabama line and seemed to be headed for the town of Gadsden. On October 17, just beyond the Georgia-Alabama border, Sherman tired of the game and halted the army. He then resumed begging Washington to let him turn around and "move through the bowels [of the South] and make a trail that would be visible for fifty years."

Sherman seemed fond of such pronunciations, probably stemming from his view even before the outbreak of hostilities that "secession was treason, was *war*." His reasoning from the outset was crouched in legal terms—specifically, that the South was breaking the law and that once war broke out, all constitutional guarantees of the Southerners became null and void. For instance, just before he resigned from the Louisiana

Military Academy and went north, Confederates seized the U.S. Arsenal at Baton Rouge and transferred its weapons around the state, including several thousand rifles that soon arrived at Sherman's school, with orders from the governor for him to take receipt and account for them. "Thus," Sherman complained, "I was made the receiver of stolen goods." Six months later, as a colonel commanding a Union brigade, he not only threatened to open up his artillery on one of his own regiments for trying to leave after their enlistments expired, but also told one of his captains he would "shoot [him] down like a dog" for going absent without leave.

A day or so after that incident—which was brought to the attention of Abraham Lincoln himself—Sherman was promoted to brigadier general. He was subsequently sent west to the Department of the Cumberland, where he got into the big brouhaha about being "insane," and for a while it looked like his military days might be over. In less than a month, though, his career was partially revived on orders for him to proceed to St. Louis and take charge of a training camp. By February 1862, Sherman had been sent down to Paducah, Kentucky, to organize men and supplies for Generals Grant, Halleck, and C. F. Smith, who were trying to dislodge the Confederates from their forts along the Cumberland River, northwest of Nashville. By the end of the month, those forts were taken, and consequently the Union armies walked triumphantly into Nashville and remained there unmolested until almost the end of the war.

Meantime, General Ulysses S. Grant had been ordered to march his Army of the Tennessee down to the Tennessee River near the Mississippi state line to destroy railroad bridges and connections. Sherman was now officially out of the doghouse for being crazy and was given a division to command. On March 10, 1862, he boarded his four brigades of green troops on transports and steamed southward—ostensibly to wreck railroad bridges at Corinth, Mississippi, and Tuscumbia, Alabama—but was forced back by heavy flooding. The place Sherman eventually debarked, in southern Tennessee, was called Pittsburg Landing—or Shiloh—where he received the momentous opening blow of the trap the Confederates had laid there.

Confederate commander Albert Sidney Johnston had disguised the

movements of his army so carefully the five divisions of encamped federals had no idea they were facing anything but a troop of cavalry. In fact,
the Southern army had arrived less than a mile from Shiloh the day
before but were unable to get organized for attack until too late in the
afternoon. Shortly after sunup on April 6, a Sunday, some forty thousand Confederate infantry came screaming out of the woods, line after
line, overrunning Union camps, driving the surprised blue-coated soldiers before them and, in some cases, even stopping to eat their enemy's
unfinished breakfast or loot his tent. Sherman's division was posted all
around the little log Shiloh church. By midmorning, he had been flanked
and driven back half a mile. The grizzled redhead was holding on for
dear life without the help of one of his brigades, which had run away at
the first of the fight. At 10 A.M. Grant, having rushed to the battlefield
from a sickbed upriver, joined Sherman, who by now had been twice
slightly wounded. Sherman told his commanding general he thought he
could hang on but was worried about running out of ammunition. By
noon, he had been forced back again but was giving ground very stub-
bornly. Still, when sundown ended that day's battle, Sherman and the
rest of Grant's army had been driven more than two miles and were
clustered with their backs to the foreboding bluffs at Pittsburg Landing,
dropping away behind them.

Grant might have lost the whole Army of the Tennessee when the
Confederate attack resumed next morning but for one thing—or perhaps two. While the surgeon's saws and probes were busy late into the
night, General Don Carlos Buell with the Army of the Ohio was hustling
down from Nashville to join the fray. This would give Grant thirty
thousand more men with which he could then counterattack instead of
withdraw.

Unbeknownst to most of the Confederates and none of the Union
soldiers huddling beneath a frightening spring thunderstorm, General
Alfred Sidney Johnston was dead—bled to death after a bullet cut a leg
artery. The new commander was Pierre Gustave Toutant Beauregard.
Unaware that Buell was arriving on the field at that very moment, the
Creole general went to sleep, relying on an intercepted telegram that
claimed that Buell was marching in an entirely different direction.

General John Bell Hood

Unless otherwise noted, all photographs are printed courtesy of
the Prints and Photographs Division of the Library of Congress.

The Confederate High Command

President Jefferson Davis

General P. G. T. Beauregard

General Joseph E. Johnston

The Confederate Corps Commanders

General Benjamin Franklin Cheatham

General Stephen Dill Lee

General Alexander Peter Stewart

The Confederate Division Commanders

General Edward C. Walthall

General William Wing Loring
(courtesy of Culver Pictures, Inc.)

General Samuel French

General John C. Brown (courtesy
of the Chicago Historical Society)

General William Brimage Bate

General Edward Johnson

The Confederate Generals Killed at Franklin

General Patrick Ronayne Cleburne

General States Rights Gist

General Otho French Strahl

General Hiram B. Granbury

General John Adams

General John Carpenter Carter

General William Tecumseh Sherman

General George H. Thomas

General John M. Schofield

Before going to bed, Beauregard telegraphed Richmond that the army had achieved "a great victory, driving the enemy from every position."

As a cloudy dawn broke behind the federal lines, Confederates were startled to see massive ranks of blue-coated soldiers marching toward them out of the mists. Sherman halted his division near his original camps, where he remained, he said, "patiently awaiting the sound of General Buell's advance upon the main Corinth road." When, about 10 A.M., he heard the sound of heavy firing that marked Buell's arrival, he formed a line of battle and marched forward again. He hadn't gone far when one regiment, he said, "advanced upon a point of water-oaks and thicket, behind which I knew the enemy was in great strength, and entered it in beautiful style. Then arose the severest musketry-fire I ever heard."

This was about five hundred yards east of the Shiloh Church, and Sherman concluded, "It was evident that here was to be the struggle." All that morning and into the afternoon his division slugged it out, with Sherman personally directing his artillery fire and organizing new attacks. By midafternoon, Beauregard, now fully aware that he was outnumbered three to two and that the future of the fight looked grim, ordered a withdrawal. Grant's and Buell's men were too worn out and used up to follow, and then a huge sleet storm descended on the countryside, foreclosing all possibility of close pursuit. Sherman led his division out next morning and discovered abandoned Confederate camps and hospitals; the Army of Tennessee was gone.

Sherman's first taste of major combat—he had been at Bull Run, but that was child's play compared with this—had given him a sobering revelation on how the war must be fought. Thirteen thousand Union soldiers had fallen and more than ten thousand Confederates, and, aside from spilling blood by the barrelful, nothing much had been settled. If it didn't occur to him at that moment, it surely did shortly afterward, that the North could not win the war merely by locking horns with the Confederate armies on some meaningless killing ground. No—the only way to save the South for the nation was to first destroy it, a notion that ironically became unofficial American policy a hundred years later in Southeast Asia.

Soon after the battle, Sherman was at it again with the press—with which he was still irate for calling him a nut—for publishing "wild and damaging reports" of the engagement at Shiloh. "It was publicly asserted at the North that our army was taken completely by surprise; that the rebels caught us in our tents, bayoneted the men in their beds; that General Grant was drunk," and so forth, Sherman wrote, railing that "the danger of sudden popular clamors is well illustrated by this case."

Possibly the most important feature of Sherman's service at Shiloh was the close personal relationship he made with Grant. While it seemed that every other Union commander—McDowell, McClellan, Pope, and, later, Burnside, Hooker, and Meade—was allowed to have his star both rise and fall in the east, these two determined old soldiers were socked away in a remote theater of the war far from the glory (and shame) that befell those fighting close to Washington. Through all their trouble they grew to trust and rely on each other's abilities. Two years later, when they finally emerged as commanders of the two huge Union armies converging on the remains of the Confederacy, Sherman could sit back and say, "Well, Grant, you supported me when I was crazy and I supported you when you were drunk."

Meantime, Grant had gotten himself on the bad side of the theater commander, General Henry Halleck, who, apparently believing the stories in the press, came down from St. Louis after the battle and took charge of all the western armies himself, making Grant second in command, a do-nothing job sort of like vice president. Sherman recorded that while his friend suffered the affront without complaint, "I could see that he felt deeply the indignity, if not insult, heaped upon him." Grant had decided to leave the army, but Sherman persuaded him to bide his time and wait for "some happy accident to restore him to favor"—as in fact had happened with Sherman following the accusations that he was crazy.

The army—now swelled to more than one hundred thousand—began to move on Corinth, Mississippi, thirty miles to the south, where Beauregard had reformed the Army of Tennessee. When the federals arrived, however, they found that Beauregard had withdrawn further south again. And as the army languished in and about Corinth, Sherman's "happy accident" occurred for Grant. Halleck—known popularly as "Old Brains"—was ordered to Washington to become chief of staff for all the federal armies, and Grant was restored to command of the Army of the Tennessee. Soon afterward, on the 21st of July, Sherman was sent to occupy Memphis with his division, and this effectively placed him in the role of military governor.

It was Sherman's first taste of control over civilians, and he exercised it with a stony harshness tempered by a chilling logic. Entering Memphis, he found the city all but closed down, and he immediately ordered everything—businesses, schools, churches—to begin operating again. He rounded up all the fugitive slaves he found in the city and put them to work on his fortifications. Next, he began expelling the wives and families of Confederate soldiers and sympathizers from their homes in reprisal for Confederate fire on Union gunboats operating on the Mississippi. On September 24, he ordered the town of Randolph, Tennessee, burned to the ground in retaliation for firing on U.S. vessels and also commanded the destruction of all homes, farms, and farm buildings for fifteen miles down the Arkansas side of the river opposite Memphis.

These seem the earliest of Sherman's pyromaniacal urges in connection with southern civilians and their property, but by a long shot they were not his last. He had by now refined his philosophy regarding the civilian population of the South, which he expressed bluntly in a letter to U.S. Treasury Secretary Salmon Chase three weeks after taking over in Memphis. Noting that the war was thus far "complicated with the belief on the one hand that all on the other side are *not* enemies," Sherman branded this a "mistake" and declared, "The Government of the United States may now safely proceed on the proper rule that all in the South *are* enemies."

By early 1863, the principal Union objective in the west was to reclaim the Mississippi River, the main artery of commercial transportation in the heartland. To that end, federal troops had secured the river from its source down to near Vicksburg and from its mouth north, to above Baton Rouge. But there still remained hundreds of twisting river miles in between that were firmly in Confederate hands, and Washington was determined to wrest them away, splitting the Confederacy in

two. It was a tall order. Vicksburg was stoutly defended by a Confederate army under General John Pemberton, and its two-hundred-foot
bluffs were frowning with sinister artillery of all sizes and shapes. Be that
as it was, Vicksburg had to be taken, and to that end, in December,
Grant ordered Sherman to steam downriver and land a dozen miles
above the city along the Chickasaw Bayou, then move on Vicksburg
from the rear.

By the day after Christmas, Sherman had landed his thirty-three-
thousand-man task force and during the next week floundered southeastward through the tangled swamps of the Mississippi Delta harassed
by snipers, the weather, and unfordable streams and bogs. Two days
before New Year's Sherman encountered a steep ridge called the Wal-
nut Hills, manned by what he estimated to be a Confederate force at
least half his size under General Stephen D. Lee. He immediately ordered an attack, which quickly turned into a disaster.

Sherman spread his four divisions opposite the Confederate-held
ridge, sending about half of them to feint an attack while the others actually charged across the bayou and overran the hills—or so it was
hoped. As the attack opened, it was met with a furious artillery blast
from the Southerners astride the hills. One of Sherman's brigades hid
behind the bank of the bayou and would not go forward, while another
lurched off in a wrong direction. Those that did reach the base of the
hills suddenly came under a galling crossfire by artillery on their flanks
and rifle fire from above, and wound up cringing beneath the bluffs, trying to scrape out holes to hide in. It was only after nightfall that they
managed to escape, one at a time.

Sherman's army—minus some seventeen hundred killed, wounded,
or captured—were loaded back on the transports to try to find another
way, but Sherman was soon astonished to learn that he had been relieved of command. The new leader was to be General John McCler-
nand, a politician who arrived with orders from Lincoln in person,
putting him in charge. Naturally, when the press got wind of this, they
"raised the usual cry of 'repulse, failure and bungling' " and, as well,
renewed the old accusation that Sherman was insane. Fact was, Sherman
had learned a valuable lesson at Chickasaw Bayou—which was to be

very wary of attacking high, heavily fortified positions head-on—and he put this firsthand knowledge to good use when he opened his Atlanta campaign the following year.

In late January 1863, Grant put Sherman to work on a stupendous project. He ordered him to excavate a huge canal in the marshy Mississippi River swamps opposite Vicksburg so that Union navy gunboats and transports could move past the Confederate batteries unmolested. Such an undertaking would have been difficult enough under the best of circumstances—the canal would have to be nearly a mile long and wide and deep enough to accommodate the big deep-draft warships, supply vessels, and troop transports of the federal fleet—but to try with only axes, picks, and shovels to dig out anything of that magnitude, and during the rainy season when the river was at flood, was indeed a colossal chore. All through January and February the men heaved up the thick delta soil, "fighting off the water of the Mississippi, which threatened to drown us," Sherman complained. Frequently, the men had to clamber up onto the levee or jump aboard steamboats to keep from being swept away. After they had toiled for nearly two months, the river hit a new flood tide, crushing the dam at the north end of the canal and inundating the countryside for miles around. The soldiers were evacuated, the project abandoned, and Sherman sourly branded the whole business "fruitless."

Next Grant set in motion another elaborate scheme for getting around the Vicksburg defenses, and again Sherman became the goat. Twenty land miles above the city was a point at which the Yazoo River—which flows into the Mississippi—intersected with a body of water called Steele Bayou, which in turn connected to half a dozen backwater rivers, bayous, streams, and creeks that ultimately led to a spot behind the harsh Confederate fortifications near Chickasaw Bayou, where Sherman had come to grief a few months before. The same high water that had cursed the canal project had providentially made all these normally shallow streams navigable—even for huge ironclad gunboats—and the plan was to load up Sherman and his troops and sneak them on a two-hundred-mile roundabout voyage through this labyrinth of snake-infested jungle to a spot where they would emerge on dry land

and overwhelm the surprised Vicksburg defenders from the rear. If anything, this machination was even more ambitious than the ill-fated canal,
but Sherman gave it a go, and on the 18th of March embarked his troops
in an armada of ironclads, tugs, mortar boats, and transports to weave
through the trackless delta swamp.

In the beginning it wasn't so bad. The sturdy ironclads in the lead
simply smashed their way through the overhanging trees and rude
bridges they sometimes encountered; in other cases, Sherman's men
armed with axes and saws would cut a path through. The first day they
made better than sixty miles. But the second day the head of the flotilla
ran into trouble in the form of Confederates drawn up in their front
with artillery, who shot down any sailor venturing outside of his iron
shield to fend off the boats. To the rescue came Sherman (informed by a
courier) leading a column of infantry, marching them by candlelight
through, to use James Weldon Johnson's words, canebrakes and thickets dark as a "hundred midnights in a cypress swamp." Twenty-odd
miles downstream Sherman reached the beleaguered gunboats and
drove off the Confederate sharpshooters, but the naval officer in charge
had already turned back. The Confederates had set work gangs to felling
trees into the river, and at a crucial turn in the route, the channel was so
obstructed it was impossible to go on. It took Sherman's task force three
days to back out of the morass, with Sherman muttering over "the most
infernal expedition I was ever on."

Having made half a dozen unsuccessful attempts on Vicksburg,
Grant finally decided to play his last card—he persuaded the navy to attempt to silently drift the supply ships past the dreaded Vicksburg fortifications in the dark. The army would cross over to the Louisiana side
of the river and stealthily make a wide sweep south, then recross, to
come up in the rear of the city. Sherman's role in this was to stage a
diversion near his old bugaboo, Chickasaw Bayou, to confuse the
Confederates, and this he did, before crossing the river himself and joining Grant forty miles below Vicksburg at a place called Hard Times.

From there, the federal soldiers pushed quickly inland another
forty miles to Jackson, the rail center and state capital, where, on May
14, they routed a Confederate army under General Joseph E. Johnston

that had been sent to support General Pemberton's defense of Vicksburg. Sherman was immediately employed to destroy anything of possible military value in the city, and within a day or so he had torn up all its rail lines and torched factories, warehouses, shops, and depots. Next the army turned back toward Vicksburg and on the 16th of May, halfway between the two cities, it met Pemberton's army in the battle of Champion's Hill. Sherman did not take part in this engagement but marched on toward Vicksburg, where, on May 19th, the Union army finally confronted the bastion from the rear. Grant immediately launched an assault, but it was repulsed. Next day he tried again, twice—with the same result—and at last he decided that his only alternative was the laying of a siege.

For six weeks Vicksburg held out, completely surrounded by Grant's army on one side and the federal gunboat flotilla, which had run the Vicksburg defenses, on the other. Meantime, Johnston's Confederate army was reinforcing to the east in hopes of attacking Grant in the rear, and Sherman was sent out with what amounted to a corps to forestall any such designs. During this time a poignant incident occurred. After positioning his corps to defend against Johnston, there wasn't much for Sherman to do but sit and wait out the siege. Learning that a Mrs. Wilkerson, whose son had attended the Louisiana Military Academy while Sherman was superintendent, was staying nearby, Sherman rode over to the house, where he found "quite a number of ladies sitting on the porch." When he inquired after her son, Mrs. Wilkerson replied that he was an artillery captain, now besieged inside Vicksburg; when he asked about her husband, whom he had also known, "she burst into tears and cried out in agony, 'You killed him at Bull Run, where he was fighting for his country!' " Taken aback, Sherman later wrote, "I disclaimed killing anybody at Bull Run; but all the women present burst into loud lamentations, which made it most uncomfortable for me, and I rode away." Afterward, Mrs. Wilkerson came to Sherman with a request that she be allowed to pass through the Union lines to visit her son at Vicksburg, and the stern Ohio general immediately wrote her a note to take to Grant himself, requesting permission, which was given.

On the 4th of July, 1863, Vicksburg surrendered with its entire army—the first and only surrender of a whole Confederate army until Appomattox—thus "fatally bisecting the Southern Confederacy," as Sherman put it. On that same day, Lee's battered army began retreating southward from Gettysburg with the shattered Hood in an ambulance. Though few on either side were convinced of it at the time, the high-water mark of the Southern bid for independence had been reached, a couple of weeks short of two years after the contest opened in earnest.

For the next three months the Union army relaxed in its camps near Vicksburg while Sherman further honed his philosophy of how to deal with the South. On September 27 he responded to a request from Halleck to provide his views on the future of the conflict to President Lincoln—specifically, his view on whether the Lincoln administration should attempt to reconstruct the Southerners under its control at this stage of the game, or subjugate them, or was there something else.

In a three-thousand-word document, Sherman defined the problem as he saw it, sorting the Southerners into four social and economic classes. "First," he wrote, "are the large planters, owning lands, slaves and all kinds of personal property." Describing this class as "educated, wealthy and easily approached," Sherman ventured, "If this country were like Europe, crowded with people, I would say it would be easier to replace this class than to reconstruct it"—just how, he did not say. But he went on to suggest that there were more battles to be won before these aristocrats could be reconstructed, and only then should they be "allowed to adjust their minds to this new order of things."

Next, Sherman described his "second class": the small farmers, workers, and merchants who made up three-fourths of the population. Essentially, he considered those people stupid and foolish. "The Southern planters, who understand this class, use them as the French use their masses—[and] seemingly consult their prejudices, while they make their orders and enforce them. We should do the same," he wrote cynically.

For his third division, the Union men of the South, Sherman expressed only contempt. "I have no respect for this class," he said, branding them cowards for not standing up to the Confederates. "Their sons, horses, arms, and everything useful, are in the army against us, and they stay at home, claiming all the exemptions of peaceful citizens. I account them as nothing in this great game of war."

Finally, he turned his rage on his fourth class—the "young bloods of the South: sons of planters, lawyers about town, good billiard-players and sportsmen, men who never did work and never will. War suits them, and the rascals are brave, fine riders, bold to rashness. . . . This is a larger class than most men suppose, and they are the most dangerous set of men that this war has turned loose upon the world. They are splendid riders, first-rate shots and utterly reckless." Sherman cited Confederate generals J.E.B. Stuart, John Morgan, Bedford Forrest, and Stonewall Jackson as "the types and leaders of this class," concluding, "These men must all be killed or employed by us before we can hope for peace."

Having thus classified the people of the Confederacy, the feisty Ohioan scoffed at the idea of establishing any kind of reconstruction government in the conquered states at that point. Calling for total subjugation of the entire South, he went off on another of his florid proclamations: Southerners, he declared, must be made to understand that even if it took twenty years, the Union army would "take every life, every acre of land, every particle of property, every thing that to us seems proper; that we will not cease till the end is attained; that all who do not aid us are our enemies, and that we will not account to them for our acts."

Duly impressed by Sherman's reasoning, Lincoln wanted the letter published, according to Halleck, but Sherman demurred, claiming that he did not want any further controversy with the press.

In October, a tragedy befell General Sherman and his family. After the battle of Vicksburg, Sherman brought his wife and children down from Memphis, including his son, nine-year-old Willie, and they stayed on with him in his encampment until the end of September, when word came of the Union disaster at Chickamauga. Reinforcements were being rushed from all quarters to Rosecrans's Army of the Cumberland, which Bragg had now bottled up in Chattanooga, and Sherman was ordered by Grant to take his corps back into eastern Tennessee. As Sherman's party was boarding the steamer north, Willie fell sick, and a regimental doctor diagnosed typhoid fever. The river had fallen, and the passage upriver took several days, during which time Willie's condition worsened. When they finally reached Memphis, and the best doctors, it was too late; the little boy died the next day. Sherman was heartbroken, but in the military emergency attending at Chattanooga he had no time to lose. Willie had been made an honorary sergeant in the Thirteenth Battalion of United States Regulars, and it was those troops who escorted the small body aboard a steamer bound north for burial in Illinois. Years later officers and men of the Thirteenth Battalion designed and carved a marble monument for Willie's grave.

A few days later, Sherman was en route for Chattanooga aboard a train that was loaded with orderlies, clerks, horses—and the Thirteenth Battalion of regulars. Two dozen miles out of Memphis the train suddenly ground to a halt near the Collierville depot, and a Confederate officer rode up under a white flag. Identifying himself as the adjutant of General James Chalmers, the Confederate demanded surrender of the depot, train, and Union troops, but Sherman refused and began deploying the battalion of regulars and arming the clerks and orderlies. The Confederate attack came swiftly, isolating the train by tearing up the tracks and then blasting the locomotive to bits with artillery. The fight seesawed back and forth until dark; the Southerners managed to capture the rear of the train and stole Sherman's favorite horse, a mare called Dolly, and also set the cars afire using as fuel a suitcase of shirts belonging to Sherman's aide-de-camp. But Sherman's unlikely little band held fast, and the Confederates eventually drew off, leaving them to repair the damage and continue toward Chattanooga next day.

About halfway there a telegraph came for Sherman with big news. Grant had been promoted to theater command, comprising the armies of the Ohio, Cumberland, and Tennessee, and Sherman now became the commanding general of this last. Furthermore, for letting Bragg whip his Army of the Cumberland, Rosecrans was fired and replaced by George H. Thomas, the "Rock of Chickamauga."

When Sherman reached Chattanooga, he was astonished to behold Lookout Mountain, "with its rebel flags and batteries" frowning down upon the town. "Up until that time I had no idea how bad things were," he said, adding, "Rebel sentinels, in a continuous chain, were walking their posts in plain view, not a thousand yards off."

"Why, General Grant, you are besieged!" he exclaimed to his cigar-chomping riding companion.

"It is too true," was Grant's solemn reply.

Bragg's siege was taking a fearful toll, and for the second time, as at Chickamauga, Grant was in danger of losing an entire army. Horses were so starved they were too weak to haul artillery, and to feed themselves the men were actually stealing corn intended for the animals. Worse, the soldiers had become so demoralized over their humiliation at Chickamauga, it was "feared they could not be got out of their trenches to assume the offensive." But the state of affairs that was permitted to exist under General Rosecrans was not going to continue for long under General Grant.

Within two weeks an attack was launched. "Fighting Joe" Hooker had arrived on the scene with four divisions from the Army of the Potomac and combined with Thomas's six and Sherman's four for a total of nearly seventy-five thousand men to throw against Bragg's Confederate army of forty thousand. The design was for Sherman to clamp on to Bragg's right flank, Hooker his left, while Thomas attacked his center. As Sherman later explained it, "The object of General Hooker's and my attacks on the extreme flank of Bragg's position was, to disturb him to such an extent, that he would naturally detach from his centre as against us, so that Thomas' whole army could break through his centre." Bragg's entrenchments along Missionary Ridge were a tough nut to crack, but as it turned out, it was easier than anyone thought—except Sherman.

Holding the north end of Missionary Ridge at Tunnel Hill was Confederate General Pat Cleburne. The tough Irishman had anchored his division into the steep hillside without the least intention of being the nut that cracked, and when, at daybreak, Sherman hit him head-on he recoiled as if snakebit. Sherman threw more and more of his divisions into the all-day fray but never gained even a toe-hold against Cleburne's stubborn men, who even heaved large rocks down on their blue-clad assailants. All the while he was watching his columns repulsed, Sherman was listening impatiently for the noise that would indicate Thomas had begun his attack on the Confederate center. Not until 3 P.M. did he breathe a sigh of relief when the racket of Thomas's tardy assault came echoing across the valley.

Grant's plan had worked like a charm. To the surprise of everybody, Thomas easily pierced Bragg's line, capturing many prisoners and supplies and forcing the Confederate army to evacuate backward into Georgia. Sherman was mightily disgruntled that he had been denied a share in the limelight of this repulse, but he had little time to worry over it because Grant immediately sent him and his corps up to Knoxville, where Longstreet—who had been detached from Bragg's army—was besieging the city. Before Sherman could arrive, however, Longstreet became aware of his moves and withdrew back toward Virginia.

After a little well-earned rest, Sherman was again on the move. In early February 1864, he organized a march from Vicksburg of seventeen thousand men and descended on the Mississippi city of Meridian, a rail and supply center close by the Alabama line. After cutting a fifty-mile-wide swath of destruction and blackened ruins from one side of the state to the other, Sherman reached Meridian on the 14th and immediately set about wrecking it so thoroughly that he could report later, "It no longer exists." The Meridian march was merely practice for what Sherman envisioned next. Before setting out, he broke his usual silence to the press with the publication of a letter to the people of the South, which he declared they should use "to prepare them for my coming." In it, among other things, he threatened everybody involved in the Confederacy—men (and) women—with death and dispossession of their lands and property.

In March a momentous event overtook Sherman. Congress passed a law reviving the rank of lieutenant general, highest post in the army, and the first recipient of this rank was Ulysses S. Grant, who was promptly ordered to Virginia to see—after all the previous failures—what *he* could do about Robert E. Lee and his army. On March 17, Sherman met with Grant in Nashville and was informed that he would now be in charge of the military division consisting of the armies of the Ohio, the Cumberland, and the Tennessee. With this new responsibility, Sherman began to turn his attention to plans for a push on the Confederate army now drawn up in Dalton, Georgia, and which, two weeks earlier, had been joined by John Bell Hood.

7

To Conquer the Peace ✭

From the lovely valley of the Chattooga, where Hood made his fateful judgment to enter Tennessee, the Confederate army marched westward through a brilliant autumn landscape on October 19, 1864, until it reached Gadsden, Alabama, and the waiting Confederate supply train. It was there that Hood met with Beauregard for the second time, and the commanding general of the Army of Tennessee unfolded his plan to march northward to Nashville, Cincinnati, and all the rest. At first the little Creole general was skeptical, but after two days of deliberations and interviews with officers of the army, on October 22 he authorized the expedition.

That was great news for the soldiers, more than half of whom were Tennesseans who had not set foot in their native state since Grant expelled them so rudely nearly a year before in the battle of Chattanooga. As word spread that they were at last going home, great cheers rose from the campfires, and next morning Hood confidently marched them north toward Guntersville, where they were to cross the Tennessee River.

There was a lightheartedness at the beginning of this trek. The weather was good, and the soldiers had filled their bellies, and some even had been issued shoes and clothing before setting out. No longer

did they resemble the scarecrow army that had been fighting almost continuously since May. Just outside of Gadsden, the Army of Tennessee
filed past the home of a then famous southern heroine, young Emma
Sansom, who stood on her porch most of the day waving to them.

The year before, sixteen-year-old Emma had figured prominently
in Bedford Forrest's celebrated bagging of an entire federal brigade that
had come flying through north Alabama on what was supposed to be a
raid on the Confederate foundries at Rome, just over the Georgia line.
Culled from General Grenville Dodge's division, a two-thousand-man
blue-coated force under the command of Colonel Abel Streight left
from Tuscumbia, Alabama. No horses being available, they set out
aboard mules, many of them half-broken, and followed the Tennessee
River toward Lookout Mountain. Forrest, with about half as many men,
caught up with them about five days out, whereupon a running battle
took place for the next four days until the Confederate pursuers arrived
just outside Gadsden to discover that Streight and his men had burned
the only bridge across Black Creek. Forrest was in danger of losing contact with his prey when, in the midst of a hot fight near the burning
bridge, Emma Sansom called out from a farmhouse that she knew an old
cow-path ford to the other side. With no time to waste, Forrest hoisted
the girl behind him and dashed off to find the ford, which he quickly
ordered his cavalry to cross. Returning the dark-haired young lady to
her mother, Forrest hastily penned a note to her:

> Hed Quaters in Sadle
> May 2, 1863

> My highest regardes to Miss Ema Sansom for hir gallant conduct
> while my posse was skirmmishing with the Federals a cross Black
> Creek near Gadsden Allabama

> N.B. Forrest
> Brig. Genl,
> Comding N. Ala—

Forrest kept the pressure on Streight and his raiders all the way to
the Georgia line, where he finally captured them with a trick. Reduced

by broken down horses to six hundred men, Forrest wanted to avoid an out-and-out fight. About fifteen miles from Rome he approached Streight with a truce flag, demanding his surrender. Streight met him between the lines, saying that he would surrender only if Forrest could convince him that he was completely superior in force. Forrest declined to do that—and wisely, since he was actually outnumbered more than two to one—but he had secretly arranged with his artillery men to haul the only two artillery pieces he had around and around, in a circle, across and below a rise in the road, so that it would appear to Streight that whole batteries of guns were being brought up to the front.

Finally, Streight couldn't stand it any longer. "Name of God! How many guns have you got?" he exclaimed. "There's fifteen I've counted already!"

"I reckon that's all that has kept up," the wily Confederate replied.

Streight still wasn't quite convinced, but after Forrest threatened to attack him then and there, the federal colonel decided prudence was the better part of valor and handed over 1,466 soldiers with all their arms and equipment, the victims of a ruse.

So more than a year later—a year that had seen the fall of Vicksburg, the carnage at Gettysburg, and the loss of Atlanta—the grateful Army of Tennessee marched past Emma Sansom's doorstep on their way to Nashville—and possibly the Ohio—and the regiments cheered and felt good about her and about themselves.

But almost from the first, things started to go wrong.

Hood's battle plan assumed that he would take with him at least half of Wheeler's cavalry to guard his flanks, sending the rest back into Georgia to watch and harass Sherman—whatever he did next. But Beauregard insisted that all of Wheeler's men be returned to the Sherman watch and, in their place, offered Hood the use of Nathan Bedford Forrest's cavalry divisions, which were roaming around in west Tennessee, smashing up things in Sherman's rear. Hood readily acceded to this stipulation—who wouldn't have accepted the legendary Forrest?—but when he neared Guntersville, Alabama, the disturbing word was received that Forrest was then operating all the way at the other end of the

Tennessee River, nearly two hundred miles northwest between Jackson and Johnsonville, near the Kentucky line. And rains had so flooded the river that he could not cross it.

This was dire news, for Hood needed Forrest's cavalry to protect his army from a federal attack while he crossed the river at Guntersville. Worse, if the whole plan was to evolve, time was of the essence before Thomas could combine all the Union forces then rushing toward him at Nashville. Reluctantly, but with what he felt was no other choice, Hood turned the army westward again, toward Florence and Tuscumbia, Alabama, about midway between Forrest and himself. There he hoped at least to take advantage of the repaired Memphis and Charleston and Mobile and Decatur railroads to bring up all the supplies he would need for the Tennessee adventure, but again he was disappointed. "Notwithstanding my request as early as the 9th of October that the railroad to Decatur be repaired, nothing had been done . . . towards the accomplishment of this important object," Hood fumed.

Mercifully unaware of these developments, the army trooped over Sand Mountain into the Tennessee River Valley, but it quickly turned into a hard march. "We have had nothing to eat since [yesterday]," wrote diarist Sam Foster, in Cleburne's division. "Today a wagon drives through camp and issues two ears of corn to each man. We are living on parched corn. Have had no meat for several days." They tromped past the Union garrison at Decatur with little more than an artillery demonstration, prompting Foster to huff, "Came away and left the Union flag flying in full view of us."

The march continued toward the setting sun, following the Tennessee River. "The richest country I have seen since I left Texas," Foster marveled, but he quickly added, "Now it is a desert waste. Fences burnt, large dwelling houses burnt, leaving two chimneys and their shade trees to mark the place, and as many as fifty negro cabins—but no sign of life unless an occasional old negro came out of a hut—No cattle, horses, hogs, chickens nor people—nothing but desolation on every hand."

Leading elements of the army reached the area of Florence and Tuscumbia on October 30 to find more evidence of Sherman's intent to drive the South into rack and ruin. Captain Thomas Key, who commanded an artillery battery in Cleburne's division, received permission to ride into Tuscumbia to stay overnight with some friends. "As I passed down the valley of the Tennessee I saw nothing but the wrecks of palaces and devastated plantations," he wrote in his diary. "I visited the business part of Tuscumbia and found a large portion of the town burned and all the streets looking weather-worn and dilapidated," said Key, who had previously owned a newspaper in the city. He blamed this "fiendish" handiwork on "the Federal General, Dodge" (the same General Dodge who had unleashed Streight's unfortunate raid against Rome) and contented himself with imagining the "fiery torments that justice will heap upon his guilty soul."

Meanwhile, Hood received more disturbing news. Jefferson Davis, it seemed—despite all his passionate rhetoric about Hood's soldiers' feet soon "pressing the soil of Tennessee"—was under a different impression of the way things should be done. Hood had telegraphed Davis on November 6, outlining the movement toward Nashville, and the following day Davis wired back telling Hood he should have kept after Sherman and should still do so now.

"If you keep his communications destroyed," said Davis, "he will most probably seek to concentrate for an attack on you. But if, as reported to you, he has sent a large part of his force southward, you may first beat him in detail, and, subsequently, without serious obstruction, or danger to the country in your rear, advance to the Ohio River."

This was a tall order, for Hood was now more than a hundred miles westward from Sherman's army and communications. He reasoned that Davis was not, at this point, "acquainted with [the army's] true condition." He immediately sought out Beauregard for support, and several days passed before Hood responded to Davis, saying that until now, "I did not regard this Army in the proper condition for a pitched battle." He went on to reiterate his plan to leave Sherman behind and move into Tennessee. There was some logic to Hood's position; after all, he had fewer than forty thousand men with which to fight double that many under Sherman, who had already beaten him once face to face at Atlanta. Furthermore, Hood's commanders remained of the opinion that the men were in no mood to tangle with Sherman's army again. And finally, he had the Tennesseans to consider. They made up a majority of his army, and they were ready to go home.

Beauregard added his own two cents' worth, telling Davis in a letter shortly after Hood moved out that he did not "countermand" Hood's proposal because the weather and condition of the railroads back to where Sherman was in Georgia were such that Hood could not have caught up with Sherman anyway and because if Hood moved back east, Thomas would soon have taken his army into Alabama and removed that state from the Confederacy. Last, Beauregard said he was under the impression that the Georgia state militia could raise twenty thousand men to oppose Sherman's advance. While this last assumption was much overblown, Beauregard nevertheless added the final weight of his authority for Hood to proceed.

Up in Richmond, surrounded by Grant's army and with the Confederacy in distress, Davis privately complained of Hood's intentions, calling them "ill advised," but he did nothing to stop him. It showed something of the deterioration of the once indomitable Davis, who, in earlier days, if he thought a thing "ill advised" would have brought it to a screeching halt. By now Davis had become almost as embattled personally as Lee was in the field, buffeted by rebellious congressmen, governors, and newspapers. As Confederate territory shrank, crops were lost and Confederate money dwindled practically to nothing. When the war began, a paper dollar issued from the Richmond mint was presumed to be worth a dollar of gold. Two years later it took three paper "shinplasters" to buy one gold dollar, and by the end of the year it took twenty. Now, in the fall of 1864, a gold dollar, if it could be found, cost forty or more Confederate dollars. People of wealth were selling their silver, jewelry, paintings, and other family treasures to questionably scrupulous "auctioneers"—often from Europe—in exchange for gold enough to buy food, clothing, and fuel for heat. The poor, as usual, often went without. The Richmond government couldn't pay its debts, nor could it pay its army, which actually didn't matter too much anyway, since its money was becoming worthless. Some state politicians were making ominous noises about establishing a separate peace with the Union, and by now Davis's cherished hope of recognition by England or France was a faded dream.

In any case, the beleaguered Davis seemed, if not overjoyed, at least content that somebody like Hood was willing to take the bull by the horns and attack the Union army someplace, maybe taking a little pressure off him, five hundred miles to the east in Richmond. Two days after Hood's telegram to Davis, Forrest finally arrived with his cavalry. Captain Key recalled that his entrance into town was marked by a "band playing lively airs, interluded with vociferous cheering."

While all of this was going on, another indelible milestone in the war was reached: Abraham Lincoln was reelected. The Democrats—or Peace Party—could muster only the electoral votes of Delaware, Kentucky, and New Jersey; the Republicans won the rest. The popular vote was closer—2,200,000 for Lincoln to 1,800,000 for "Little Mac" McClellan—but any remaining Southern hopes that the war could end in a peaceful settlement were finally dashed.

In the North, George Templeton Strong rejoiced in his diary, "The crisis has been passed. . . . The American people can be trusted to take care of the national honor." But in the South a pall of gloom drifted over the Confederacy. "The victory of the Constitution was postponed, and its triumph reserved for another and uncertain time," the Richmond *Examiner* moaned. And also, at this news, the bottom dropped out of the Confederate dollar; people could hardly give them away.

The defeat of the Northern Peace Party was in some measure laid at the feet of Hood and Johnston. "If only Atlanta had not fallen . . . ," and so forth. If Hood ever had a chance to redeem himself of these accusations, it was gone now—and had been gone from the moment he decided against crossing the Tennessee River at Guntersville back in October. Possibly a swift march and a quick victory over Thomas's as yet unorganized forces and the recapture of Nashville could have changed the outcome of the election. No one would ever know.

Captain Thomas Key, standing in the cheering crowd as the band serenaded the newly arrived Forrest and his troopers at Tuscumbia, made the unpleasant forecast, "With [Lincoln] the executive we may now expect the War to continue for another term of four years unless we shall be able to conquer the peace."

Conquering the peace was precisely what John Bell Hood was now preparing to do—he put no stores by politics or politicians. Besides, even if Lincoln had lost the election, it would have been three months before his opponent was installed, and in war—especially this one—three months was an eternity. On November 21, a week after Forrest and his command arrived, Hood set his army in motion, north, across the Tennessee River.

Back in the velvet-draped drawing rooms of the Chesnut family, a different kind of drama was being played out. Beautiful Sally Preston was "so sad, so utterly depressed," Mary Chesnut wrote in her diary the same day Hood's final, fateful telegram to Jefferson Davis was received. "She does not hear from Hood. Every insanity has entered her head, even that J.B. may be tired of his engagement."

It was indeed true—Hood and Buck Preston were engaged. For Hood it must have been the culmination of his dreams: In four short years he had gone from being an obscure lieutenant in the U.S. Army to a full general of the Confederacy at the age of thirty-three—right up there with Robert E. Lee. Before the fall of Atlanta, glory and acclaim were heaped upon him; newspapers sang his praises; Southern society—including Jefferson Davis himself—welcomed him as a hero and a peer. And now he was engaged to be married to one of the most beautiful and sought-after women in the South, the great-grandniece of Patrick Henry; she and her sister had been described as "goddesses upon a heaven-kissing hill, tall and stately, with brilliant fresh complexions, altogether the embodiment of physical health." Not only was Buck the "sweetest woman I ever knew," as Mary Chesnut recorded, she had "a mischievous gleam in her soft blue eyes; or are they gray, or brown, or black as night?" She went on, "I have seen them of every color varying with the mood of the moment."

Mrs. Chesnut's description might have been more telling than she realized, for, as Buck's eyes changed color with her moods, so her moods changed as quickly as the leaves of autumn. It was later suggested that Hood's romance with Buck Preston was actually a kind of metaphor for the plight of the Confederacy—the knight in shining armor goes out to slay the dragon but in the end does not get the girl. There is truth in this, and Hood—while he was no aristocrat, he was no backwoodsman, either—must have felt some hint of this as the affair progressed.

On the day he had been formally introduced to Buck by his surgeon, John Darby, when his men marched through Richmond the year previous, Hood had returned to the Chesnut house for dinner, and there the courting began in earnest. Before supper they played cards—Hood, Buck, Buck's sister Mary, and Mary's fiancé, Dr. Darby. "Certainly," Mrs. Chesnut wrote, "never did a game of casino cause so much uproarious mirth."

Hood was quickly on the move again, south, down to Suffolk with Longstreet and then on the long march to Gettysburg. After his wounding there, he was treated at hospitals in the Shenandoah Valley and then in early September brought to Richmond, where he resumed his courtship of Buck. The day he left for Chickamauga he proposed to her. "She would not say yes, but she did not say no," he remembered later, "but she half-promised me to think of it."

After his wounding at Chickamauga, Hood said he "gave it up," but by November he was back in Richmond, recuperating from the loss of the leg, and tried again. Mrs. Chesnut recalled that Buck "saw me sending a nice pudding to the wounded man" and remarked, "I would not marry him if he had a thousand legs instead of just one." Not long afterward, Hood visited the Chesnuts. Buck's sister Mary called out, "Look here Mrs. C. They are lifting General Hood out of his carriage, here, at your door. Neither Mrs. Chesnut, nor Buck, had been to visit Hood since his wounding, so he came to them, but Buck was either ill or feigning illness and would not come downstairs. The conversation was amicable enough until other people began to arrive, and Hood became uncomfortable. "This is the first house I had myself dragged to," he groaned. "I mean to be as happy as a fool, well, as a one-legged man can be. Send me off now. So many strangers scare me always. I can't run now, as I did before." Whether this was real self-pity or jesting, Mrs. Chesnut does not tell, but it was clear that he was back on the track of Buck Preston. The next day he went to see her again, and this time she received him with tears in her eyes.

By this time people were beginning to gossip about Hood behind his back, hinting that he was making a fool of himself with Buck. Charles Venable of Lee's staff called Buck a flirt. "She can't help it," he told Mrs. Chesnut. "She does not care for the man. It is sympathy for the wounded soldier." In this, Venable was doubtless correct. Buck seemed to enjoy tormenting her suitors, including Hood—perhaps especially Hood. She made a point of correcting his diction and his manners, even yawned in his face. There was a strong aura of Scarlett O'Hara about Buck; she might even have been the model for Scarlett O'Hara—bright, fickle, strong, stunningly beautiful, and with no illusions about her power over men. On Christmas Day, 1863, Hood proposed to her again. She turned him down.

This might have been enough for most people, but not Sam Hood, clearly a man in love who knew how to set his star in motion. During the next six weeks he somehow was invited to practically every place Buck might show up—parties, dances, dinners, amateur theatricals, even church—and slowly a relationship of sorts developed, strained though it was. He was using his crutches more easily by then and was even able to ride his horse, with some help mounting it. He would take Buck for carriage rides, after which she would usually come back complaining about him.

At the end of January 1864, Hood, again at the Chesnuts, announced he had been promoted to lieutenant general and given a corps in Joe Johnston's Army of Tennessee. "Suddenly his eyes ablazed as he said this," Mary Chesnut recorded. "I said to myself, 'All that ambition still—in spite of those terrible wounds.' " At that point Hood declared, "This has been the happiest year of any, in spite of all my wounds."

Buck was there, at the other end of the sofa, with Hood sitting between them. "When I am gone, it is all over. I will not come back," he remarked—ostensibly to Mary Chesnut. "Are you not threatening the wrong end of the sofa?" she replied.

Before the evening was over, Buck had taken a diamond star from Hood and promised to sew it on his new hat, an encouraging sign, at least for the general. By now Buck's friends, including the Chesnuts, were becoming alarmed that the affair might be getting too serious. "How I want him to go back to the army," puffed Henry Brewster, a Confederate politician. "These girls are making a fool of him."

But Hood persisted, and Buck was more and more in his company, often "guarding" him in public, shielding him with her body from the rush of crowds. Privately she would tell people, "Engaged to that man—never—for what do you take me?" But publicly they had become—at least to much of Richmond society—an item.

In mid-February, Buck announced that she and Sam Hood were engaged. It was not a clean change of heart for her—not by any means. Her version of the story to Mrs. Chesnut was that she had gone down to his carriage to say good night, and he had held out his good hand and asked her to marry him once more. "Say yes or say no," the tall young general told Buck. "I will not be satisfied with anything else—yes—or no is it?"

"Well, he would *keep* holding out his hand," Buck told Mary Chesnut. "What could I do? So I put mine in his. Heavens, what a change came over his face."

"Now I will speak to your father," Hood declared. "I want his consent to marry you at once."

So he had become engaged, but almost by default. When Buck told her parents about the engagement, they went into shock, forbidding her to make a public announcement in the evident hope the thing would break of its own weight. But this seems only to have set off something rebellious in Buck. A few days later the engagement was announced in the Charleston *Mercury*. Buck blamed Hood for leaking it, but she now not only admitted it openly, but warmed to it as well. Richmond society seemed stupefied. Some gossiped that Hood had no property in Kentucky, that West Point was a "pauper's school," that there was "nothing in him"—only the military glory. Others stoutly defended him. Burton Harrison, Jefferson Davis's private secretary, retorted, *"Only the military glory! The glory and the fame that he has gained during the* war—that is Hood." The subject of Hood—his engagement to Buck, his spectacular rise in rank—was in the air of every salon and parlor in Richmond that winter.

General John C. Breckinridge, prewar U.S. vice president and former Kentucky senator and a boyhood friend of Hood's, asked Mary Chesnut at a party one evening, "What's the name of that fellow who has gone to Europe for Hood's leg?"

"Dr. Darby."

"Suppose it is shipwrecked?"

"No matter—half a dozen are ordered."

At this point Buck's mother raised her hands. "No wonder the general says they talk of him as if he were a centipede," she huffed, "his leg is in everybody's mouth." The elder Mrs. Preston was to prove a formidable obstacle in the romance.

Hood was destined to have only a few days with his new fiancée. Orders were delivered for him at the Spottswood Hotel, telling him to report to Dalton, Georgia, and his new corps command. On February 16 he boarded his baggage and horses on a train and set out west, first stopping in Columbia, South Carolina, to visit Major "Willie" Preston, Buck's brother, who was stationed there with his artillery battery. Willie was later killed under Hood's command during the battle of Atlanta.

It had to have been a bittersweet parting for Hood. At long last love, but now war called him back. Whatever his feelings were, he also must have somehow sensed that he was not meant for the silver tea sets and velvet drapes and polished marble and mahogany of Richmond society, so far removed from the grime and smoke and horror—and, probably, the exhilaration of the battlefield—after all, his whole life, he had been a warrior.

The night before he left Richmond, Hood was at the Chesnuts' with Buck, and he said to her, "You look mighty pretty in that hat. You wore it at the turnpike—where I surrendered at first sight." Mary Chesnut, recording that Buck was wearing "last winter's English hat with the pheasant's wing," turned to Hood, who had hobbled over to the window, and said to him, "Actually, if you stay here in Richmond much longer, you will grow to be a courtier."

8

Go On As You Propose ★

Through the end of that long 1864 October Sherman hung around the Alabama-Georgia line watching Hood—who was still at Gadsden—and resumed his agitated plea for permission to begin what he now referred to as "the big raid." One of his corps commanders, General David Stanley, remembered his mood in those days:

> Sherman, like the rest of the ranking officers, lived in a tent. He was nervous and sleepless. Long after the rest of the company had gone to bed he would remain sitting on a camp stool, wrapped in a well worn army overcoat, leaning over the remains of the evening fire and seemingly pondering over the tremendous campaign before him. At times, for want of company, he would join the sentinel, walk alongside of him on his post, and, despite regulations, enter into long conversations with him. He used to say that these sentinels always knew someone away back home whom he knew.

As the days passed, Sherman fumed and boiled and was more nervous and sleepless than ever. His nervous tics began to recur as he plotted his march to the sea, and he continually telegraphed Washington for permission to get on with it. "This movement is not purely military or strategic," he wired Halleck, "but it will illustrate the vulnerability of the South." In the same vein he sent Grant a long telegram outlining his overall views of the political situation, in hopes of shaking something loose. All had been to no avail. Grant's chief of staff, John Rawlins, was still dead set against the idea, as were Halleck and the Lincoln government. Sherman may have conquered Atlanta, but he had failed in his main objective, which was to destroy Hood's army, and now he proposed to abandon that mission altogether and go off in a different direction. "This is not war, but rather statesmanship," Sherman argued to Grant.

But to the feisty Sherman's extreme annoyance, Grant was not convinced. "Do you not think it is advisable," Grant telegraphed him back the same evening, "now that Hood has gone so far north, to entirely ruin him before starting out on your proposed campaign? With Hood's army destroyed, you can go where you please with impunity." Finally, the commanding general went on to more or less *order* Sherman to follow after the Confederate army.

The exasperated Sherman wired back the moment he received Grant's reply.

> If I could hope to overhaul Hood, I would turn against him with my whole force; then he would retreat to the southwest, drawing me a decoy away from Georgia, which is his chief object. . . . No single army can catch Hood, and I am convinced that the best results will follow from defeating Jeff. Davis' cherished plan of making me leave Georgia by manoeuvering. . . . I regard the pursuit of Hood as useless. Still, if he attempts to invade Middle Tennessee, I will hold Decatur, and be prepared to move in that direction but, unless I let go of Atlanta, my force will not be equal to his.

When he sent this telegram, Sherman was in transit to a command post more closely between his divided armies, down to Kingston, Georgia, all the destructive activities against his Atlanta-to-Chattanooga railroad by Hood's army having been miraculously repaired in the space of two weeks. On the ride down, still fuming, he penned an afterthought, which he fired off to Grant later in the day. "If I turn back the whole effect of my campaign will be lost. . . . I am clearly of opinion that the best results will follow my contemplated movement through Georgia."

He probably needn't have bothered—though perhaps this last little communiqué pushed Grant over the edge in his favor. In any case, he had barely arrived in Kingston when he got another wire from Grant—the one he'd been waiting for these many weeks: "I do not see that you can withdraw from where you are to follow Hood, without giving up all we have gained in territory. I say, then, go on as you propose."

Sherman had been working out his plan in his head and on paper from the time he occupied Atlanta, and now he put it in action. To counter the threat of Hood's advancing into Tennessee, he had recently sent back to George Thomas at Nashville the Twenty-third Army Corps under General Schofield and the Fourth Army Corps under David Stanley. In addition to a corps of garrison troops at Nashville, Thomas had the equivalent of another corps in the three divisions of the Nashville District that he had stationed at Murfreesboro, Decatur, and Chattanooga. Not only that, but most of General A. J. Smith's Sixteenth Corps was supposedly on the way to Tennessee from Missouri to complete the picture. Thus, when all was said and done, Thomas would have on hand twelve divisions of infantry plus three divisions of cavalry—some seventy-five thousand men—to undo whatever Hood was planning to do to him.

But all was not said and done. First, Smith's Missouri force was delayed, owing to some mischief created on the other side of the Mississippi by the Rebel General Sterling Price. Second, one of Thomas's corps—the one he organized out of the Nashville garrison—was composed of noncombatant quartermaster troops who probably wouldn't be worth much in a fight. Finally, it was conceivable that Hood could somehow bottle up, delay, or destroy the three spread-out divisions at Murfreesboro, Decatur, and Chattanooga, thus subtracting yet another Union corps from the equation. All in all, then, Thomas might conceivably have more problems on his hands than Sherman knew, or cared to think about.

What Sherman did know of his old West Point classmate Thomas was that he was dependable—slow perhaps, cautious certainly—but dependable, and Sherman was perfectly content to leave the fate of the entire western theater of the war to "the Rock of Chickamauga" while he went on his big raid.

Having brought down from Tennessee all the supplies he needed, Sherman sent back his sick and wounded and anything he could not take with him and then proceeded to re-destroy all the railroads and telegraph lines leading back to Tennessee, utterly cutting himself off from his sources of communication and supply. He had organized his remaining army into two "wings" led by Generals Howard and Slocum, and by mid-November he was prepared to embark on a three-hundred-mile southeastward march across hostile territory to Savannah, Georgia, and the sea.

Two long months before, when the mayor and two councilmen of Atlanta begged Sherman to rescind his order expelling the citizens from the city, the general had replied with his usual florid bluntness, that war is hell: "You cannot qualify war in harsher terms than I will," he said. "War is cruelty, and you cannot refine it; and those who brought war into our country deserve all the curses and maledictions a people can pour out. . . . If the United States submits to division now, it will not stop, but will go on until we reap the fate of Mexico, which is eternal war. . . . You might as well appeal against the thunderstorm as against those terrible hardships of war.

Now Sherman was prepared to put this philosophy into practice on the grandest scale yet imagined in any war: His sixty-thousand-man army would cut a sixty-mile-wide swath through the breadbasket of the South, systematically destroying practically everything in its path. Not since the depredations of Attila the Hun and the Duke of Alva had such an adventure been conducted in Western civilization, but Sherman's reasoning was definitely nineteenth—if not twentieth—century in character. So far, it had been the border states—Virginia, Tennessee, Maryland, Kentucky, and parts of Mississippi and Louisiana—that bore the brunt of the war. Now it was Sherman's intention to bring down its horrors on the very heart of the Confederacy—from Atlanta to Savannah and, in particular, South Carolina, which had started the whole thing in the first place, then northward, seven hundred miles up to Richmond itself. His campaign would ruin the South militarily, physically, *and* psychologically.

Warring against civilians and quasicivilians had become commonplace by the middle of the following century—Hitler's bombing of London and other English cities, for example, and the Allied carpet-bombing missions over Germany—though the military consensus subsequently showed that in most cases such strategies merely tended to stiffen resistance. Sherman was not the first Civil War general to adopt such a policy. General David Hunter burned schools in Virginia, and there was Phil Sheridan in the Shenandoah, who bragged that when he was through with the valley even a crow would have to look somewhere else for its food. To Sherman it was all expedience: the sooner the war was over, the sooner the bloodletting would stop; and that justified everything.

Sherman's marching orders to his generals were specific regarding the destruction of private property and the molesting of citizens, which was forbidden unless mandated by some military need. But in the event, this turned out to be mostly lip service. Later, in his after-action report, he shrugged off what happened by saying that some of his men "did some things they ought not to have done," which was one of the understatements of the war.

On November 16, Sherman started out from Atlanta with his four corps, three thousand supply wagons, and artillery. Even years later he was able to describe the scene vividly: "Behind us lay Atlanta, smouldering and in ruins, the black smoke rising high in the air, and hanging like a pall over the ruined city." Before they left, he had ordered that anything militarily useful be destroyed and to that end sent his engineers to burn down the offending structures. Afterward, he characterized as more or less "accidental" the fact that nearly two thousand buildings had gone up in flames, most of them private homes and shops. He continued: "The day was extremely beautiful, clear sunlight, with bracing air, and an unusual feeling of exhilaration seemed to pervade all minds—a feeling of something to come."

Thus, with Sherman now on the march south and Hood embarking north, an extraordinary spectacle was introduced to the war: two armies that had been locked in a death embrace for four bloody years now moved off in opposing directions—despite the serious misgivings of the governments of both sides—each to a singular destiny.

Pap Thomas did not at all like what his old West Point roommate had gotten him into. Here was Sherman traipsing off with the bulk of the western army to face nothing more than some old men and boys of the Georgia militia, while the onus fell on Thomas to fend off Hood's entire army of forty-thousand combat veterans. Time and again, Sherman insisted that Hood would not try to enter Tennessee, but Thomas correctly believed otherwise. Actually, he had proposed to Sherman that *he* be allowed to go off to the sea with his much smaller army, leaving Sherman and the bulk of the Union forces to hold Atlanta and Tennessee and go after Hood, but the red-haired Ohioan waved off this proposal and, despite Thomas's opposition to his plan, ordered his old friend north to hold the line on his own.

When Sherman first sent Thomas to the defense of Tennessee, "the Rock" had requested that the Army of the Cumberland, his old command, be sent with him. This also was denied, however, for Sherman picked only the choicest of divisions for his march to the sea and left Thomas to settle for an amalgam of troops from various quarters, including raw recruits and the sick and lame that Sherman had directed back to him. Furthermore, many of the regiments Sherman promised to Thomas were in fact nonexistent because their terms of enlistment had expired, while still others had been shipped back to their homes en masse to vote in the presidential election. There were about twelve thousand cavalry under Thomas's jurisdiction, but most of them, because of a scarcity of horses, were dismounted and scattered all over Tennessee. In short, what Thomas commanded at this point was a lot of people, not an army.

And there was Forrest, too. One main factor Thomas was counting on to thwart Hood's expected movement into Tennessee was the barrier of the Tennessee River held by a strong flotilla of Union gunboats. These heavily armed ships could move swiftly to almost any point on the river and blast a crossing army with a deathly rain of shells the caliber of which no land artillery could hope to match. But while Hood was languishing around Tuscumbia waiting to ford the river into Tennessee, Forrest and his cavalry were wreaking havoc with the proud Union navy and its fancy gunboats.

The Tennessee River curves like a big letter U stamped about in the center of the state of Tennessee, and about midway up the left side of the U is the port town of Johnsonville, where the federals had established a strong main terminal for river traffic. Fresh from a remarkable raid into downtown Memphis, where his men literally chased Union generals from their bedrooms, Forrest now descended on the unsuspecting environs of Johnsonville, destroying forty federal gunboats, transports, and barges and disrupting movement all along the river. Sherman branded him a "devil," but when Thomas asked for reinforcements, what he received instead were suggestions and advice. All in all, Thomas didn't like the looks of things and wasn't ashamed to say so, wiring Sherman, "There is one thing, however, I don't wish—to be in command of the defense of Tennessee, unless you and the authorities at Washington deem it absolutely necessary." This sentiment fell on deaf ears as far as Sherman was concerned. In any event, on November 12, a couple of days before Sherman embarked on his "big raid," the telegraph lines between Atlanta and Nashville went dead for good. Thomas was on his own.

Pap Thomas was a methodical man of the old school of military science. He was also an old-line Virginian, which, at least in the early stages of the war had caused his loyalty to the United States to be questioned in the North and, at the same time, cast him as a pariah in his native Southland; he was one of the few Southern officers of the old army who refused to join the Confederacy.

Born in Southampton County, Virginia, in 1816, Thomas was the scion of a prosperous plantation family and might have led the life of a

Southern cavalier but for an independent, if not rebellious, streak that led him into such frowned-upon activities as teaching school and giving church lessons to slave children. He was a meticulous boy who taught himself the patience to make fine saddles, boots, and other leather goods, as well as furniture. Undoubtedly, this methodical and painstaking nature was partially the cause of Grant's later description of him as "slow beyond excuse."

Thomas graduated from the Military Academy in the class of 1840, standing twelfth of forty-two cadets, six places behind William Tecumseh Sherman. He had developed into a tall, square-shouldered, handsome man with blue eyes and brown hair. He served in Florida during the Seminole War and in 1846–47 was an artillery officer in the Mexican War in a unit that included his future enemies Braxton Bragg and Sam French. His conduct there won him renown both in the army and in his native state. Southampton County presented him with an ornate sword of gold, silver, and precious stones.

In 1855 the Second Cavalry was formed by then U.S. Secretary of War Jefferson Davis, and Thomas became a major in it. The regiment was largely officered by Southerners—in fact, of the seventeen generals the Second U.S. Cavalry furnished during the Civil War, twelve served the Confederacy—leading many, including Thomas, to suspect that Davis had deliberately organized the unit with a future war between North and South in mind. As one of his junior officers, Thomas had a young Kentucky lieutenant, John Bell Hood.

In 1860 Thomas took a year's leave of absence from the army, and in early 1861, with many Southern states seceding, he applied for the post of commandant of the Virginia Military Institute. The post had already been filled, but Thomas was then offered a position as chief of ordnance for the state of Virginia, which, of course, would require him to resign from the U.S. Army. He replied, "As long as my native State remains in the Union it is my purpose to remain in the army, unless required to perform duties alike repulsive to honor and humanity." Thus, a conclusion can be fairly reached that on the eve of war Thomas was certainly toying with the idea of placing his loyalty with the South. But in the end he took the oath to the Union, forever dissolving his ties of family and friends in Virginia, who not only never spoke *to* him again, they never even spoke *of* him.

After the outbreak of hostilities Thomas was promoted to brigadier general and, along with his old pal Cump Sherman—who, in fact, had interceded with the government to get him promoted—was sent to Kentucky, where he commanded a training camp. It wasn't long afterward that Sherman supposedly went crazy, and Thomas was ordered to lead a force into the southeastern part of the state to contend with a Southern army under General George Crittenden that was anchoring the eastern end of a Confederate line stretching from the Cumberland Gap to the Mississippi River. While Grant was hammering the opposite end of the line, Thomas, in early January 1862, advanced on the brigades of General Felix Zollicoffer, who had unwisely posted his men in a fairly untenable military position with their backs to the rain-swollen Cumberland River. When Crittenden discovered Zollicoffer's mistake, he sent an order for the Tennessean to remove to the south bank; but when he personally took the field, he discovered to his consternation that the order had not been carried out. Thomas, by now encamped in a driving rainstorm, had divided his force on opposite sides of Fishing Creek, and Crittenden decided to launch a sneak dawn attack on the left wing.

From the Confederate standpoint, the battle was a series of disastrous errors and ill luck. First off, Thomas was not surprised as intended because a cavalry patrol he sent out detected the advance of Crittenden's army. This allowed him time to unite his divided forces and rout the cold and muddy gray-clad attackers. In the melee, Zollicoffer was shot down when he mistakenly rode into the Union lines, and Crittenden, a West Point man, afterward was convicted of drunkenness during the battle. It was the first Union victory of the war, and Pap Thomas had won it. In its gratitude, the government promoted him to major general.

At Shiloh, next spring, Thomas did not take part in the battle but commanded a division of Buell's army that arrived after the fight was over. By this time the reports of Grant's incompetence and intoxication had reached the ears of the department commander, Halleck, and that was when he personally took charge and placed Grant in the humiliating vice commander position. Thomas was installed in Grant's place as commander of the Army of the Tennessee.

Thomas occupied that position for several months, after which Halleck restored Grant, and Thomas returned to his old division under Buell. By late summer 1862, he was made second in command of Buell's Army of the Cumberland. That September, Washington had become disenchanted with the ponderous maneuvering of Buell and ordered him replaced by Thomas, but Thomas himself had the order rescinded, saying it was fair neither to Buell nor to him at that time. When the War Department really got around to canning Buell a month or two later, Thomas was passed over in favor of General William S. Rosecrans. That incensed the Virginian to the extent that he filed a protest to Washington, but Halleck persuaded him to withdraw it.

All this time Thomas was establishing himself as a soldier of proven field merit, an earnest and methodical workhorse who was absolutely indifferent to danger but without the flair of a "Rosy" Rosecrans or Don Carlos Buell. He served as Rosecrans's assistant commander without further complaint.

On New Year's Eve, 1863, one of the bitterest battles of the war exploded about forty miles south of Nashville, near Murfreesboro, beside a stream called Stones River, where Confederate General Braxton Bragg had drawn up the three corps of the Army of Tennessee and, in essence, dared Rosecrans to attack him. The night before the battle, bands on both sides struck up their favorite tunes, "Dixie," "Yankee Doodle," and so on, finally ending the evening with "Home, Sweet Home," which was played by both sides. Thomas commanded three divisions in the center of Rosecrans's army, opposite some names that would become increasingly familiar to him as the war dragged on— Bishop Polk, Frank Cheatham, Pat Cleburne, William Hardee.

At sunrise the Confederates emerged from woods and flew into the Army of the Cumberland, causing the two corps of Thomas and General A. M. McCook to recoil on the rest of the army. It was an even bloodier day than the day at Fredericksburg, Virginia, had been three weeks earlier. That night, as the exhausted armies tried to rest beneath a frigid rainstorm, the grim Union generals gathered for a council of war in a house beside the Nashville Pike. Retreat to Nashville was being discussed when Thomas, who had fallen into a half sleep in a chair, perked up and grumbled, "This army doesn't retreat." With this pronunciation in mind, they stuck it out for three more days, until Bragg and the Confederate army sullenly drew off southward to a position about midway between Nashville and Chattanooga.

All through that winter and spring Rosecrans's army remained inert, but finally in June, after much prodding by Washington, the Army of the Cumberland, with Thomas's corps in the lead, began to move southward in a series of drenching rainstorms, pushing Bragg's Army of Tennessee before it. In early September, Bragg abandoned Chattanooga and moved his army south beyond Lookout Mountain to an area defined by Chickamauga Creek. Going for the kill, Rosecrans pushed after him, advancing his army in three widely separated columns, with Thomas in the middle. What he did not know was that Bragg had finally divined a scheme to wreck him. With reinforcements expected any day from Longstreet's corps of the Army of Northern Virginia—including the division of John Bell Hood—Bragg designed a trap he hoped would destroy the Army of the Cumberland. While parts of his army held up Rosecrans's two farthest separated corps, the bulk of it would pounce on the unsuspecting Thomas as he emerged from a gap in the mountains, grind him up, and then turn on the other two corps in similar fashion.

But the plan did not work out that way. Through confusion in some orders and failure to carry out unconfused orders, the trap was sprung, but the bait was not taken. Thomas quickly realized his peril and drew back. An angry Bragg ordered a similar attack on the northern wing of Rosecrans's army, but it, too, pulled back before any damage was done. The two armies faced each other for a week, until Longstreet arrived. The federals had drawn up their four corps with Thomas's occupying the left center. The Confederates hit them with a fury on September 19, but by day's end nothing much had been gained except the spilling of a great amount of blood. Thomas had held fast but braced for a renewal of savagery in the morning.

It came not at sunrise—owing to more confusion on the part of Confederate commanders—but about 9:30, when Bishop Polk's screaming divisions swooped out of the woods on the left of Thomas's line, which he had been trying without success to get Rosecrans to reinforce all morning. As Thomas contended with this threat, and begged again for reinforcements, Longstreet launched his assault on Thomas's right. Here Hood received his mutilating leg wound but not before he saw his troops smash through the Union lines and rout the enemy in front. At this point, half the Army of the Cumberland seemed to melt away, including Rosecrans himself, who, along with his staff, scrambled back toward Chattanooga. But George Henry Thomas, after even his commanding general had fled the field, defiantly kept his corps fighting all through that long hot Sunday afternoon, saving the Army of the Cumberland from a total rout.

For this heroic effort he became idolized as "the Rock of Chickamauga" and a month later was promoted to command of the Army of the Cumberland, which, by the spring, would become the anvil for Sherman's pulverizing attacks on the road to Atlanta.

No matter how loud Sherman crowed to Washington about giving Thomas all the troops he needed should Hood march on Nashville, Thomas didn't see it that way at all. Reports came filtering up to him that Hood was beginning to advance across the river with forty to fifty thousand men, while he had barely more than thirty-one thousand effective infantry available. He had sent most of his cavalry up to Louisville to meet shipments of animals and equipment, and the divisions of A. J. Smith had still not shown up. More disturbing was information that the Rebel General Kirby Smith was on his way to Hood with up to twenty thousand fresh troops from the trans-Mississippi theater. And now his old pal Sherman had taken the bulk of the army and marched totally and unalterably out of reach.

Thomas was said to be imperturbable, a virtual man-mountain who inspired universal confidence. But it was also recorded that in times of stress—such as the battles at Murfreesboro and Atlanta—he had a habit of roughing up his whiskers with his hands, then smoothing them out when things calmed down again. In those early days before Nashville, with the gathering storm of Hood on the horizon and his own forces in disarray, Pap Thomas's whiskers remained for him irritatingly ruffled.

9

★ It Is Almost Worth Dying

Way back in July, when Hood took command of the Army of Tennessee, Buck Preston had received the news not as a proud fiancée might but with a good deal of apprehension: "Things are so bad out there," she said. "They cannot be worse, you know . . . they have saved Johnston from the responsibility of his own blunders—and put Sam in. Poor Sam."

And it continued to be "poor Sam" as the days wore on. With the arrival of Grant's army at the gates of Richmond, Buck and Mary Chesnut had fled home to South Carolina, but that was not far enough to escape the unflattering gossip and carping that came at Hood's expense. He was "too rash," or he "lacked refinement," or he "intrigued to be put over Joe Johnston's head," or he was "Jeff Davis's pet." Even worse were the snide remarks about Hood and Buck: "Will she marry that man? He has no manners, no fortune. He is only a lucky soldier," or, "She is throwing herself away—to marry a maimed man," or, "Her family are mute as mice. They know he is unfit for this high command."

Naturally it got worse when Atlanta fell. There were calls for Hood's removal, accusations that he had butchered his army, and so on. Even his old friend Dr. John Darby—after returning from France with

Hood's new wooden leg—reportedly expressed shock at Hood's ''lack of *refinement*.'' Not that he didn't have his defenders; there were many—including Mary Chesnut, who always took up for him—and men of high and low rank in and out of the army. In her diary, Mary Chesnut recorded the story of one, a maimed old veteran on his way back to the front:

> One man had hair as long as a woman's. A vow, he said. He has pledged himself not to cut his hair until war [is] declared [over] and our Southern country free.
> Four of them had made this vow. All were dead but himself. One was killed in Missouri, one in Virginia, and he left one at Kennesaw Mountain. This poor creature had one arm taken off at the socket. When I remarked that he was utterly disabled and ought not to remain in the army, he answered quickly.
> ''I am First Texas. If old Hood can go with one foot, I can go with one arm.''

When it became plain that Hood was going after Thomas in Tennessee, leaving Sherman an open door to the heartland of the South, there arose another public outcry. One day, Mary Chesnut recorded, she ''found Buck in bed, with a diamond ring from Hood. She needs something, for her beloved's star is under a cloud.''

It may have been so, but John Bell Hood did not see it in those terms. Cloud or no cloud, he was embarking on the greatest march of his star-studded career—the youngest of the eight full generals of the Confederacy leading forty thousand-odd men northward to fame or destruction, nothing less momentous was on the table for this roll of the dice.

On Sunday, the 20th of November, 1864, Hood sent Stephen Dill Lee's corps across the newly constructed pontoon bridge over the Tennessee, and at dawn the next day the entire army went into motion, with cheering and the music of many bands. Hood had lost nearly a month waiting for the railroad repairs that would bring him twenty days' supplies and ammunition, a dangerous but necessary decision, for he was well aware that Thomas would not be idle in the preparations for his unstringing. But he was immensely heartened by his perception that the army "had entirely recovered from the depression that frequent retreats had created." When they reached the Tennessee state line, they were greeted by a sign that read, TENNESSEE—A FREE HOME OR A GRAVE, and they cheered again.

It was Hood's immediate campaign plan to outflank by rapid movement the federal army at Pulaski, about thirty miles to the northeast, which he now knew was under the command of Major General John Schofield, his old friend and West Point classmate. Once that was accomplished, Schofield's only choice would be to fight a battle with Hood, which the Southern commander was confident he would win because his army was nearly a third larger than Schofield's, or to retreat hurriedly to Thomas at Nashville, in which case Hood proposed to cut him off and wipe him out. With Schofield's force disposed of, the Army of Tennessee could then march unopposed to defeat Thomas's divided forces at Nashville. An important part of this plan was that Schofield should be dispensed with *south* of Columbia and the barrier of the Duck River, and Hood had set his army moving with this in mind.

Various participants recorded their feelings as they crossed the high swirling river, many back into their native state. Tennessee boasted thirty-two regiments of the army; Alabama was next with thirty-one; Mississippi had twenty-eight; Georgia fifteen; Arkansas thirteen; Texas seven, plus seven of cavalry; Louisiana seven; Missouri four, plus eight of cavalry; Florida five; South Carolina four; and North Carolina two. Of the Confederate states, only Virginia went unrepresented; all of her sons were fighting with Lee up around Richmond. The march of Hood's army is a soldiers' story, told in soldiers' words.

Captain Thomas Key, an artillerist with Cleburne's division: "The whole army this morning with steady steps bends its way northward towards the fruitful lands of the gallant Tennessee. There is now a snow storm raging. . . . The wind howls mournfully from the west."

Captain Sam Foster, Granbury's Texas brigade: "We left camp this morning at sun up and started for Tenn."

Dr. D. G. Owen, surgeon with Major General John Calvin

Brown's division, Cheatham's corps: "I think we will have a severe fight before a month. Sherman will endeavor to keep us out of Tenn. Hood intends going. That is the question before the contending armies at present."

Sam Watkins, of Cheatham's corps: "We walked over this floating bridge, and soon found ourselves on the Tennessee side of the Tennessee River. In driving a great herd of cattle across the pontoon, the front one got stubborn, and the others, crowding up all in one bulk, broke the line that held the pontoon and drowned many of the drove. We had beef for supper that night."

Ralph Neal, private, 20th Tennessee Infantry: "For several days we had marched through a very poor country, and on very short rations, three sinkers per day—to those who don't understand, a sinker is a biscuit made from unbolted wheat flour without milk, grease, salt or soda."

Captain Joseph Boyce, Sam French's division, Cockrell's Missouri brigade: "We were obliged to leave behind at Tuscumbia and Florence many men who were so badly shod and clothed they could not make the march towards Nashville. Presently a snow storm set in, the first heavy snow of the season. The men set up a shout and hurrahed for Missouri. 'This is the kind of weather we want, regular old Missouri weather. This is none of your southern rains; this is something decent.' "

Dr. Owen, surgeon: "Gen'l Cheatham issued an order for all bare-footed men to sew them up shoes out of beef hides, put the hair next to the feet & stitch them close around the feet. I saw several pairs of them & they did fine to walk around in but did not smell well after a day or two."

Captain James L. Cooper, 20th Tennessee Regiment: "About the 22nd of this month we commenced our march from Florence into Tennessee. It was a terribly cold day and the rain as it fell froze in a hard mass on my horse's mane. We marched through Wainesboro and in a day or two began to see evidences of the Yankees, in the dead horses and men along the road, where Forrest's cavalry had been skirmishing with them."

Captain Sam Foster: "Today came to Waynesboro, a very nice little town, but nearly ruined by the war. Several houses burned down, some torn down, gardens destroyed.''

Surgeon Owen, to his wife: ''When this reaches you I expect to be in Mid'l Tennessee. My boots were worn out & I had to buy me a pair of old pontoon shoes from the government & they don't suit me in this muddy weather. . . . Have you made me any shirts of your old dress yet? I would like very much to have a couple. . . . I would like very much to have something to line my grey coat with, for the lining has all torn out.''

Thomas Key: ''Through the laziness of a sergeant, two wagons last night were driven into a pond, drowning one mule and near drowning a freezing negro teamster. His clothes froze on him and it was with strenuous exertion that his life was saved.''

E. T. Eggleston, Lee's corps, artillery: ''Came through some of the finest and most beautiful country I ever beheld, passed by the residence of Gen Pillow and Wm Polk, brother to the late Lt. Gen Polk, two magnificent structures.''

Sam Foster: ''Came past Mount Pleasant today and strike the richest country we have seen yet—Land rich, very rich. Water good and plenty of it, and the finest timber we have ever seen. To day we pass the Polk place in Maury County. The prettiest place I have ever seen in my life.''

Chaplain Charles L. Quintard, Cheatham's corps: ''In consequence of the wretched condition of the roads and the rough weather, we had a hard time of it. I made my way with all possible speed through Mount Pleasant to Ashwood and to the house of my dear friend, General Lucius Polk.''

Over at Pulaski, about twenty-five miles northeast, John Schofield was justifiably alarmed. From the day Hood's army began marching into Tennessee, he had gotten reports from his cavalry that the Southern commander's intention seemed directed at getting between him and the Duck River crossing at Columbia. But Schofield wasn't sure; he worried that Hood might be planning to swing around and attack him at or near

Pulaski. Schofield's orders from Thomas were to prepare for either possibility, and so he dawdled around Pulaski with his twenty-eight-thousand-man army for a couple of days longer than he should have, trying to divine Hood's designs.

John Schofield was an odd sort of bird for the army. By the time he arrived in Pulaski he was thirty-three—the same age as Hood, stocky and bald-headed, with a long, full black beard and drooping mustache. Except for the actions in Missouri and the fight around Atlanta, he had not spent much time on the battlefield, and, at least according to one observer, he was not too keen on battle itself. He had started out life as the son of a traveling Baptist missionary and was engaged in the study of pre-law when, at the age of seventeen, the West Point cadet appointed from his district in Illinois dropped out of the academy, and Schofield got the vacancy. He did well enough in his studies to tutor his present-day nemesis, Sam Hood, through mathematics, and though he remained religious, managed to pick up on the way a few vices such as smoking and playing cards. While at the Point a curious event befell Schofield that would figure in his later career, particularly in the defense of Nashville. As a senior, he was nearly expelled from the academy for refusing to name the participants in an incident of horseplay that he witnessed. A court-martial was eventually ordered, and one of the members of the court was none other than George Thomas, the cavalry instructor, who voted against him. Even though he was eventually acquitted, Schofield apparently harbored a grudge against Thomas thereafter.

After graduation, Schofield served in Florida, helping to subdue the Seminole Indians, and eventually returned to West Point as an instructor. In 1857 he married the daughter of his boss at the academy, but by 1860 he had decided to get out of the army. "My taste for service in the line of the Army, if I ever had one, was gone," he recalled. He was on the verge of resigning when he received some "timely advice" from the former secretary of war, Jefferson Davis, who gave him a prescient "hint that promotion might be better in a year or two." When war broke out some months later, Schofield was posted to Missouri on the staff of General Nathaniel Lyon, where he was soon promoted to brigadier general, commanded the Missouri state militia, took part in the battles of Wilson's Creek and Prairie Grove, and, ultimately, was given command of the entire Department of the Missouri. He joined Sherman's army as it launched the Atlanta campaign.

As Hood's men moved menacingly northward, Schofield arrived in Pulaski on November 13, took command from General Stanley the following morning, and began organizing his army. At this time the federal camps were a beehive of activity, troops arriving, and drilling, ammunition and supply trains chugging into the depot hourly from Nashville. Also, about this time, there was a certain amount of spying going on by both armies. General Stanley recorded one incident in which a "funny little fellow," shoeless, tattered, and driving a rickety wagon containing a bale of cotton, drove into the Union camp. He was trying to sell the cotton to the federal soldiers—a common practice at that time, since they were the only ones to sell cotton to—and after completing the sale he lingered for a while, speaking with soldiers. He was about to leave when he was recognized by someone and brought to Stanley, who discovered "concealed in that old shirt a very perfect drawing of all our lines and fortifications at Pulaski." Noting that this was a "very bright and intelligent spy," Stanley added that he "intended to hang that fellow but in the confusion of our retreat he escaped, and I am not sorry." On another occasion a double agent arrived at the federal camp offering to scuttle the boats of Hood's pontoon bridge at Tuscumbia for the sum of ten thousand dollars. Terms were agreed to, and the saboteur actually cut loose Hood's bridge; but "as it was caught and preserved, he never claimed any reward."

By his own account, Schofield soon became "apprehensive" that Thomas, up in Nashville, would be too "slow" to react to whatever surprises Hood had in store for him. At that point, Schofield and Thomas both believed that Hood's army numbered up to fifty-five thousand. Before long, Schofield concluded that Thomas's orders for him to fight Hood at Pulaski were not only wrong but "embarrassing" and began a correspondence with his commander to give himself more flexibility. This was granted, but even after he had sure information that

Hood was on the march, Schofield dallied several days before coming to the realization that "Hood is nearer Columbia than I am" and frantically ordering the concentration of his forces below the Duck River at Columbia.

The fact that he got there first is remarkable, accomplished as it was by a frenzied day-and-night forced march, and even when the federal army entered the Lawrenceburg Pike, it was only a few miles ahead of Hood. Nevertheless, Schofield had won the first leg of the race for Nashville and thwarted Hood's plan for his destruction south of the river.

It was by now the 26th of November. The Confederate army had been marching for almost a week by parallel mud-rutted routes. After crossing the Tennessee, they moved simultaneously north, with Cheatham's corps on the right via the Waynesboro road; A. P. Stewart's corps, with much of the artillery and baggage wagons, by way of the crushed-stone, or "macadamized," Lawrenceburg Pike; and Lee's corps in between on country roads. By the time they all converged near Mount Pleasant, they had come sixty miles and were less than half a day's march from their immediate objective, Columbia. Trouble was, of course, that because of bad weather, John Schofield's federal army had beaten them there.

As Hood's division began to set up opposite the Union army, things began to assume a festive air. At Hamilton Place, the mansion of General Lucius Polk, Chaplain Quintard recorded, "All day long there was a constant stream of visitors. . . . General Hood and [the exiled Tennessee] Governor [Isham] Harris came early in the day, as did General Cheatham. Then came General John C. Brown, General [Randall L.] Gibson, General [William Brimage] Bate, handsome Frank Armstrong, and General [Edward C.] Walthall. . . . I offered a special prayer of Thanksgiving to God for our return to Tennessee."

The hospitality of the Polks and Pillows and other gentry of Columbia turned into an extended fete for the Confederate officers as they waited for the battle to develop. There were dinner parties, serenading, and bands playing and much welcoming and gaiety. The elegance of the surroundings deeply impressed even one Union soldier who had passed by just ahead of the Confederates on his way into the town proper. "The well-kept farms and spacious lawns, with long, straight lanes bordered with trees, leading up to the handsome mansions, gave us the impression of peace and comfort. But," he added, "how quickly there was to be a change."

At this stage of the game, Hood was supremely confident. He had lost the race to Columbia but still had under him a superior army and the superb divisions of Forrest's cavalry to throw against Schofield's outnumbered command. That he was vigorous in spirit is undoubted, but in health there were questions. He had recovered from the loss of his arm—or the use of it—but carried it in a sling. And the leg still caused him trouble; amputated so close to the hip, it must have been excruciatingly painful even after a year. Everywhere he walked he used crutches, and to mount a horse he needed the assistance of aides and had to be strapped into the saddle. He used at least two artificial legs—one of hardwood and the other of cork. Mary Chesnut, without identifying which one, recorded, "The Charlottesville leg is much better looking than the French one." The result was that Hood simply could not perform some of the duties of a healthy commanding general, such as dashing rapidly to observe the action or traversing rough terrain or moving rapidly as a situation changed. Furthermore, his mutilations were bound to have produced some lingering emotional trauma, though to what extent remained anybody's guess.

The catalyst in Hood's advance against Nashville was the cavalry corps of Nathan Bedford Forrest. Forrest's exploits had become legendary by this time; his raids into Kentucky, Tennessee, and Mississippi had frustrated many a Union commander's plan of operations. "The wizard," as Forrest had become known in the South—"the devil" in the North—was sent ahead of Hood's army with his six thousand troopers to clear the path of federal cavalry, and this he did in spectacular fashion.

Forrest was a forty-year-old Tennessean who had become a successful planter before the war and in his younger days in Memphis was a slave trader. Unlike J. E. B. Stuart and Joe Wheeler, the other two Confederate cavalry corps commanders east of the Mississippi, Forrest had not attended West Point; in fact, he had no formal military training of any kind. He enlisted as a private in the Tennessee cavalry in 1861 but was quickly commissioned and given a regimental command, where he proved to be a soldier of remarkable ingenuity, smuggling arms and supplies for his new regiment from under the very noses of Union forces in Kentucky. He was also a man of daring and schemes and almost unimaginable courage. After the battle of Shiloh, as Sherman's men attempted to pursue the Confederates, Forrest turned on them with a vengeance and drove them back. In his fury, at one point he outraced his own men to charge a line of federal foot soldiers and found himself surrounded. As the blue-coated enemy closed in, shouting, "Kill him!" Forrest demonically struck out with saber in one hand and blazing pistol in the other, until one man stuck the barrel of his rifle against his side and pulled the trigger, sending a bullet tearing into his back. Enraged, Forrest reached down and snatched one of his tormentors by the collar and hoisted him up behind him on the horse; then, employing this ill-fated passenger as a shield, he galloped through the mass of seething guns and bayonets back to his own lines, where he unceremoniously dumped the amazed enemy soldier on the ground.

With this kind of cavalryman pointing the way, Hood need not have worried, and, in fact, he was able to march his entire army by the outmatched federal cavalry under General James Wilson unmolested. One Union general described the federal cavalry as being driven by Forrest "like a herd in a stampede."

When James Wilson took over command of the federal cavalry of the Army of the Tennessee that same month, he found it in chaos. On paper, he had nearly twenty-five thousand troopers, but, as Hood set out across the Tennessee, he had only about five thousand effectives. The rest were scattered all over the department, many without mounts. Wilson immediately sought and received an order from Secretary of War Stanton to impress from any local citizens living below the Ohio River all horses and mules needed for the campaign. As he later recorded, "All street-car and livery stable horses, and private carriage and saddle horses were seized," and "within seven days . . . seven thousand horses were obtained in middle and western Kentucky and our mounted force was thereby increased to twelve thousand.'' They even confiscated the carriage horses of U.S. Vice President Andrew Johnson, as well as those of a traveling circus.

Wilson was a twenty-seven-year-old Illinois native who graduated sixth in his West Point class. He was sent west as an engineer to do land surveying for the army and continued in the Engineer Corps after the war broke out until 1863, when he became an inspector general on the staff of Grant. Then, from May through September of 1864 he was sent east in command of a cavalry division under Phil Sheridan in Virginia, until he was appointed major general and shipped back west to take over Thomas's cavalry. What Wilson saw when he arrived at Nashville was deeply disturbing. Years later he was to say, ''It is no slander now to say that the mounted service was looked upon as both futile and discreditable.''

Wilson was just setting about to reorganize the cavalry when Hood invaded Tennessee. He arrived at Columbia in time, to his chagrin, to witness Croxton's brigade retreating wildly through the streets before the determined Forrest and his men. He was also astounded to see at the head of one of his ''better'' regiments ''a well mounted and well clad woman, riding with the field and staff as though she belonged there.'' When he inquired who the woman was, he was informed, ''Oh, that is Mrs. Colonel Smith commanding the Eighth Michigan Cavalry,'' a further explanation being that the lady had been with the regiment for some time and ''seemed to be quite at home.''

After issuing an order relieving Mrs. Colonel Smith from further duties with the 8th Michigan Cavalry, Wilson set about posting his brigades to protect the Duck River fords from a crossing by Hood, while the Union infantry dug entrenchments in front of Columbia and Schofield looked in vain for reinforcements from Thomas, up in Nashville.

As the two armies lay opposite each other at Columbia, Schofield was in a further stew because of a faulty communications arrangement with Thomas. It seemed the War Department did not trust anyone except the telegraphic corps with the cipher to encode and decode telegraphic messages—not even Schofield or, for that matter, Grant himself—and, as the general reported, ''The work was so badly done that it took from eight to forty-eight hours in sending or delivering a despatch. The fact is," Schofield grumbled, "I was not only without any appropriate orders or instructions nearly all the time, but also without any timely information from General Thomas to guide my action." Not knowing what to do—or so he said—Schofield withdrew his army through the town and across the Duck River, establishing a line with the river to his front instead of his back, and began raising breastworks again, or, in his words, "inviting attack." This at least would fulfill the part of his mission that he understood included delaying Hood wherever possible until A. J. Smith and the Sixteenth Corps arrived at Nashville from the north.

Hood, meantime, had calculated a scheme for Schofield's unraveling, and on November 27, following one of the gala fetes at the Warfield mansion, the headquarters he occupied on the Pulaski Pike, he held a council of war with his generals during which he laid out his intentions. Later that night, as a snowstorm raged outside, he revealed these designs confidentially to Chaplain Quintard: "Hood detailed to me his plan of taking Nashville & calling for volunteers to storm the key of the works about the city." The army, Hood said, "will press forward with all possible speed" and "will beat the enemy to Nashville or make him go there double quick."

The plot Hood had concocted was to leave two-thirds of Stephen Lee's corps, and almost all the artillery, in front of Schofield while the rest of the army maneuvered to a pontoon bridge the engineers had secretly constructed about three miles upriver at Davis ford, to the northeast and around Schofield's left flank. Thus, while Lee blasted away at Schofield with his cannons and threatened an immediate frontal attack, the main body of the army, at dawn, would be sneaking around to his rear, trapping him between the two pincers—the classic turning movement, worthy, Hood said, of "the immortal Jackson" himself. In the relish of contemplating Schofield's fate, Hood described his scheme as "one of those beautiful and interesting moves upon the chessboard of war." Twice before in his career he had hoped for just this kind of chance—once at Gettysburg, when he had practically begged Longstreet to let him outflank the federal position at Round Top, and again at the battle of Atlanta, where only Hardee's lateness had thwarted his expectations. This time Hood concluded to see to it himself that the ploy was carried out to the letter; despite his physical handicaps, he would go in person and lead the army forward. "The enemy must give me a fight," he declared to his friend Chaplain Quintard, "or I'll be in Nashville before tomorrow night."

Hood delivered this singular and heavy prophecy to the chaplain before hobbling off to bed, but another prophetic episode elasped before the Army of Tennessee embarked on its swirling dreams of conquering the Ohio. Sometime during all the blustering and festivities around Columbia, General Pat Cleburne rode by St. John's, the lovely little Episcopal chapel that the Polk clan had built in a grove of magnolias near one of the Polk family mansions called Ashwood Hall. Stopping to admire its Gothic ivy-covered brick walls and tidy green graveyard, the reserved Cleburne remarked to his ordnance officer, a Captain Hill, "It is almost worth dying for, to be buried in such a beautiful spot."

Patrick Ronayne Cleburne was one of the more remarkable officers in all of the Confederate armies; newspapers called him the Stonewall Jackson of the west, but he remained only a division commander, probably because of his audacious notion that slaves should be freed and recruited into the Southern armies.

Cleburne was born in 1828 in County Cork, Ireland, of a well-to-do Protestant family of distinguished lineage. He was raised in private schools, but with the death of his father, a physician, the family fell on difficult times, and at the age of eighteen he enlisted in the British army in a regiment that was posted near Dublin. He served for nearly four years until a harsh British domestic policy prompted Cleburne and his mother and siblings to emigrate to America. He ultimately settled in Helena, Arkansas, on the west bank of the Mississippi River not far from Memphis, where he bought and ran a drugstore, later studied law, and was admitted to the bar in 1856. By the outbreak of the Civil War Cleburne had become a landowner as well as a member of the Arkansas militia, and as hostilities opened, he was elected colonel of the 15th

Arkansas Regiment, with a promotion to brigadier shortly afterward. After serving in the battles at Shiloh and Perryville, he was advanced to major general and quickly established himself as a superb combat leader in the western army, including crucial heroics at the battles of Chickamauga and Chattanooga.

By 1864, Cleburne was one of the genuine folk heroes of the Confederate army. Like Hood, he had also become engaged to be married. Just before the Atlanta campaign, Cleburne's friend General William Hardee had asked him to serve as best man at his wedding at a plantation near Demopolis, Alabama. As it turned out, Cleburne, then a bachelor of thirty-six, fell immediately in love with the maid of honor, Miss Susan Tarleton of Mobile, daughter of a wealthy cotton broker. The two became affianced during one of the leaves Cleburne was able to take. After the arduous Atlanta fight, he had planned to go again to Mobile, but Hood's decision to take the army to Tennessee foreclosed all possibility of a furlough. Learning of this, Miss Tarleton had a good cry and then wrote to a friend, "I suppose I can but wait patiently and keep up a brave heart."

And so here, two months later, Pat Cleburne stood in front of a beautiful little church up in Columbia, Tennessee, a handsome, wiry man with a thick shock of reddish hair, probably thinking of his sweetheart and musing on how this would be such a lovely spot to be buried, just the way his ancestors were, in churchyards back in Ireland.

10

★ The Best Move Come to Naught

In the cold misty dawn of November 29 Frank Cheatham's corps began to march across the pontoon bridge over Duck River. They were moving along an old wagon road lined with bare hardwoods and cedar brakes. Four miles to the east, at Columbia, the crash of Stephen Lee's artillery broke the autumn silence and swelled to a continuous roar. Riding in the vanguard of the crossing with General Mark P. Lowrey's brigade of Cleburne's division was Hood, strapped to his saddle. They could see the federal cavalry watching them from the hills to the west, but the army kept moving. By late morning, seven divisions—more than twenty thousand men—had passed over the river and turned due north toward the little village of Spring Hill, about a dozen miles away.

They were marching along poor country roads, soggy and rutted from the rain and snow, but without the artillery and supply wagons the going was not as slow as it might have been. Clear skies and a warm sun turned the morning into a beautiful fall day, and by 3 P.M. the leading elements of the army had crossed a small stream called Rutherford Creek, about two miles from Spring Hill. Hood, still riding at the head, stopped atop a low rise from which he later recalled that the advance troops and wagons of Schofield's Union army were clearly visible, retreating toward Spring Hill along the Columbia-Franklin Pike. In his memoirs Hood wrote that he sent immediately for Generals Cheatham and Cleburne and, after pointing out the federals on the pike, said to Cheatham, "Go with your corps, take possession of and hold that pike at or near Spring Hill. Accept whatever comes and turn all those wagons over to our side of the house." Then, turning to Cleburne, Hood charged him with similar duty: "General, you have heard the orders just given. You have one of my best divisions. Go with General Cheatham, assist him in every way you can, and do as he directs. Go and do this at once. [General A. P.] Stewart is near at hand and I will have him double quick his men to the front."

At least that's what he said he said. What transpired from that moment through the next twelve hours—and a great deal did—became one of the great mysteries of the war, ranking right up there with Lee's infamous "lost orders" during the Antietam campaign. From that day until well into the next century when the last of the participants was dead and buried, what became known as the Spring Hill affair prompted countless charges, countercharges, rebuttals, speculations, rumors, analyses, and acrimonious debates. What is certain is that somewhere between "I told you to do it" and "No, you didn't," "I ordered it done" and "I never understood," the federal army managed to elude the lovely trap Hood had designed. As event piled upon event, a visible truth was put to the old adage, "For want of a nail the shoe was lost . . ." and so on. The controversy over Spring Hill began there and then with the conversation among Hood, Cheatham, and Cleburne. Cheatham disputed Hood's entire account of the conversation and said later that there was not "a bit of truth" in Hood's recollection of seeing Union men and wagons moving on the pike and that even if they had been, the pike was "never in view" of the three generals as they conversed.

Whatever exactly Hood said to Cheatham and Cleburne on that magnificent November afternoon, the commander of Hood's leading corps began deploying his men toward Spring Hill with about two and a half hours of daylight remaining. At that point, Hood had on the field, or within easy support distance, two full army corps plus one of Lee's divisions and Forrest's cavalry, giving him twenty-five thousand men with which to crush what was later ascertained to be but a single division of fifty-five hundred federals that had been sent by Schofield as an advance party with the supply wagons and reserve artillery. As will be seen, that this was not accomplished remains one of the greatest might-have-beens of the Civil War, surrounded by dark accusations of drunkenness, cowardess, stupidity, debauchery, treachery, dereliction of duty, drug use, ennui, lying, failure to follow instructions, and failure to give them—characteristics thus far so foreign to Confederate armies as to inspire disbelief.

Back down in Columbia, Stephen Lee's division, with most of the army's artillery, was still smashing away at the Union position and threatening a frontal attack, and Schofield himself was in a quandary. He later claimed that his telegraph operator, who possessed the only cipher to the codes, had deserted and run away to Franklin, thus depriving him of any instructions from Thomas up in Nashville and any way to communicate his own situation to Thomas. Schofield pointedly chastised Thomas after the war for not being personally present on the battlefield, for not concentrating his forces—including A. J. Smith's divisions and those of General James B. Steedman, near Chattanooga—more rapidly, for not bridging the Harpeth River between Columbia and Nashville, and for not leaving him precise orders about what he should do.

A little past midnight of the previous day, James Wilson, the federal cavalry commander, acting on information his men had obtained from Confederate prisoners, sent an urgent message to Schofield warning that Hood's army was in the process of laying pontoons over Duck River to flank him and cut him off. Schofield's reaction to this apprehensive news was to retire to a state of perplexity. On the one hand, if Wilson's report was correct and Hood was in the process of flanking him, Schofield would have no time to lose in fleeing back to Spring Hill before Hood got there—which Wilson warned in his message could be as early as noon that day. His task would be to get his entire twenty-thousand-man army, along with nearly a thousand supply and artillery wagons, moved twelve miles north before Hood could get at him. But on the other hand, if Hood's flanking movement turned out to be a trick, the moment Schofield started his army marching, Hood could come rushing across Duck River and strike him in the rear as he moved out. The fact that most of Stephen Lee's corps was still at his front and, for all he knew, the rest of Hood's army as well, seemed to paralyze Schofield, which was precisely what Hood had intended.

Through the rest of the night Schofield waited and wondered what the morning might bring. About sunrise, when Lee's artillery opened up on him, he received word that Hood's divisions were in fact crossing Duck River around his flank, but this brought a new concern—were they destined to outrace him to Spring Hill, or would they simply turn back west once they crossed the river and attack him in flank around Columbia or on the road? Realizing that complete inaction would be disastrous, Schofield summoned General David Stanley, who commanded the Fourth Corps, and ordered him to go with two divisions—General Nathan Kimball's and General George D. Wagner's—to Spring Hill, taking all the wagons and the reserve artillery, but to drop off Kimball's division a little way up the road to guard against a direct flank attack by Hood. Thus, about 8 A.M., Stanley began the trek that may have saved the Union army.

David Stanley was a thirty-six-year-old Ohioan who grew up in a typical frontier family of farmers, dressing in buckskin and homespun clothes. He was apprenticed to a doctor to learn that profession but, like Schofield, got an appointment to the Military Academy after another cadet was found unacceptable. He graduated from West Point in 1852 in the class with Generals Sheridan and Slocum and served as a cavalry officer, fighting Indians, until the war broke out. He was actually offered a commission in the Confederate army but turned it down and served with distinction in the Missouri campaigns until he was appointed brigadier general and sent to Grant's Army of the Mississippi, where he commanded a division. A year later he was made chief of cavalry in Rosecrans's army and fought at Murfreesboro. By the time the Atlanta campaign got under way, Stanley had been promoted to corps commander, but he was faulted by Sherman for allowing the Confederates to escape in the last days of the fighting around Atlanta, which probably accounts for Sherman not taking him on the march to the sea.

Stanley now found himself in a dead earnest heat for Spring Hill, with Hood having a good head start. He had been moving about two hours when he stopped inside a "handsome house" along the road for some refreshment and was chatting up "some very pretty southern ladies" who complained to him about the behavior of Union troops, when a courier rushed up to him "breathless, saying Forrest's force was in sight of Spring Hill and driving in the pickets. . . ." Stanley reacted to this news by starting the division toward Spring Hill at a run, and by 1 P.M. he had gotten his men set up for a defense.

If Stanley's recollection of the time is correct, it puts him at odds with Hood's account of seeing Union troops and wagons hurrying up the road toward Spring Hill when he arrived on the field at 3 P.M. This recollection would also square with Cheatham's version of his meeting with Hood, because by 3 P.M. Stanley would have been off the pike and into his breastworks. Whatever the case, the first enemy troops Stanley saw that day were from Forrest's cavalry, who were on the verge of taking both the town and the turnpike when the veteran infantry division opened fire on them. According to Stanley, the Confederate horsemen were "brushed away as you would shoo away blackbirds."

They may have flown like blackbirds at that time, but Forrest's cavalry had done more than yeoman's duty from the beginning of the Columbia-to-Spring-Hill advance. First, they had chased away Wilson's federal troopers to allow Hood's engineers to lay down the pontoon bridge over Duck River. Then, as the army began to cross, Forrest's brigades drove the federal horsemen before them through the woods like a herd of sheep, actually removing them from the entire battle area until they were huddled way up north near Franklin. That is not to say this was done without opposition. Wilson, in his chagrin at being outmatched by the wizard, later contended that he had deliberately retreated, giving fight only when he had to, and indicated that perhaps he had been deceived by Forrest into thinking that the Confederate cavalry's intention was to go directly into Nashville. If this indeed were true, it does not explain how Wilson intended to fulfill his duty as the "eyes" of Schofield's army or his mission to delay and harass Hood's infantry column when he had allowed himself to be pushed nearly ten miles from the scene of the action.

In any case, with the whole Union cavalry corps now disposed of, Forrest left a small force to watch them and turned the attention of his main forces back south, toward the capture of Spring Hill. It was a near thing. Had he arrived just minutes earlier, he would have been in possession of the town and its fortifications and in control of the vital Columbia Pike up which Stanley's division was frantically marching. As it was, however, Stanley got there first and was able to brush off the Confederate horsemen with his powerful infantry brigades. Nevertheless, Forrest continued to fight until his troopers literally ran out of ammunition. Trying to perform the crucial task of identifying exactly what federal troops were around Spring Hill and in what numbers, Forrest came upon a scene of battle overseen by one of his division commanders, James Chalmers. Chalmers's troopers had just dispersed a horde of federal cavalrymen on the edge of some woods when they encountered strong fortifications, behind which was massed Union infantry, and they quickly retired. About this time Forrest rode up and saw about two hundred enemy cavalry coming into the open again.

"Why don't you drive those fellows off?" Forrest asked. When Chalmers replied that there was federal infantry in breastworks behind the cavalry, Forrest was skeptical. "I think you are mistaken," he told his trusted subordinate. "That is only a small cavalry force." Bedford Forrest was not one to argue with, so Chalmers told him, "All right, I will try it," formed his men, and yelled, "Forward, gallop!"

They raced through a beautiful grove of trees, but as they reached the woods again, all hell broke loose. Massed infantry rifle and artillery fire exploded in their faces; arms, legs, and heads were blown off; horses tumbled over each other and dashed away riderless; and "the ground was covered with limbs and bark." When the smoke cleared, only a handful of Confederates were left unharmed, including Chalmers, who returned to his lines and encountered Forrest, who had been watching the charge.

"They was in there sure enough, wasn't they Chalmers?" Forrest said to him.

"Yes sir, that is the second time I found them there," was Chalmers's sour answer.

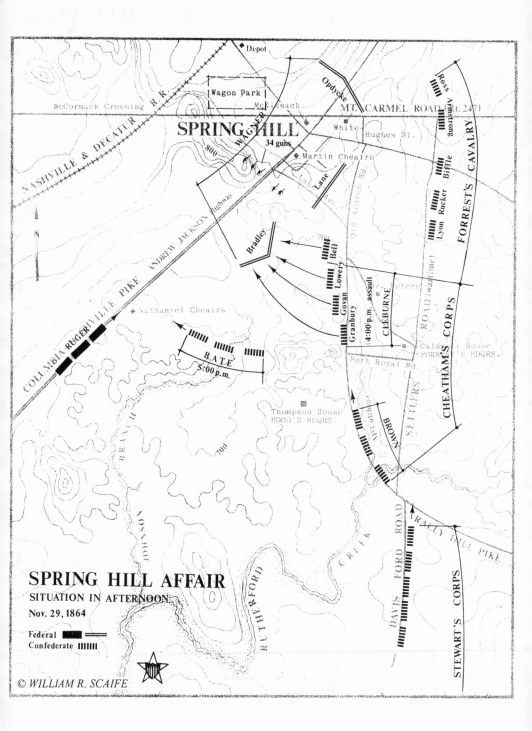

Depot

Wagon Park

McCormack Crossing R. R.

McKissack

MT. CARMEL ROAD (Rt. 247)

SPRING HILL

White   Hughes St.

34 guns

Martin Cheairs

Lane

Bradley

Bell

Lowery

Govan

Granbury

4:00 p.m. assault

CLEBURNE

Nathaniel Cheairs

BATE
5:00 p.m.

Port Royal Rd.

Thompson House
HOOD'S HDQRS.

FORREST'S CAVALRY

Ross

Armstrong

Biffle

Rucker

Lyon

FORREST'S HDQRS.

Caldwell House

CHEATHAM'S CORPS

SETTLER'S

BROWN

McCutchUUUn

RALLY HILL PIKE

DAVIS FORD ROAD

STEWART'S CORPS

SPRING HILL AFFAIR

SITUATION IN AFTERNOON

Nov. 29, 1864

Federal
Confederate

© WILLIAM R. SCAIFE

*   *   *

Presently, a little past 3 P.M., Cheatham, acting on Hood's instructions, set Pat Cleburne's division moving toward Spring Hill to see what was there and to find out from Forrest, who had been in the vicinity for a couple of hours, what the situation was. Meantime, Cheatham said later, he waited at the crossing of Rutherford Creek for Bate's division to come up, and when it did, he rode forward himself to about a mile and a half of the town and positioned Bate on Cleburne's left, preparatory for an attack on the entrenched federals. Hood, said Cheatham, waited at the bridge for the arrival of Cheatham's third division—Brown's—which he would hurry along when it arrived. If and when Cheatham's entire corps had gotten on the field, it should have been more than enough to crush Stanley, who was defending Spring Hill with only Wagner's fifty-five-hundred-man division.

But Cheatham's entire corps did not take the field. Cheatham said he sat on a knoll watching first Cleburne's and then Bate's divisions disappear over some hills toward the town, and then he heard the sinister crackle of heavy rifle fire echoed back to him indicating that Cleburne was engaged. But other evidence indicates that Cheatham did not in fact watch Bate's men follow after Cleburne's; and that, wherever he was on the battlefield, he did not hear Hood change Bate's orders to turn directly westward, seize the pike, and sweep southward toward Columbia.

In any event, Brown's division soon appeared on the scene, and Cheatham sent it off to the right of where he thought Cleburne was, so that he would have a front consisting—or so he conceived—of Bate on the left, Cleburne center, and Brown right. Meantime, as Cheatham got Brown's men in motion, a courier rode up from Cleburne with a message that his far right had stumbled on a strong entrenchment of federals and was severely mauled. The advance must halt, Cleburne said, until he had time to fall back and reorganize with a change of front. Cheatham afterward said Cleburne somehow got turned around, that from his line of departure he could not actually see either Spring Hill or the pike, and that he was attacking west instead of northwest toward the town when his far right brigade came into the direct line of fire of Stanley's federals and was struck in the flank. But Cheatham also wrote that Cleburne's westward advance was "almost parallel with the turnpike," which is an impossibility, since the pike runs northeast into Spring Hill. Perhaps he meant perpendicular, but in any case, Cleburne did get stalled for about an hour after he encountered the federal lines.

What went on there was fast and furious and very nearly accomplished what Hood had intended. After wading across Rutherford Creek, pants rolled up, their distinctive full-moon battle flags waving in the fading light, Cleburne's division marched across open fields and hills until, at half an hour before sunset, they struck the Union lines, which were spread in a semicircle facing south and east of Spring Hill. There they encountered an exhausted Forrest, who had been fighting federals since sunup, and with a dismounted brigade of Forrest's troopers Cleburne charged the Union position that was being held by the federal brigade of General Luther Bradley, severely wounding Bradley and sweeping the blue-coated soldiers from the field.

At this point, the whole right wing of Stanley's command crumbled, and the Southerners called upon their Northern brethren "with loud oaths, charging them with a Yankee canine descent, to halt and surrender." Cleburne's Confederates pressed a hot pursuit right up to the edge of town. At one point Lowrey, commanding Cleburne's right brigade, perceived that a single federal regiment that remained on the field was about to attack him and dashed over to Cleburne to tell him so. The Irishman, "with his right hand raised as though he held a heavy whip, exclaimed, 'I'll charge *them!*'" and, rushing to his favorite brigade, commanded by General Daniel C. Govan, did exactly that, driving the federals in confusion from the field.

Cleburne's men were on the verge of overwhelming Stanley's entire position when suddenly Union General Wagner opened up on them "with a furious cannonade" from at least eight guns that had been brought up from Columbia, and the Confederate charge quickly stalled. Cleburne ordered an aide to ride over to General Hiram Granbury's brigade with instructions to reform on a fence several hundred yards away, facing the pike, then set about rectifying the lines of his other two brigadiers, Govan and Lowrey. It was then that he sent the message to Cheatham saying that he had been struck in the flank and needed time to reorganize.

From the point of view in the federal lines, the situation was now desperate. William Keesy of D Company, 64th Ohio, was on Stanley's far right when Cleburne's attack burst out from some woods and across a corn field. Keesy aimed a shot at one "audacious fellow," but the rifle misfired, and his captain made him disassemble the piece on the spot and fix it. Nearby, he recalled, "I distinctly heard the unmistakable 'whack' and knew that some one of our boys was hit." The Confederates "came with a rush and a yell, and swept like a cyclone across that field. It was now far safer in the rear and the order came not a whit too soon, 'fall back.' " In the midst of all this, Keesy became overwhelmed by the trance of battle. "While this tremendous rattle of musketry was raging so fiercely," he recalled, "I noticed a flock of wild pigeons fluttering right over the smoke of battle. The scene was so contrary to anything that I could conceive, I called to a lieutenant standing by my side and said: 'Look at those pigeons there.' " The lieutenant gave the Ohioan a prod with his sword and told him, "Look at that Rebel flag. Shoot that fellow with that flag there. That is the kind of game we are after now."

Pressed by the ferocity of Cleburne's attack, Keesy's brigade drew back, trampling to death many of their unfortunate wounded. Cleburne's men were in sight of the pike and would have gained it, accomplishing Hood's plan, when the calamitous artillery barrage opened up in their faces. Captain Levi Scofield later remembered that it was Captain Alec Marshall's artillery battery and a lone regiment of infantry, the 103rd Ohio, that saved the day for the federals. What had begun as a planned withdrawal to a better position had turned into a general rout, and the officers of this brave little regiment were trying to stop the flow. "Capt. Charley Sergeant," Scofield said, "grabbed one officer who was tearing past him, who shouted, 'For God's sake, don't stop me! I'm a chaplain!' " The regimental officers had broken open boxes of ammunition and "built a little parapet of ammunition in front of the men, from which they loaded," pouring "a furious, driving storm of lead" into the Confederate ranks. This, coupled with the deathly artillery fire, caused

Cleburne to lose momentum and thus ended the second opportunity of the day for the Confederates to secure the turnpike (the first had been Forrest's failure to place himself athwart it in time).

By now it was nearly sunset, but with about an hour and a half of twilight left, Cleburne was poised to resume the attack, when an officer from Cheatham's staff arrived with instructions to halt where he was and await further orders.

Cheatham's reasoning for the delay seems to be that he was under the impression Stanley had a much larger force in Spring Hill than he actually did, and so Cheatham wanted to get all three of his divisions in line for a massed assault. To do this, he first had to find and relocate Bate—who, acting on Hood's instructions, had gone due west and was on the verge of taking the Columbia-Franklin Pike—and place him on Cleburne's left. Meantime, Brown was formed on Cleburne's right and the corps was now positioned in accordance with what Cheatham desired, which seemed to be the disposal of Stanley's Union troops, instead of securing the all important pike.

Actually, Bate had been in the perfect location to initially cut off the retreat of Schofield's army coming up from Columbia. His division was only one hundred yards from the pike when a heavy column of federal soldiers and wagons appeared, moving rapidly toward Spring Hill. This—though Bate did not know it—was the vanguard of Schofield's main force, which Schofield had not started moving out of Columbia until nearly 3 P.M., having finally satisfied himself that Hood was not in his front but well in his rear, a fact brought home to him with utmost clarity as the sounds of battle from Spring Hill began wafting down toward him.

In any case, Bate at this particular moment was a man in the right place at the right time. A lawyer and newspaper editor before the war, the thirty-six-year-old Tennessean and veteran of the Mexican conflict had established himself as a bold fighter, having been wounded several times previously, and he was spoiling for a fight now that he could see the advancing federals before him. He was about to plunge into these strung out and nearly helpless bluecoats when Cheatham's message arrived ordering him to pull back northward and join Cleburne. Puzzled,

Bate sent the messenger back with word that he was about to launch an assault and requested that Cheatham suspend his withdrawal order. Cheatham, apparently in no mood for argument, and seemingly unaware that Hood had personally ordered Bate to seize the pike, responded with word for Bate to either join up with Cleburne immediately or report to the commanding general under arrest. So, with the advancing columns of Schofield's army in plain view, Bate reluctantly withdrew his division and marched to where he had been told to go.

With this golden opportunity lost, yet another blunder soon occurred. With his whole corps on line for attack, Cheatham had given instructions that the assault on Stanley was to be carried off en echelon, right to left—Brown's division leading off, then Cleburne's, and finally Bate's. Cheatham ordered Cleburne to wait until he heard the crash of Brown's guns as the signal to begin his attack, then rode off to his field headquarters to await the opening of the battle. It never came. Not long afterward, Cheatham received a message from Brown that the Union left outflanked him by several hundred yards, and that any attempt at an assault would result in "inevitable disaster." Cheatham later said he fired off a dispatch telling Brown to "throw back" his right brigade and go ahead with the attack immediately. By now it was nearly dark, but Cleburne and Bate, battle flags flying in the dim air, were straining at the leash to get at the Union troops at their front. From his headquarters, Cheatham paced nervously and kept asking his staff, "Why don't we hear Brown's guns?" Finally, he rode to Brown's position to see what was going on.

Major General John Calvin Brown was no coward; the handsome thirty-seven-year-old lawyer had joined up as a private and taken part in every major battle of the Army of Tennessee. But just why the assault never came off remains shrouded in mystery and perhaps a deliberate cover up. Brown himself claimed that he had been told that General A. P. Stewart's entire corps was being rushed to his right flank, and so he waited for its arrival—which never came. He also contended that Cheatham visited him in position and concurred in suspending the assault. Cheatham, however, claimed that he never got to Brown's position at all, that he was waylaid en route by a courier from Hood who told him the commanding general wanted to see him. By this time, Hood had left the field and taken up headquarters at the Absalom Thompson house, an imposing columned mansion more than a mile from the battlefront. There, Cheatham said, Hood informed him that he had decided to call off the attack until morning. Later, Cheatham was to write, "I was never more astonished than when General Hood informed me that he had concluded to postpone the attack till daylight."

Others had different versions of the story, including Hood, who said that when Cheatham rode up to his headquarters, instead of ordering him to suspend the attack, he exclaimed, "General, why in the name of God have you not attacked the enemy and taken possession of that Pike?" Cheatham, according to Hood, replied that the enemy line "looked a little too long for him," and that he was waiting for Stewart's corps to form up on his right. Hood says he then posted guides to place Stewart's corps in position to support Cheatham, grumbling, "I would as soon have expected midday to turn into darkness as for [Cheatham] to have disobeyed my orders." Still others, including Captain Joseph B. Cumming of Hood's staff, remember that it was Cheatham "remonstrating with Gen. Hood against a night attack." This might well have been the real situation, and for a darker reason than Hood then realized. Brown, it seems, was drunk.

That disturbing information came from no less a source than Lieutenant General Stephen Dill Lee, who imparted it many years after the war to fellow general Ellison Capers, who had since become Episcopal bishop of South Carolina. Responsibility for not launching the attack on Stanley, Lee wrote, rests "on one not suspected. He was drunk, and it was not Cheatham either. John C. Brown, who commanded Cheatham's old Div.—either lacked the nerve on that day or was drunk—no doubt the latter." Middle Tennessee in those days was whisky country—as it is today (the Jack Daniels Distillery was established there a year after the war). Brown along with other generals had received "a great many presents of liquor" and became "too intoxicated to attend to his duties." Cheatham, Lee went on to hypothesize, was covering up for his long-time friend Brown when he urged Hood to wait until morn-

The Union High Command

President Abraham Lincoln

*General Ulysses S. Grant
(courtesy of Culver Pictures, Inc.)*

Secretary of War Edwin M. Stanton

General Henry W. Halleck

Union Infantry Commanders

General David S. Stanley

General Jacob Cox

General James W. Reilly

General Thomas H. Ruger

General Nathan Kimball

Union Cavalry Commander James H. Wilson
and His Division Commanders

General Edward Hatch

General John T. Croxton

General James H. Wilson

General James B. Steedman, who ferreted out
the plot against Thomas

Colonel (later General) Emerson Opdycke,
who disobeyed orders at Franklin but saved the
Union Army there

General George Day Wagner, who was accused of
drunkenness at Franklin

General Thomas J. Wood, who was accused of
disloyalty by his corps commander

General John M. Corse, who gave the famous reply when French asked him to surrender

Bishop-General Leonidas Polk, who baptized General Hood on the eve of battle

Emma Sansom, who was eulogized by General Forrest as a Confederate heroine (courtesy of the Alabama Department of Archives and History, Montgomery, Alabama)

Captain Theodoric (Tod) Carter, whose death expressed the tragic irony of Franklin (courtesy of the Carter House, Franklin, Tennessee)

Sally Buchanan "Buck" Preston (photograph by Alt-Lee; printed courtesy of the Historic Columbia Foundation)

The Absalom Thompson House, which served as Hood's command post at Spring Hill on the night of November 29, 1864 (courtesy of the Maury County Visitors Bureau)

The Nathaniel Cheairs House at Spring Hill, where on the morning of November 30, 1864, Hood became "wrathy as a rattlesnake" (courtesy of the Maury County Visitors Bureau)

The Carter House, Franklin, Tennessee, which served as General Cox's headquarters during the battle
(courtesy of the U.S. Army Military History Institute)

The town of Franklin, looking north from Carter's cotton gin
(courtesy of the U.S. Army Military History Institute)

ing, when Brown would presumably be sober again. There was also talk around Brown's division that whisky was at the bottom of the Spring Hill affair. One diarist, William Pollard of the 1st Tennessee, wrote down, "Rumor had it that John Barleycorn played his part in the drama."

Whatever the cause, no decisive all-out assault was ever launched against the federal army, either at Stanley or at Schofield when he showed up, and what Hood described as his "golden opportunity" was forever lost. But there was even more to it than that. By the time night finally closed in, Stewart's large corps had only begun to take the field. While three hours earlier Hood had told Cheatham that Stewart was "close by" and would soon be forming for battle, a courier from Hood had actually given Stewart orders *not* to cross Rutherford Creek but to wait there for further instructions. Thus, Brown and Cheatham, facing the Union line several miles to the north, waited in vain for the arrival of nearly half of the rest of the army. Later, Stewart said that Hood had held him in place because he said he needed a force to prevent the federals from escaping eastward toward Murfreesboro. This, in Stewart's opinion, "was the fatal error."

In any case, about dusk and exasperated that no attack had been made by Cheatham, Hood finally told Stewart to move north and ordered him to get across the pike above Spring Hill. With a "young man of the neighborhood" procured by Hood as a guide, Stewart's column groped forward in the darkness for several hours until they came upon Forrest's headquarters, where they were overtaken by a messenger from Cheatham's staff. This man brought news that Hood now wished Stewart to form on Cheatham's right, next to Brown's division. Stewart recalled it "striking [him] as strange" that Hood would send new orders by one of Cheatham's staff and not his own," and when he had time to examine the position these new instructions directed him into, "Old Straight" realized his new line would bear *away* from the pike instead of across it and, worse, would "require all night to accomplish." So Stewart put his weary soldiers into bivouac, and he and Forrest rode back together to Hood's headquarters to see if they could iron this out.

By then it was past 10 P.M. Much had been going on inside Hood's headquarters at the Absalom Thompson mansion, including, if the word of one of Hood's guides is to be accepted, excess drinking, and even drunkenness, by, among others, Generals Cheatham, Cleburne, Walthall, and Granbury. While Hood wasn't specifically singled out as a participant in this revelry, it has been suggested that he was, and also that, to ease the pain of his wounds, he might have been taking drugs such as laudanum or other opiates. Even more tantalizing, the federal cavalry commander Wilson reported having information that Frank Cheatham had been absent from his command, whiling away his time at the mansion of the beautiful Jesse Helen Peters.

Mrs. Peters had become the center of one of the Confederacy's most notorious scandals the previous year. One of the Confederacy's rising stars, Major General Earl Van Dorn, had been using the mansion of Nathaniel Cheairs as a headquarters when, on a bright May morning about 10 A.M., Dr. George Peters, on the pretext of obtaining a pass to go through Union lines, came into Van Dorn's office and—having gotten his pass—shot the dashing young general dead. This apparently had much to do with Van Dorn's attentions to Mrs. Peters; in any case, in the ensuing confusion the doctor was able to use his pass to escape to the federal lines to spend the rest of the war up north.

That the alluring Mrs. Peters was indeed receiving visitors on the day of the Spring Hill affair is attested to by a Major Tyler, of Forrest's staff, who recalled seeing a woman on the porch of a home at Spring Hill. "I was struck by her great beauty," he said. "She at once asked if General Forrest was with us, and I pointed him out to her. She then said that she would like to meet him and speak to him. I said, 'who are you, madam?' and she replied: 'Mrs. Peters. General Forrest will know me.' I took him to her and left them talking."

Whether Cheatham, a bachelor and well-known ladies' man, spent the evening with Mrs. Peters, drunk or sober, has never been conclusively proven, but it provided a good deal of speculation and gossip then and since.

Benjamin Franklin Cheatham had gained a reputation as a harddrinking, profane general whose troops were among the hardest hitting of any in the Army of Tennessee. He was a muscular, blue-eyed man

with wavy hair and a big mustache who was described by a soldier as
"one of the wickedest men I have ever heard speak." When he assumed
command of Hardee's corps after the fall of Atlanta, a New York newspaper writer described Cheatham as "only a fighter, not a general, and a
better horse jockey than either." There was both truth and unfairness in
that assessment. Indeed, he was both a fighter and a "horse jockey,"
having bred and raised some of the finest thoroughbred horseflesh in
Tennessee before the war. He had been born forty-four years earlier on
an imposing plantation called Westover on the Cumberland River near
Nashville—the eighth generation of American-born Cheathams, who
originally descended from British stock.

As a young man he joined a militia company called the Nashville
Blues, was promoted captain, and when war was declared with Mexico
fought with distinction in several major battles, emerging as a colonel of
volunteers. Although not West Point educated, Cheatham showed an
aptitude for the military and after he returned home was promoted to
major general of the Tennessee militia. Meantime, he had developed a
sort of wanderlust that took him to various jobs and businesses from
Philadelphia to the California gold rush country, but he was back home
farming and dabbling in politics when civil war broke out. He commanded a division early on, taking part in the bitterest battles in the
west: Shiloh, Perryville, Stones River, Chickamauga, and Atlanta.
Whether he had the mettle to command an entire army corps no longer
remained to be seen; it *was* being seen moment by moment as Hood's
chances slipped away into the cool Tennessee darkness. First Forrest's
chance, then Cleburne's, then Bate's and Brown's—four so far, and all
gone awry.

By the time Stewart and Forrest finally arrived at the Absalom
Thompson home, they were informed that Hood had gone to bed.
Stewart had him awakened and asked if Hood in fact had "changed his
mind" and sent the orders for Stewart's corps to be formed on Cheatham's right. Hood "replied that he had," but when Stewart pointed
out to him the difficulties he envisioned, Hood waved him off and said
just to let the men rest where they were, and they would all continue
the fight at daylight. Then, apparently still unaware that Schofield's

whole army was already marching rapidly across his front, Hood asked Forrest if his exhausted troopers could throw a barricade over the pike north of Spring Hill. Forrest, always the good soldier, reminded the general that his men were nearly out of ammunition and had been in the saddle fighting continuously for nearly twenty hours, but the old wizard said that he would try. On the strength of this inconclusive response, the commanding general bade Stewart and Forrest good night and went back to sleep, whereupon the fifth opportunity to seize the pike and cut off Schofield's army began to fade away.

The boots of twenty thousand Union soldiers on their way to Spring Hill and Franklin trudged by Hood's army unmolested that night, passing thousands of glowing Confederate campfires, some so close to the road that the federal troops occasionally wandered into them, thinking they were their own. Colonel Isaac Sherwood, commanding the 111th Ohio, remembered that the night was clear, with stars but no moon. Seeing the encampment of an army by the pike, he halted his men and rode over to investigate. Not able to ascertain who occupied the camp, he called out to a figure on horseback in the darkness, "Whose division is that on the left?" When the response came back, "General Cleburne's," the astonished Union colonel replied, "All right" and dashed away at a gallop.

The federal column had been instructed to move at a steady pace of four miles an hour, but soon that broke down as wagons and artillery clogged the roads. Captain Levi Scofield, riding with the head of the army, remembered that as they approached Spring Hill, a colonel was posted by the road and cautioned them "with a finger to his lips, not to speak above a whisper, and pointed to the camp-fires on the rolling slopes within sight of the road." Private Tillman Stevens said that a little before midnight, as they neared Spring Hill, they passed by "thousands of campfires burning brightly, and [they] could see the soldiers standing or moving around the fires." "It was a rare and grand spectacle to behold," Stevens went on. "We were one company of thirty-five men passing right through Hood's army."

One Confederate officer remembered, "We were actually so close to the pike that many Federal soldiers came out to our fires to light their

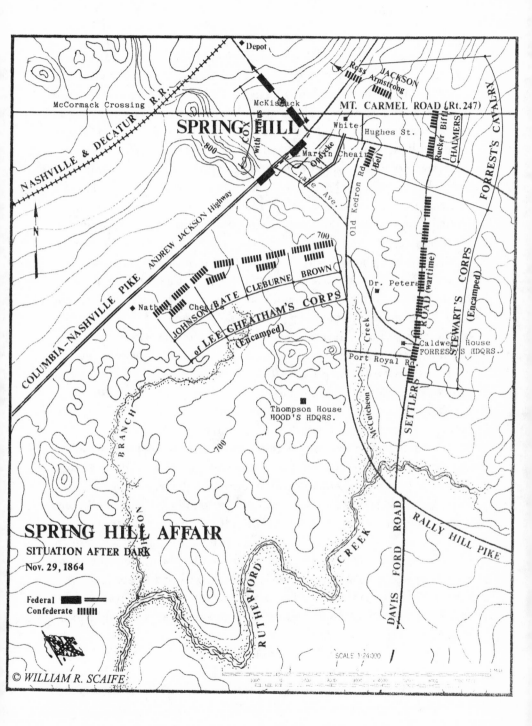

Depot

Ross JACKSON
Armstrong

McCormack Crossing R.R.

McKissack

MT. CARMEL ROAD (Rt. 247)

SPRING HILL

White

Hughes St.

Rucker Biff CHALMERS

FORREST'S CAVALRY

Martin

Queen Cheair

Bell

Lane Ave.

Old Kedron Rd.

800

700

Nath

Cheair

JOHNSON'S

BATE

CLEBURNE

BROWN

of LEE CHEATHAM'S CORPS

(Encamped)

Dr. Peters

STEWART'S CORPS
(Encamped)

Creek

Caldwe House
FORREST'S HDQRS.

Port Royal Rd.

McCutcheon

SETTLER'S ROAD (wartime)

Thompson House
HOOD'S HDQRS.

700

BRANCH

RUTHERFORD CREEK

DAVIS FORD ROAD

RALLY HILL PIKE

SPRING HILL AFFAIR

SITUATION AFTER DARK

Nov. 29, 1864

Federal
Confederate

© *WILLIAM R. SCAIFE*

SCALE 1:24000

pipes and were captured.'' A few enterprising Confederates waylaid unsuspecting blue-coated stragglers in the dark and took their gear and
food, but those were only small incidents. The bulk of Schofield's huge
column snaked right past Hood's whole army, their flank utterly exposed, for six or seven uninterrupted hours. They did not even stop at
Spring Hill but marched on through it, north toward Franklin.

There was yet another chance for Hood. Sometime after midnight
a lone barefoot Confederate private somehow found his way to Hood's
headquarters and reported seeing massed columns of federal infantry,
baggage wagons, and gun carriages clogging the pike toward Spring Hill
in Cheatham's vicinity south of the town. Hood, rubbing the sleep from
his eyes, ordered his adjutant, Major A. P. Mason, to send an immediate
order to Cheatham to have a regiment move out and fire on anybody
marching on the pike. Cheatham contended that he directed General
Edward Johnson—commanding the single division of Lee's corps that
had come north with the army, which was posted near Bate's earlier position near the pike—to check this out. Johnson, who was only temporarily under Cheatham's supervision, was none too happy that he—and
not one of Cheatham's command—was the one who had to roust out in
the dark of night. But he claimed he did as he was told yet found the pike
empty and desolate in both directions and so retired to camp.

It could have been that Johnson arrived after the last of Schofield's
army passed by, or perhaps he encountered a gap in the Union column.
Also, it is possible the federals had detoured off the pike onto a country
road leading to Spring Hill. Or perhaps Johnson did not go at all. In one
of the queerest contradictions in a night filled with queer contradictions,
Adjutant Mason the next day confessed that he had fallen back asleep
before he could get Hood's order sent to Cheatham, yet Cheatham
oddly claimed that he indeed received this never-sent-order and commanded Johnson to move out in compliance with it. Whichever was the
truth, here was a *sixth* opportunity for the undoing of Schofield squan-
dered.

There was one last hope for Hood to thwart Schofield's retreat,
and that was Forrest, who had sent General W. H. (''Red'') Jackson's
division of his cavalry about four miles north of Spring Hill to try to

block the pike. While the rest of the army slept, the Confederate horse-men attacked the Union column that was marching toward Franklin around midnight. They halted the retreat, burning a few wagons and creating havoc until the big blue infantry columns came up and drove them away. That the cavalry was brushed off was almost a foregone con-clusion, it being a military axiom that unsupported cavalry alone cannot not withstand massed infantry fire, yet that was exactly what Hood had ordered.

So when Hood arose a little before dawn, eagerly expecting to re-sume the battle and crush Schofield in place, all he found were empty camps and a few smouldering fires. The whole federal army had es-caped, bag and baggage, right under his nose. He was infuriated, and when his generals assembled by invitation for breakfast at the mansion of Major Nat Cheairs alongside the pike, he "lashed out" at them for the failure to contain Schofield's army. It was said that voices were raised, fingers pointed, accusations made and denied, and at some point the whole thing threatened to turn violent. Brown, upon whom at least some of the commanding general's maledictions were heaped, described Hood to one of his staff as "wrathy as a rattlesnake this morning, strik-ing at everything." Hood himself put it this way: "The best move in my career as a soldier I was thus destined to behold come to naught . . . never was a grander opportunity offered to utterly rout and destroy the Federal army." And then he went into a tirade about his pet peeve—breastworks. Ever since taking over the army back in Atlanta, this had been on his mind. "The discovery that the army, after a forward march of one hundred eighty miles, was still, seemingly, unwilling to accept battle unless under the protection of breastworks, caused me to experi-ence grave concern. In my innermost heart, I questioned whether or not I would ever succeed in eradicating this evil." He could not have known it then, but in a few short hours he would at last find out that he had.

11

★ Franklin, Tennessee

And so the Army of Tennessee followed behind Schofield, angry, sullen, and frustrated. Private Bill Pollard, of the 20th Tennessee, felt "desperate" and was hoping "the enemy would run upon us so that I could fight to the death-spent." In stark contrast to the army's mood, it was a pleasant autumn morning, the final day of November 1864. The pike wound through lovely pastoral valleys glowing with the last reds, yellows, and browns of dying foliage. On the hillsides sat white farmhouses with a few grazing cattle and sheep and fields of corn and wheat, and streams shimmered in the sunlight.

Stewart's corps, with the enraged Hood at its head, led the way, followed by Cheatham and by Lee, who was struggling to catch up from Columbia. Captain Joseph Boyce, near the front of the column, remembered that citizens, "nearly all old people or boys too young for military service, and any number of enthusiastic young ladies, lined the fences, cheering [them] and crying out: 'push on, boys; you will capture all of the Yanks soon. They have just passed here on the dead run.' " This might have heartened the men somewhat, but in the high command there was rancor and unease and hard feelings.

Hood gave stern instructions that morning: "If there is but a company in advance, and if it overtakes the entire Yankee army, order the captain to attack it forthwith.'' Back down the column, Pat Cleburne, wearing a new gray uniform and his favorite old cap with faded gold braid, was riding apart in the fields with General Brown, who had already endured a personal dressing down from Hood that morning. In a letter to Cheatham after the war, Brown remembered the Irishman telling him ''with much feeling'' that he had heard Hood was trying to put the blame on Cleburne for the Spring Hill business. Brown replied that he had ''heard nothing on that subject'' and said that he hoped that Cleburne was mistaken. But Cleburne told him, ''No, I think not; my information comes through a very reliable channel.'' Cleburne, Brown remembered, was ''quite angry and evidently was deeply hurt'' and stated that he would demand a full investigation. At this point a courier from either Hood or Cheatham arrived with orders, ending the discussion. On parting, Cleburne told Brown, ''We will resume this conversation at the first convenient moment.''

The enigma of the Confederate failure at Spring Hill was to remain in deep and seething controversy long after the war. At the time, Hood blamed his generals, specifically Cheatham, Cleburne, Bate, and Brown, as well as the soldiers themselves for what he believed was an aversion to attack breastworks. The generals, in turn—as well as many of the men—blamed Hood; after all, he was in command. Schofield himself, many years later, summed up his fortunate escape this way: ''Hood was in bed all night and I was in the saddle all night.''

In the end, there was enough blame to be shouldered all around. Cleburne seems not at all guilty for failing to make a second attack on Stanley; his orders, after all, were to wait for Brown to go first, and Brown never did. But Hood apparently did not know this, and so early on censured Cleburne. Brown's failure was more pernicious. He was a major general in command of an infantry division and should have known that the actions of the entire corps—and ultimately the army— depended solely on him. Being drunk was certainly no excuse for failing to make his attack, and if Hood had known this, he would surely have had him court-martialed. After the war was over, and before he died, Brown wrote a full personal account of his actions at Spring Hill, but his family refused to make it public, and presumably it was destroyed.

Cheatham also shared the onus. Apparently, he was not very communicative with Hood for most of the afternoon and evening regarding the situation on his front. Hood had ordered the seizing of the turnpike as Cheatham's main objective, but Cheatham seemed more interested in fighting Stanley's men instead. Also, there were the rumors that he had been intoxicated or had strayed into the seductive arms of Mrs. Jesse Peters. The fact is that Cheatham neither attacked the federals in Spring Hill with his full force nor secured the pike.

Neither Bate nor Forrest was responsible for the failure. Bate earnestly tried to attack the head of Schofield's column as it approached him on the pike but was recalled by Cheatham under threat of court-martial. And after driving the entire Union cavalry corps out of the battle area, Forrest then attacked Spring Hill, but timing—through no fault of his own—had allowed Stanley to arrive with his bristling infantry division. Later that night, Forrest did the best he could with what he had to hold back Schofield's retreat.

Finally, there was Hood. Altogether he had six opportunities to seal off the Columbia-Franklin Pike: Forrest's attack at Spring Hill, Cleburne's assault on Stanley's troops, Bate's lost chance at heading off Schofield, Brown's failure to set into motion a general assault on Spring Hill, Cheatham's failure to have Johnson or one of his other commands close off the pike late that night, and finally Forrest's outmatched attempt to hold off Schofield's retreat north of town. Some of these failures were understandable, but others were not because of possible misfeasance or malfeasance on the part of the officers in command. But Hood ultimately was the man in charge. He wasn't on the field to see that his orders were carried out, and this was the Army of Tennessee, not the Army of Northern Virginia, where he had served so long. And too bad, because Robert E. Lee did not have to personally supervise the activities of Stonewall Jackson or Longstreet or Ewell or A. P. Hill. It is not to say that the Army of Tennessee was materially or morally inferior to Lee's army. In strength, courage, and audacity it was certainly on a par, but in leadership experience it was lacking. Spring Hill was Cheatham's first major battle since being promoted to corps command; Stewart and Stephen Lee had led their corps only in the last days of the

Atlanta campaign. And Hood was equally inexperienced. To make matters worse, Hood's physical condition severely limited him. The night he went to bed at his headquarters near Spring Hill, he had been up since three o'clock that morning and spent an agonizing day in the saddle—including taking a fall—with a throbbing stump of the leg that had been amputated only a year before. He might have been just too exhausted to keep a proper eye on things.

Riding back at the tail of Cheatham's column was the chaplain, Dr. Quintard, astride a ''splendid horse named Lady Polk,'' which had been given to him as a present that same morning by General Otho Strahl. While they were still at Columbia, Hood had confidentially predicted to Quintard that the federals ''must give me a fight or I'll be in Nashville by tomorrow night.'' Now they were plodding up the pike in Schofield's rear, outwitted and undone by their own bungling and the vague fortunes of war. Years later, Quintard, trying to unravel the botched-up Spring Hill disaster, wrote to former Tennessee governor Isham Harris, who while in exile had been traveling with Hood's army, asking if he could shed any light on the subject. Harris answered, ''I was there and know much, if not all that occurred, and yet I cannot fix the responsibility upon any one officer. . . . Let's not open an old sore, and cause it to bleed again.''

It had been a frantic afternoon and night behind the Union lines. Schofield arrived in Spring Hill about 9 P.M. and around midnight got his army hustling on the twelve-mile march toward Franklin, leaving Wagner's division in a two-mile-long defensive perimeter around Spring Hill. All was hush-hush—at least as much as an army of twenty-five thousand men and enough horses and mules to draw a thousand wagons and artillery caissons could make it. The men marched ''left in front'' so if attacked they could simply face to the right and still be on line. They continued the long-strided pace of four miles an hour, so that the head of the army reached the Winstead Hills, just below Franklin, about 3 A.M. The tail, consisting of Wagner's division, did not finally leave Spring Hill until nearly 6 A.M., with the whole Confederate army in hot pursuit. As Private William Keesy of the 64th Ohio recalled, "Often, as we were coming over a hill and started down the descent we could see the enemy's advance coming up over a distant hill. The anxiety and excitement became intense."

Up in Franklin, Captain Levi Scofield of the engineers had been instructed to place the arriving divisions in their defensive positions. He had been with the first of the federals to get into the town, along with General Jacob Cox and his staff. On the outskirts of Franklin, beside the pike, they found the imposing brick home of Fountain Branch Carter, an elderly cotton farmer with two sons now in the Confederate army. General Cox decided to make the Carter house his headquarters, and the aged Carter was unceremoniously rousted out of bed and informed of this. Visiting home at this time was one of Carter's sons, Colonel Moscow Carter, who was on "parole" after his capture in an earlier engagement. A second son had been severely wounded two years before. The youngest son, Captain Theodoric ("Tod") Carter, was an adjutant on the staff of General Thomas Benton Smith, the twenty-six-year-old "boy brigadier" in Bate's division. Three families of young grandchildren were also in the house, and a couple of female servants, Cox recalled, "making a household of seventeen souls."

Cox and his exhausted people had just about fallen asleep on the downstairs floors and furniture of the Carter house when Schofield burst into the room, back from an inspection of the bridges crossing the rain swollen river to their rear. Red-eyed and pale, the worried commanding general exclaimed, "The pontoon are not here. The county bridge is gone and the ford is hardly passable." He told Cox that he must take command of the Twenty-third Corps and put it in position to "hold Hood back at all hazards" until the bridges were repaired and they could get across the river.

The river in question was the Harpeth, a not very wide but rather deep stream that snaked up from the southeast and enclosed the northern boundary of Franklin in a sort of semicircle before turning north again. It was the principal terrain feature in the peaceful little valley that was just now beginning to glow with the first pinkish rays of dawn. Some lamps were beginning to come on in the misty first light; alarmed

and curious citizens were peeking out of their windows to the noise of
tin cups rattling against bayonet clasps as the leading divisions of Schofield's army began streaming into town. Franklin, a village of about
twenty square blocks, with farms and plantations in the outlying fields,
had seen its share of fighting during the war but nothing to remotely
compare with what was about to be visited upon it. Sallie Carter, who
grew up there, remembered in her diary that Franklin was a lovely
place, with fresh peaches and apples to be picked and cool swimming
holes. About the most violent thing that had occurred there until the
war was a duel fought between an Andrew Jackson aide and the brother
of future U.S. Senator Thomas Hart Benton, and even then nobody was
hurt badly.

Schofield at this point was nearly beside himself with apprehension. First, he had not heard from Wilson and his cavalry since Forrest
chased them out of the Spring Hill vicinity the previous day. He was undoubtedly upset over this, because about two hours later he acidly telegraphed Thomas up at Nashville, "I do not know where Forrest is.
Wilson is entirely unable to cope with him." Furthermore, his telegraph communications with Nashville had been either nonexistent or
unreliable ever since Columbia when his decoder ran away; afterward,
Forrest's men had cut his wires north of Spring Hill. Before leaving Columbia, Schofield had wired an urgent request to Nashville asking
Thomas to send down pontoon bridges so he could cross the Harpeth,
but the wires were down, and Thomas never got it. Thus Schofield was
understandably agitated when he finally got to Franklin to find the
bridges wrecked and no way to get across. Finally, he didn't know
whether Thomas wanted him to fight or run—nor did he know himself.
In Cox's words, "In all my intimate acquaintance with him, I never saw
him so manifestly disturbed by the situation as he was in the glimmering
dawn of that morning."

So Schofield did the only thing he could in the circumstance, which
was to start rebuilding the bridges over the river from whatever materials he could scrape up in town. One burned wood wagon bridge had to
be entirely reconstructed, while a narrow iron railroad bridge was
planked over its crossties for troops to use. Meantime, Schofield en-

gaged in a frantic telegraphic correspondence with Thomas to ascertain his next moves. He had believed that the fifteen thousand fresh troops of A. J. Smith would certainly have arrived in Nashville by now and called for them to be sent immediately to his aid. Thomas, however, replied that Smith's troops were only then beginning to arrive by steamboat and could not be dispatched that quickly. Then he added, "I do not wish you to risk too much. I send you a map of the environs of Franklin." So Schofield was left with only a map and a wonder about how much risk was "too much."

Worse, Thomas asked if Schofield could hold Hood at Franklin "for three more days," while Schofield at that point didn't even know if he could hold him for three more hours. He wired back: "I cannot prevent Hood from crossing the Harpeth whenever he may attempt it." He also told him, "I am satisfied that I have heretofore run too much risk to hold Hood in check. . . . The slightest mistake on my part, or failure of a subordinate during the last three days might have proved disastrous. I don't want to get into such a tight place again." Years later, Schofield was to charge that Thomas "expected me, with two corps, to fight the entire hostile force until he could complete his concentration at Nashville."

Meanwhile, the citizens of Franklin were waking up to the chilling realization that a cataclysmic event was about to be unleashed on their sleepy little town.

Frances McEwen, a schoolgirl at the Franklin Female Institute, remembered, "Our teachers' faces looked unusually serious that morning." All through the village federal officers were galloping "hither and thither." Finally, she recorded, "The bell called us to chapel. We were told to take our books and go home, as there was every indication that we would be in the midst of a battle that day."

To fifteen-year-old Harding Figures, who lived with his widowed mother and brother in a house on the main street of Franklin, it was the scene of a lifetime. That morning, General William Grose, commanding a brigade of the Fourth Corps, arrived in the Figures yard and asked Mrs. Figures if he could pitch his tent there, saying, "In my opinion a great battle will be fought here today." Young Harding, a Tom Sawyerish sort of boy, later declared, "No mortal can tell with what a thrill of excitement I heard this announcement." Mrs. Figures and General Grose were in a "more serious mood," he reported, "and with her usual tact, my mother said: 'General, instead of pitching your tent in the yard, you can use my parlor for your headquarters, and breakfast is just announced. You and your staff come in and take breakfast.' "

There might have been more to this seeming hospitality than met the eye. Federal soldiers frequently made a practice of stealing from the occupants of Southern homes, and having a Union general using the house for headquarters might just prevent such mischief. Mrs. Sallie Carter, a widow who lived down the street from the Figureses, remembered, "Two mounted Federal officers came to my house and asked for breakfast. I told them that I would give them breakfast willingly, but I had no flour, that their men had taken my flour as it was being brought from the mill. These men belonged to the commissary department, and offered to sell me a barrel of flour, and I gladly paid their price—ten dollars."

Over at the Fountain Carter house, now Cox's headquarters, the elder Carter asked the general, "with some anxiety," whether he should move his family and abandon the house. Cox advised him to stay there until the battle was imminent, saying, "For whilst my headquarters tents were in his door-yard, there was no danger of annoyance from the men of my command." Eight-year-old Alice McPhail later reported, "[I would never forget how frightened I was when they told us children to keep in the house, for the Yankees were coming. We were afraid of the very name of Yankee." Alice remembered "Granpa and the negroes digging a big hole out in the middle of the North cellar floor." She wrote, "They brought all the meat from the smokehouse, potatoes, lard and big sacks of ground meal and everything else they could pack into that hole, then built a plank floor over it and laid the bricks all back and set a big table over it, and I was told it was done to keep the Yankees from getting it."

*   *   *

As the sun rose into a cloudless blue sky and warmed the valley of the Harpeth and the town, exhausted federal soldiers "worked like beavers, tossing houses, fences, timber and dirt into their breastworks." Lieutenant William Mohrmann, of General Thomas H. Ruger's division, Twenty-third Corps, "arrived about 8 in the morning, hungry and tired out, half dead with want of sleep." He said, "We drew rations, made coffee, were given an allowance of whisky—ominous sign—and then set to fortify. I showed my men where to dig a line of small pits and when the bright sun warmed up the side of a stump I located my headquarters right there and fell asleep at once."

Schofield, in apparent worry over the safety of his supply trains, spent his morning personally supervising the rebuilding and repair of the bridges north of town, while Cox was girding for the defense against a Confederate attack. Stanley, with the rear guard of the army, still had not arrived.

Thirty-six-year-old Jacob D. Cox was descended from an old New York Dutch family, graduated from Oberlin College, and became an Ohio lawyer and politician. He was a staunch abolitionist and one of the organizers of the Republican party in his state. Through his political connections—namely former Ohio governor Salmon P. Chase, now Lincoln's treasury secretary—he entered the army as a brigadier general less than two weeks after the war began. He fought in the early battles in West Virginia and in 1862 was assigned to General John Pope's Army of Virginia in time to take part in the embarrassing defeat at Second Manassas. Soon afterward he commanded a division in the Antietam campaign. The next year found him commanding the district of Ohio, and in the spring of 1864 he joined Sherman's Army of the Tennessee for the Atlanta campaign.

Not being an engineer himself—nor for that matter having any formal military education—Cox skillfully utilized the skills of those who did, including young Levi Scofield, in constructing the impressive line of fortifications around Franklin. More than twenty thousand men with picks and shovels feverishly threw together breastworks up to five feet high and capped by a "head log," which prevented exposure of everything but a few inches of the face that peeked beneath it.

At first light, Cox and his staff "carefully examined the ground" around Franklin. Standing on Carter's Hill, just in front of the Carter house, and looking south, Cox saw the Columbia Pike coming straight at him. Carter's Hill itself, he recognized, would be a salient point in any attack, as would the Carter cotton gin, located about one hundred twenty yards south and eighty yards east of the pike. The Winstead Hills, two miles south, which they had retreated over several hours earlier, formed the southern barrier of the valley of the Harpeth, and the land in between was a clear broad plain of fields and grass, smooth except for a long gentle roll or dip about a half mile away, which could "hide men or teams."

If Cox had had a balloon to go up in, he would have observed the approaches to Franklin as a series of lines converging on the apex of a divided triangle. To the west was Carter's Creek Pike, in the center the Columbia-Franklin Pike, and to the east the Lewisburg Pike. In between these last two were the tracks of the Alabama-Nashville railroad. Instead, Cox described it from his own point of view, looking south, as "the left hand extended with separated fingers. The little finger and thumb at right angles represent the Harpeth River and its course from left to right, whilst the three fingers spread in the midst indicate the three turnpikes diverging southward from the village."

Just northeast of town and across the Harpeth River was Figures Hill, with an old earthen fort built during an earlier battle. This was Fort Granger, named for Union General Gordon Granger, and this was where a federal artillery battery including several long-range three-inch rifles would be positioned after a tortuous fording of the river. From the heights of Figures Hill, these guns could sweep the approaches of the southern plain for more than a mile, firing well over the heads of any Union soldiers in their breastworks. "Such was the field as it lay before us under the level beams of the rising sun," Cox said.

So Cox set to work laying out his lines with the help of "an efficient engineer battalion, made up of intelligent mechanics," in the charge of Captain Twining, chief engineer. Meantime, a steady stream of federal troops and wagons from the remainder of the army continued to pour into town from the Columbia Pike. All morning this monster line of entrenchments grew until it stretched in a two-mile half-moon arc from the river southeast of town to the bend of the river northwest of town—including six well-placed artillery batteries containing about thirty guns. But the most heavily fortified works were along a one-mile front facing due south, toward the Winstead Hills, over which Hood's army was soon expected to appear.

All morning Hood's army toiled along the Franklin Pike, with Forrest's cavalry nipping at the heels of Schofield's retreating column. Joseph Boyce of the 1st Missouri, Stewart's corps in the advance, remembered passing a great many abandoned federal commissary wagons. "The enemy was too hotly pressed to have time to unhitch the mules," Boyce said. "We found the poor creatures dead in their harnesses, having been shot through the head by the drivers or rear guard. Their bodies were still warm and smoking."

By midday, Hood and the head of the army reached the near side of the Winstead Hills. The white crushed stone of the pike bent upward and over the top, and alongside the road on the upward slope Schofield's rear guard could be seen. It was the brigade of Colonel Emerson Opdycke of Wagner's division. Like Cox, Opdycke was an Ohioan with no formal military background and fierce abolitionist zeal. A dry goods salesman before the war, he overcame his lack of military training and turned into a fine combat leader, distinguishing himself at Shiloh, Chickamauga, Chattanooga, and Atlanta. At the tail end of the federal army, Opdycke had fought all day, with Hood's men close at his heels. Later he recollected how the pike from Spring Hill to Franklin was filled with stragglers, "mostly new men with immense knapsacks . . . so worried as to seem indifferent to capture." Infuriated, Opdycke ordered his soldiers to "bring along every man at the point of the bayonet, and to cut off the knapsacks," estimating that he "saved 500 men from capture by these severe measures." As Hood's skirmishers spread out and advanced toward him, Opdycke opened fire with a section of artillery, but it soon was apparent that Hood had divided his main column and was going to flank him, and the Ohioan quickly retreated his seven regiments down the opposite side of the hills and on into Franklin.

Hood was indeed flanking Opdycke's little rear guard. From his temporary headquarters at the Harrison mansion beside the pike, he ordered Stewart to move his whole corps by the right toward the Lewisburg road east of Franklin, while Cheatham's corps would come straight up the pike over the Winstead Hills—except for Bate's division, which moved off left through a gap in the hills to emerge close to the Carter's Creek Pike at the western edge of town.

As the columns moved out, Hood and his staff rode up to the crest of Winstead Hill for their first look at Franklin, below and across the plain, two miles away. Before them, the valley of the Harpeth spread out like a great oriental fan, bluegrass still green, bisected by the white-stone pike and scarcely a tree amid a patchwork of open fields. In the distance was the town, with a few white church steeples rising out of the late-autumn foliage. Off to the east and curving around behind the town was the winding Harpeth, shimmering in the midday sun. The scene would have been peaceful as a landscape portrait, were it not for the dark line of Union breastworks and the frowning guns that could be seen plainly, even without field glasses. As the Confederate troops crested the hill and filed down onto the plain, which one described as "level as a floor," they began to cheer. For most this was native soil, and the elusive enemy was finally before them.

The sun did not rise high into the sky on that short winter day but made a low sullen arc southeast to west and glared down on the valley with a rarefied hue. Particularly visible from the point of view in the federal entrenchments was the bright white line of the Columbia-Franklin Pike extending from town straight across the plain and then rising through the cut between the green-cedar Winstead Hills. A little past 1 P.M. a near hush stilled all work in the Union fortifications, and the men looked southward. Where the pike descended the slope of the hills, long lines could be seen toiling down it. From that distance, the lines appeared black against the stark whiteness of the crushed stone, like columns of thousands of black ants. Captain Levi Scofield recorded that Confederate officers on horseback could be plainly seen in the distance, "as though studying our position."

12

★ Seeing the Elephant

At the top of Winstead Hill, Confederate Sergeant-major Sumner A. Cunningham of General Otho Strahl's brigade was halted "near where General Hood, leaving his staff on the southern slope of the hill, rode over a crest and down to a linden tree—the only tree near in any direction—and with his glasses examined the area to Franklin—the breastworks in front of the town and the Fort Figures across the Harpeth River." Cunningham later recalled, "I watched him closely while there, meditating on his responsibility. When he returned to the top of the hill and near where I happened to be standing, a general officer—I thought [Lowrey] or Loring, but have never known what officer—dressed handsomely and riding a magnificent black horse, met him and Hood said, 'General, we will make the fight,' and the two clasped hands. Orders were speedily dispatched to various commanders, a band of music on the slope across the pike began to play, and the Army of Tennessee was soon in motion."

Whatever the troops may have thought, this news of Hood's proposed attack was received with less than bounding enthusiasm among his generals. Forrest, for one, soon rode up after his all-day skirmish with Schofield's army and spoke out against the plan. "Give me one strong division of infantry with my cavalry and within two hours time I will agree to flank the Federals from their works," he told Hood, adding that he would march east to the Harpeth, cross over, and swing around against Schofield north of Franklin. Hood shook his head. The enemy was there, and there he would attack him. Hood instructed Forrest to put his cavalry on both flanks so "if the assault proved successful, to complete the ruin of the enemy by capturing those who attempted to escape in the direction of Nashville."

When he learned of Hood's plan, Frank Cheatham—who had been studying the Union position—also rode up to register a protest, worrying that the army "would take a desperate chance if we attempted to dislodge them."

"I don't like the looks of this fight," he counseled Hood. "The Federals have an excellent position, and are well fortified."

Hood replied, "I would prefer to fight them here where they have only eight hours to fortify, than to strike them at Nashville where they have been strengthening themselves for three years and more." Still smarting from his chastisement over the debacle at Spring Hill, Cheatham argued no more and gave the order for Bate to move his division west through a gap in the hills, then down onto the valley floor.

Presently Pat Cleburne came along. As he waited for his troops to ascend Winstead Hill, he had been enjoying a game of checkers with his staff, using a board drawn out on the ground with a stick and with colored leaves for men. Earlier, from the crest of the hill, Cleburne had rested his field glasses on a stump and carefully examined the Union lines. "They are very formidable," was his only remark. Now he and Brown met Hood and threw their weight into the argument, with Cleburne asserting that a direct attack would involve "a terrible waste of life." Like Forrest before him, Cleburne urged a flanking movement to turn Schofield out of his entrenchments, but Hood was having none of it. Brown recorded that Hood told them, "The country around Franklin for many miles is open and exposed to the full view of the Federal Army, and I cannot mask the movements of my troops so as to turn either flank of the enemy, and if I attempt it, he will withdraw and precede me into Nashville."

So they, too, rode off in frustration to give the fateful orders. General Govan, commander of one of Cleburne's brigades, remembered that the Irishman "seemed to be more despondent than I ever saw him." He "fully realized," Govan said, "as did every officer present, the desperate nature of the assault we were about to make. He informed us that by the direction of Gen. Hood, he had called us together to impress upon us the importance of carrying the works of the enemy *at all hazards.*" Govan, an old friend of Cleburne's from Arkansas days, later recalled, "Looking over and beyond the bare common over which we had to move, you could see behind the heavy earthworks the bristling bayonets of the enemy, and flitter of Napoleon guns, as they peeped through the embrasures." As Govan saluted and started to ride off, he remarked, "Well, General, few of us will ever return to Arkansas to tell the story of this battle." To which Cleburne responded, "Well, Govan, if we are to die, let us die like men."

As the Confederate army began to pour onto the valley floor and take battle formation, over in the federal lines Schofield's men began their final preparations to receive the attack. Up until then, not a single Union general—including Schofield and his two corps commanders, Cox and Stanley—had believed that Hood would actually assault them in the front. Now as the sun sank low in the clear winter sky, it was apparent that that was precisely what he intended to do. By this time, Schofield's hard work and personal supervision of the bridging of the Harpeth had paid off—all of the thousand or so wagons were already on the far side of the river, and Schofield sent orders for the troops to begin retreating across by 6 P.M. if Hood did not attack before then.

Cox's strenuous supervision of the defensive front had also paid off. He had laid out a line of fortifications nearly two miles long, anchored more or less on both ends by the Harpeth, and most of it was contained behind a deep trench line in back of which was a mound of dirt five feet high capped with headlogs. In front of the trench the troops had hastily fashioned abatis of sharpened stakes, mostly from the locust grove at their front, on the west side of the Columbia Pike, and a thick hedge of Osage orange that grew near the entrenchments on the east side of the pike.

Facing Hood's army behind this formidable position were three divisions of Union infantry. On the left of the pike was the Third Division, Twenty-third Corps, temporarily under command of General James W. Reilly, a thirty-six-year-old Ohio lawyer and politician. The immediate right of the pike was manned by the Second Division, Twenty-third Corps, commanded by General Thomas H. Ruger, a thirty-one-year-old New Yorker and West Point graduate who had served back east in the Antietam, Chancellorsville, and Gettysburg campaigns. The far right of the federal line was occupied by the First Division, Fourth Army Corps, commanded by forty-two-year-old General Nathan Kimball, an Indiana physician before the war. In reserve on the far side of the Harpeth was the Third Division, Fourth Corps, under General Thomas Wood. Interspersed along the lines were sections of artillery containing some thirty guns.

Out in front of the whole federal line was the rear guard, Second Division, Fourth Army Corps, led by thirty-five-year-old General George Day Wagner, an Indiana politician with a receding hairline and a goatee. This was where the trouble began.

Wagner's division consisted of three brigades commanded by Colonels John Q. Lane, Joseph Conrad, and Emerson Opdycke. They had borne the brunt of the Union retreat all the way from Columbia and were the first to arrive at Spring Hill, saving it—and most likely the entire federal army—from capture. In the fierce fighting there, Luther Bradley, formerly commanding Conrad's brigade, was severely wounded, and after the rest of Schofield's army had passed through on its way to Franklin, Wagner's division had to fight the pursuing Confederates all the way up the pike.

Now, after failing to check Hood's army at the Winstead Hills, the brigades of Lane and Conrad were posted in an exposed and hastily drawn-up position astride the Columbia-Franklin Pike, about a quarter mile in front of the federal entrenchments, with orders to skirmish with and delay any general Confederate assault, then withdraw up the pike and into the Union lines, but *by no means* to stand and try to give battle.

Wagner was no doubt feeling pretty good about himself that afternoon. After all, he had "saved" Schofield's army from destruction by holding Spring Hill against Hood's whole force and then fought them hammer and tongs all the way back to Franklin. As Opdycke's tired brigade trudged back up the pike after Hood's initial flanking movement, Wagner rode up and accosted his young brigadier, ordering him to place his men in the forward position with Lane and Conrad. To this order, Opdycke "strenuously objected." Captain John K. Shellenberger, commanding a company in Conrad's brigade, said that Opdycke complained to Wagner that the position was untenable. "He also pleaded that his brigade was worn out, having been marching . . . in line of battle in sight of the enemy, climbing over fences, passing through woods, thickets and muddy cornfields, and was entitled to a relief." Finally, Wagner gave up, grousing, "Well, Opdycke, fight when and where you damn please; we all know you'll fight," then turned and rode off. Opdycke marched his men inside the federal lines and took position as a reserve, by the Carter house, two hundred yards inside the breastworks. As things developed, this turned out to be the crucial troop disposition of the battle, but it did nothing to help the brigades of Lane and Conrad, which were still hanging out there, half a mile in front, exposed to the advance of the entire Confederate army.

What began to transpire down in the valley of the Harpeth was a military spectacle to behold. Two Confederate army corps—more than twenty thousand men—began to align themselves for battle on an open plain in full view of the enemy. While A. P. Stewart's corps was forming to the east, Cheatham had delayed bringing Cleburne's and Brown's divisions over the crest of Winstead Hill in order to wait for Bate's division to swing into position way around to the west. He sent word that a prearranged signal flag would be the order for them to move out. After he satisfied himself of Bate's progress from the crest of the hill, Cheatham ordered that the flag be dropped, "and the line moved forward steady as a clock." Twenty years later, Cheatham revisited the battlefield with his former chief of staff, James D. Porter. "Don't you recall, Porter, that as they wheeled into line of battle in full view of the enemy, their precision and military bearing was as beautiful a sight as was ever witnessed in war?" Porter nodded his head. "It was the greatest sight I ever saw," he said, "each division unfolding itself into a single line of battle with as much steadiness as if forming for dress parade."

Along a three-mile front across the Franklin fields six Confederate divisions moved into line, the battle flags of more than 125 regiments fluttering in the breeze of an Indian summer afternoon. Cheatham's corps was placed with two divisions astride the Columbia Pike, Cleburne on the right and Brown to the left. Bate's division, which had gone marching around west through a gap in the hills, now reappeared on the far left of the line near the Carter's Creek Pike.

A. P. Stewart's corps occupied the far right, between the river and the cut of the Nashville-Alabama railroad. From right to left it consisted of the divisions of one-armed General William Wing Loring, mostly Mississippians and Alabamians; the Tennessee, Arkansas, and Alabama brigades of General Edward C. Walthall's division; and the North Carolina, Texas, and Mississippi regiments of Sam French's division. Forrest anchored the Confederate far right with two divisions of his cavalry, while Chalmers's cavalry division had gone around to anchor the far left next to Bate. Hood had with him only two six-gun artillery batteries; the rest of the guns were with Stephen Lee's corps, which still had not caught up to the main army. These field pieces were placed in position on the right and left of Columbia Pike, one for each corps.

It was nearing sunset when this vast panorama began to take shape across the peaceful Harpeth valley; in the lengthening shadows the long gray and butternut lines merged with their battle flags flying, officers dashing up and down on horseback, couriers coming and going, while to the north were the sullen frowning lines of the federal army, their own flags planted atop their breastworks. A surgeon in A. P. Stewart's corps recalled that "during the time while the lines were forming it was perfectly still; no sound jarred upon the ear," while a Tennessee private remembered that "a profound silence pervaded the entire army; it was simply awful, reminding one of those sickening lulls which preceded a tremendous thunderstorm."

In the ranks, various little dramas were being played out. James M'Neilly, a chaplain in Walthall's division, was surrounded by men who fully understood the implications of the coming fury. "Several of them came to me bringing watches, jewelry, letters and photographs, asking me to send them to their families if they were killed," M'Neilly said. "I had to decline, as I was going with them and would be exposed to the same danger. It was vividly recalled to me the next morning, for I believe every one who made this request of me was killed."

As Brown's division formed up on the right of the pike, Sergeant-major Cunningham was in position as guide of the 41st Tennessee, about four paces in their front. Here he met his brigade commander, thirty-one-year-old General Otho French Strahl, a handsome black-haired Northerner who came south to study law after graduating from Ohio Wesleyan University and threw his lot in with the Confederacy. Marching on foot this fading sunny afternoon because he had that morning given his horse to Chaplain Quintard, Strahl told his brigade, "Boys, this will be short and desperate," but other than that he rarely spoke, and Sergeant-major Cunningham said of him, "a sadder face I have never seen."

One brigade back, the commander—whose given name was the epitome of the lost cause—was riding up and down his lines with inspiring words for his troops. He was thirty-one-year-old Brigadier General States Rights Gist, a South Carolinian who had graduated from Harvard Law School and fought conspicuously in the Chickamauga, Chattanooga, and Atlanta campaigns. Gist was followed into battle by his slave and body servant, "Uncle Wiley" Howard, who had been with him all through the war.

Over in Sam French's division of Stewart's corps some officer made the mistake of quoting to a regiment of Irishmen Lord Nelson's famous remark before the battle of Trafalgar: "England expects every man to do his duty." Sergeant Denny Callahan raised a huge laugh by saying, "It's damned little duty England would get out of this Irish crowd."

On the floor of the Harpeth valley less than a mile from the Union lines was a small rocky knob called Merrill's Hill, where some of Cheatham's sharpshooters had been stationed, making a hell on earth for federal officers and artillerymen. Pat Cleburne rode out and asked if he could borrow a telescope. The lieutenant in charge "quickly detached the long telescope from his gun, adjusted the focus and handed it to General Cleburne, who . . . looked long and carefully over the field, and remarked, 'They have three lines of works,' and then, sweeping the field again as if to make himself certain, said, 'And they are all completed.' " Riding back to Hood, Cleburne asked permission to form his division in a column of brigades, so as to expose his front as little as possible to federal fire. Hood granted the request and further instructed Cleburne, "Give orders to your men not to fire till you drive the Federal skirmishers from their works to your front. Then press them and shoot them in the backs. Then charge the main works." Cleburne replied, "General, I will take the works or fall in the attempt."

In bizarre contrast to practically everybody's recollections of Cleburne's frame of mind at this time, Hood recalled that his premier division commander was practically ebullient at the prospect of attacking headlong into the federal lines. "Expressing himself with an enthusiasm which he had never before betrayed in our intercourse," Cleburne, Hood said, told him, " 'General, I am ready and have more hope in the final success in our cause than I have had at any time since the first gun was fired.' " Hood said, "I replied, 'God grant it!' He turned and moved at once toward the head of his division." There is such a contradiction between this and other accounts it can only be explained by assuming that Hood was not telling the truth or that his memory was faulty, or that in the time between his original orders and Cleburne's formation of his division on the field the Irishman somehow had worked himself up into a frenzied pitch of confidence and aggressiveness.

After Hood rejected Nathan Forrest's proposal to take his cavalry and one "good" infantry division across the Harpeth and flank Schofield from his position, the Confederate cavalry commander set about to do what he could—as Hood had ordered—to protect the Confederate flanks and block Schofield's anticipated retreat. About 2 P.M., just as the Army of Tennessee's brigades were beginning to form for battle on the Franklin plain, Forrest took the two cavalry divisions he had on the Confederate right, "Red" Jackson's and Abraham Buford's—totaling about three thousand men—and crossed to the east bank of the Harpeth. From there he turned north, driving the federal cavalry of Generals John T. Croxton and Edward Hatch before him.

But then Forrest hit a snag. For the first time in the campaign, Wilson had all the available cavalry in the Army of the Tennessee with him, six thousand troopers on the press-ganged civilian horses he had been so feverishly confiscating. In addition, Schofield had given Wilson use of the infantry of T. J. Wood's division, which was posted across the river north of Franklin in reserve (although Wilson said he was never told this, and the first time he heard it was weeks later when he read Schofield's official report). In any case, the vaunted Wilson, who in the week since joining the Army of the Tennessee had been nothing but humiliated and embarrassed by Forrest's "wizardry," now had on hand a force twice superior to his opponent.

Schofield, of course, was in no way convinced that Wilson could hold Forrest; after all, only that morning he had grimly telegraphed Thomas up in Nashville, "I don't know where Forrest is. Wilson is entirely unable to cope with him." And even as Wilson's troopers were moving out to meet Forrest's new threat, Schofield was replying pessimistically to a query by Thomas as to whether Wilson could hold the Confederate general in check: "I think he can do very little. I have no doubt Forrest will be in my rear to-morrow or doing some greater mischief."

Jackson's division moved on the cavalry of Croxton and pressed it back, while Buford attacked, dismounted, the division of General Edward Hatch, who had recently inspired much Southern enmity by personally looting paintings, china, and silverware from the Mississippi mansion of the former U.S. Interior Secretary. It was a sharp and vicious fight, but after about three hours Wilson's superior numbers finally began to tell on Forrest, and he was forced to fall back across the river to resupply his ammunition.

Although both Wilson and Schofield maintained that Forrest's horsemen always outnumbered them two to one, Wilson later said it had been a "fatal mistake" for Forrest to divide his cavalry by sending Chalmers's strong division way over on Hood's left flank and effectively out of the action. "Instead of driving me back and getting on Schofield's rear as he might have done with his whole corps," Wilson wrote, "it made it easy for me not only to beat his two divisions in actual battle but to drive them north of the river in confusion."

In any event, for once Forrest had not lived up to his reputation or, for that matter, to Hood's expectation. Schofield's route of retreat toward Nashville would remain unmolested.

It was now 3:30 P.M., Wednesday, November 30. The sun was a reddish biscuit "going down behind a bank of dark clouds" in the western sky. The afternoon was still warm and a little hazy. Hood had ridden forward about a half mile on the Franklin Pike to a little straw pen by a toll gate, where his staff helped him to dismount and placed him down on some blankets they had spread out on the ground over the straw. Here he reclined, using a saddle for a backrest, when word came that the Army of Tennessee was formed for battle. Precisely how he responded is not recorded, but whatever his words, they set in motion one of the most breathtaking infantry charges in the history of warfare.

Captain Joseph Boyce, of General Francis Marion Cockrell's Missouri brigade, observing that "this was no boy's play," remembered the "clear, ringing tones of the final commands: 'Shoulder arms! Right shoulder shift arms! Brigade forward! Guide center! Music! Quick time! March!' "

It must have been the incongruity of the music that struck so many of the soldiers in the line. "Our brass band, one of the finest in the army," Boyce said; there were tunes of glory, tunes of death, twenty thousand bayonets gleaming on a lovely autumn afternoon, an army of veterans with the veteran's understanding of what they were about to face. "This was the first and only time I ever heard our bands playing upon a battlefield, and at the beginning of a charge," said Dr. G. C. Phillips, of Stewart's corps. During the twenty or so minutes it took the lines to reach the outermost defense works of Schofield's army, the tunes resounded across the level valley floor, all the old Southern favorites—"Bonnie Blue Flag," "The Girl I Left Behind Me," "Dixie."

"For once, and only once," said a lieutenant in the sad-faced Strahl's brigade, "we went into battle cheered by the sound of martial music. It was the grandest sight I ever beheld."

Behind the Union lines over in Franklin there was music, too; the blue-coat bands retaliated with "Yankee Doodle" and the "Battle Hymn of the Republic." As the Confederate army advanced, Schofield's artillery began firing, but at the range of nearly a mile and a half it did little or no damage. Meantime, the Confederates answered with artillery of their own.

Franklin resident John McEwen found his home occupied as the headquarters of Union General Nathan Kimball. After lunch a federal colonel on Kimball's staff lingered in the parlor and asked McEwen if his daughters would sing and play for him. Asked what he wished to hear, the colonel replied that he didn't know one piece of music from the other, so McEwen's daughters began to play the new tune "Just Before the Battle, Mother" when suddenly a Confederate shell burst outside. McEwen wryly commented, "Colonel, if I am any judge, it is just about that time now" as the federal officer sprang to his feet and rushed outside toward his regiment; but before he reached it he "was shot through the lungs, the bullet passing quite through him."

McEwen hustled his family into the cellar, where, his daughter Frances recorded, "A few minutes later there was a crash! and down came a deluge of dust and gravel. The usually placid face of our old black mammy, now thoroughly frightened, appeared on the scene. She said a cannon ball had torn a hole in the side of the meat house and broken her wash kettle to pieces." Over at the Carter house, things were much the same. Fountain Branch Carter, the grandfather, put rolls of rope in the cellar windows to "keep the bullets out," and Alice McPhail Nichol, who had been living there, later recalled, "Now I remember the first sound of the firing and booming of the cannons, we children all sat around our mother and cried."

Out in the federal trenches, Private Adam J. Weaver was writing a letter as the Confederate lines approached: "The air is hazy. I can hear bands playing, and I see a few rebels being deployed in line of battle in the far distance. Cousin Rhody tells us it is 3:30 P.M.''

Half a mile in front of the main Union line, General George Wagner's two rear-guard brigades were still toiling frantically to throw up some sort of breastworks against Hood's advancing army.

Conrad's brigade had only two picks and two shovels to the company, and, according to Private Bill Keesy, ''They were worked by willing men for all that was in them. Every man tried to get a root, chunk, log, rail, or anything he could to help strengthen the protection we realized would soon be sorely needed.'' Captain Shellenberger added, ''Whenever a man working showed the least sign of fatigue, a comrade would snatch the spade out of his hands and ply it with desperate energy.''

Wagner's advanced position astride the Columbia Pike was in an abandoned cotton field, directly in the path of Hood's army—three thousand Union men against twenty thousand Confederates. Despite the orders for Wagner to ''give the men a few volleys'' and then bring them ''in behind the works in good order,'' Wagner had arbitrarily decided to stay and fight it out—or at least to have his *men* stay and fight it out; Wagner himself remained safe behind the main Union breastworks. Captain Levi Scofield was standing atop the fortifications beside the pike in conversation with Wagner, who was ''reclining on his elbow, his feet hanging over the works, with a staff or a crutch in his hand; he had fallen with his horse and was lame.'' As Hood's army pressed down on Wagner's little rear-guard force, a staff officer from Conrad's brigade galloped up to Wagner and said excitedly, ''The enemy are forming in heavy columns; we can see them distinctly in the open timber and all along our front!''

Wagner merely looked at the officer and ordered, ''Stand there and fight them,'' then, turning to Scofield, he roared, ''And that stubbed, curley-headed Dutchman [meaning the argumentative Opdycke] will fight them too.'' Scofield, who was on Cox's staff and aware of the instructions given Wagner, said, ''But General, the orders are not to stand, except against cavalry and skirmishers, but to fall back behind the main line." Wagner, however, did not respond. A short while later, another courier from the imperiled brigades dashed up, and this time several other officers of Cox's staff had gathered around Wagner and Scofield. This rider informed Wagner that the Confederates were "advancing in heavy force" and "would overlap the two brigades on both flanks and he did not think they ought to remain there any longer." But Wagner blithely replied, "Go back, and tell them to fight—fight like hell!" When the astonished messenger protested that "Hood's entire army is coming," Wagner "struck the ground with his stick and barked, 'never mind, fight them.' "

Among other events, Wagner's unusual behavior went to show that unsoldierly conduct was by no means confined to Hood's army, for, like the Rebel General Brown at Spring Hill, Wagner, it seems, was drunk that afternoon. No less an authority than his corps commander, General David Stanley, was to testify, "Wagner was, to say the least 'full of whisky' if not drunk. . . . He was in a vainglorious condition, though it was not known at the time by General Scofield or myself." Captain Marshall Thatcher remembered that "a staff officer was sent a second time to see if Wagner understood the order, but the poorest charity we can extend him is that he must have been drunk."

In any case, as soon as word of Wagner's sacrificial intention was delivered to the two little brigades, a near panic erupted. In Conrad's brigade, an orderly came with orders for Captain Shellenberger, he said later, to "hold the position to the last man, and to have my sergeants fix bayonets and to instruct my company that any man not wounded who should attempt to leave the line without orders would be shot or bayonetted by the sergeants. The indignation of the men grew almost into a mutiny. Even the green drafted men could see the folly of our position. One of them said to me: 'What can our generals be thinking about in keeping us out here?' " From Lane's brigade, Private W. W. Gist wrote, "The suspense and the nervous strain became greater and greater. Nearer and nearer the Confederates approached with the precision of a dress parade. We wondered why we were not moved back. It was plain that someone had blundered."

As the weight of Hood's army bore down on the exposed rear guard, Private Bill Keesy described "the swords glistening and bayonets flashing." And went on, "They are moving into close order now. See those lines closing up! Now our picks and shovels are thrown aside. Every man carefully examines his gun. Our orderly sergeant is calling very imploringly to the captain: 'Captain, for God's sake, let us get in behind the works. Why, just see them coming! Enough to swallow us up!' But the captain, poor fellow, is under orders too, and all that he can say is, 'Sergeant, keep your place, sir, and not another word.' "

By now it was nearly four o'clock, and the sharp crack of rifles was added to the roar and crash of artillery in the town of Franklin. Young Harding Figures had impishly "spent the entire afternoon upon the top of the barn and woodshed, in a tree top and other high places, seeing all that could be seen." But now, he said, "The bullets were flying and whizzing around everywhere to such an extent that I concluded I was as liable to be hit as a soldier, and I retreated to the cellar."

In the Confederate line that was steadily advancing toward the breastworks, the veterans knew exactly what a clash of this scale meant. They even had an expression for it. As the sun closed slowly over the low hills, they were going to "see the elephant."

13

★ An Indescribable Fury

Colonel Ellison Capers was a twenty-seven-year-old regimental commander in States Rights Gist's brigade. As Cheatham's corps advanced to pierce the federal center, Capers described the battlefield from the point of view of an officer in the front line:

> Just before the charge was ordered the brigade passed over an elevation, from which we beheld the magnificent spectacle the battlefield presented—bands were playing, general and staff officers and gallant couriers were riding in front of and between the battle lines. 100 battle flags were waving in the smoke of battle and bursting shells were wreathing the air with great circles of smoke, while 20,000 brave men were marching in perfect order against their foe. . . .
>
> General Gist ordered the charge in concert with General Gordon. In passing from the left to the right of the regiment the general waved his hat to us, expressing his pride and confidence in the twenty-fourth, and rode away in the smoke of the battle, never to be seen by the men he had commanded on so many fields. His horse was shot and, dismounted, he was leading the right of the brigade when he fell, pierced through the heart.

Uncle Wiley Howard had followed his owner into the battle, for what purpose is not clear, but, as the Gist family recorded him later, he remembered the following: "De last time I seen Marse States he was on foot, nigh er sugar maple tree, still leading hiz men. Joe [Gist's horse] had been shot through de neck, en was rearing and plunging so he had ter dismount. . . . When it got so hot, I went back ter our tent."

From the other side, Union Captain Scofield could also give a graphic description of the Confederate onrush and its clash with Wagner's vulnerable little brigades out in front of the works:

Soon we noticed the right of Stewart's command wrapping around Conrad's left, and then our men rose up and the break commenced. It was a grand sight! For the moment we were spellbound with admiration, although they were our hated foes. . . . The day had been bright and warm, reminding us of the Northern Indian Summer; the afternoon sun, like a ball of fire, was settling in all its southern splendor in a molten sea of bronze, over the distant hills, and in the hazy, golden light, and with their yellowish-brown uniforms, those in the front seemed to be magnified in size, one could almost imagine them to be phantoms sweeping along in the air.

On they came, and in the center their lines seemed to be many deep and unbroken, their red-and-white tattered flags, with the emblem of St. Andrew's Cross as numerous as though every company bore them, flaring brilliantly in the sun's rays. . . . Scattered along in front of them were our men, bent almost to the ground, with their heads turned to see if the enemy were gaining on them. It was every man for himself and devil take the last man over the works. As forerunners well in advance, could be seen a line of rabbits, bounding along for a few leaps, and then would stop and look back and listen, but scamper off again . . . and quails by the thousands, in coveys here and there would rise and settle, and rise again to the warm sunlight, until finally they rose high in the air and whirred off to the gray skylight of the north.

The corps of Cheatham and Stewart simply steamrolled over the brigades of Lane and Conrad with bayonets fixed, firing at will. Captain Shellenberger's company had only time to fire five or six rounds before they gave way despite Wagner's orders to stand and fight. "They were coming on a run," Shellenberger said, "emitting the shrill rebel charging yell and so close that my first impulse was to drop flat on the ground and let them charge over." In Conrad's brigade Bill Keesy reported, "[There is] a wall of blazing guns all along our front. Every second some one is killed. We are working like demons ourselves, loading and firing till the gun-barrels burn our hands with every touch. We are all mixed up in hand to hand conflict. The order is faintly heard above the din, 'fall back.' To stay means imprisonment or death. To attempt a retreat over that open field at this short range is taking a risk equally as great."

Like a gigantic gray dragon, the surging Confederate line swept the field, and as the break turned into a general rout, Confederate officers began shouting, "Go right on into the works with them, boys!" Most of the panicked bluecoats headed straight back up the pike to the gap in the federal lines, but hundreds were shot down or captured and sent to the rear. The scene was a combination of melee and half-mile sprint and posed a chilling dilemma from the aspect of Union soldiers behind the main breastworks: a whole Confederate army was rushing toward them, but they could not fire at it for fear of killing their own men.

Captain Shellenberger had nearly reached the Union line when his legs and lungs simply gave out. Thinking that his "time had come," he suddenly remembered his mother's parting words to him, "Well, if you must go, don't get shot in the back," and turned around to face a Confederate soldier looming up on him. "He was coming directly toward me on a dog trot, and was withdrawing the ramrod from the barrel of his gun . . . he stopped to prime and then aimed and fired at a little squad of our men on my right. I heard the bullet strike and an exclamation from the man who had been hit. The rebel then started to trot forward again, at the same time reaching back with one hand to draw a fresh cartridge." Somehow, Shellenberger managed to reach the safety of his lines.

The exhausted Keesy found himself running for his life over knap-

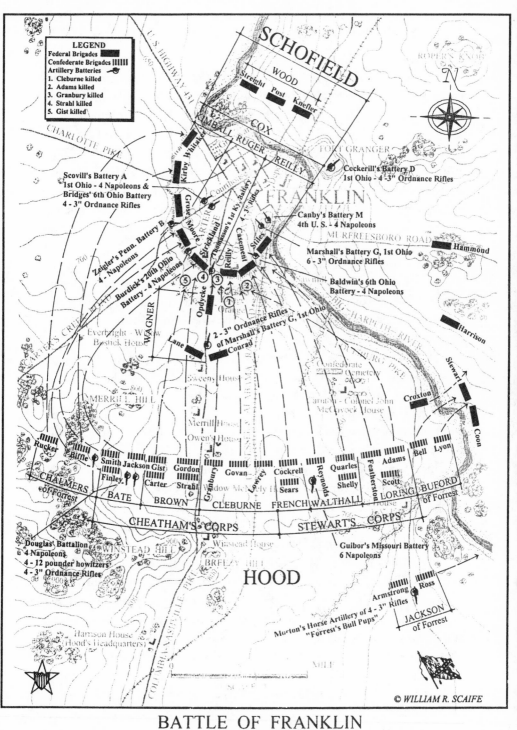

BATTLE OF FRANKLIN
November 30, 1864

sacks, haversacks, overcoats, canteens, blankets, and guns thrown away in the mad rush to escape. "Inspired by ten thousand flying bullets," he staggered toward the works, while all around him "wounded men would topple over, while some would waddle onward, or pitch head-long and bullets would go shrieking through the air." He wrote, "The cotton stalks were dropping off around me as the bullets would zip, zip, zip through them. On coming to our line of works, a man ahead of me had jumped across the outside ditch and was mounting the bank when a ball struck him in the head. He rolled back into the ditch and was dead."

All along the Union line, those blue-clad soldiers of Wagner's rear guard who had so far escaped Hood's advance scrambled breathlessly over the breastworks, and some were trampled to death by their com-rades as they slipped into the four- or five-foot ditch on the outside of the fortification.

When most of the federals were across in safety, "the long line of blue-coats within the trenches rose, and a flash of flame shot out in a sinuous line, and the white smoke rose like the foam on the crest of a breaker. The few straggling blue-coats and the long line of gray went down like over-ripe grain before a blast of wind and hail." So said Bill Keesy, who had managed to haul himself over the breastworks and was watching from a location just behind the lines. But then, he reported, "Another long line came beating up and yet another; and the long line of blue gave way, while the greycoats came pouring over the embank-ment like a flood." When that happened, a Confederate general re-membered, "All hell broke loose in our faces."

What had happened was that the gap in the federal line where the Columbia Turnpike ran through it had been breached by the onrushing Confederates of Brown's and Cleburne's divisions as they swept into the Union works on the heels of Wagner's fleeing brigades. When Wag-ner's men got inside the breastworks, they did not stop but kept on run-ning into and through the town, and, from either confusion or fear, several federal regiments holding the sides of the pike abandoned their positions and began running, too. With this development, the trium-phant Confederates began pouring into the Union lines, and a savage hand-to-hand brawl spread up and down the lines.

Seeing his division fleeing, Wagner—in spite of his inebriation—managed to mount his horse and was "riding backward and facing the disorganized brigades, trying as hard as ever a man did to rally them. With terrible oaths he called them cowards and shook his broken stick at them; but back they went to the town and nothing could stop them," said Levi Scofield, adding, "Oh what a mistake the brave Wagner made."

For a moment it seemed the Confederates had won the victory. Thousands were streaming in over the embankments and the gap at the pike. Tom Thoburn, a lieutenant in the 50th Ohio, just west of the gap, recorded, "Rebs were pouring over the works all the way along and from the direction of the pike the enemy was sweeping along the rear of our lines in a solid mass. I quickly said, 'Boys, we must get out of here; every man for himself.' " Levi Scofield, trying to help the hapless Wagner corral his panicked brigades, had his horse shot from under him and was wounded in the leg. With the whole Union line seemingly about to break, the Confederates had also driven away the members of a crucial federal artillery battery just east of the pike. They had turned the guns around to use them on the bluecoats but could not find any primers. Just then, Scofield recalled, the battery commander, Lieutenant Charles W. Scoville, "cracked his blacksnake whip round the ears of his artillerymen, and drove them back to the guns. At it they went with pick-axes and shovels, splashing all around them with a ferocity of demons." Meantime, Scofield said, two reserve federal regiments composed of soldiers from Tennessee and Kentucky soldiers who had remained loyal to the Union cause "sprang over the low rifle-pits like tigers" and "went pell-mell into the mass of Confederates who had taken [their] line but did not know what to do with it. It was right in those few minutes that the fate of one or the other of the armies was to be decided."

The Confederates who had rushed into the gap behind Wagner's fugitives were eight regiments of Tennesseans commanded by Brigadier General John Gordon, who held down Brown's right on the west of the pike, and nine regiments of Texans belonging to Brigadier General Hiram Granbury, who anchored Cleburne's left on the opposite side of the road.

As the Confederate line surged across the plain, Pat Cleburne met several times with General Brown, and as the line closed on the federal breastworks he sent for his aide, L. H. Mangum, who was off positioning an artillery battery. When Mangum rode up, Cleburne hollered at him to forget the battery. "It is too late. Go on with Granbury," the general roared, then galloped off to the right where Govan's brigade was making its charge. Moments later Cleburne's horse was shot out from under him a few hundred feet from the breastworks, and while he was mounting another, it too was killed by a cannonball. As Govan watched, the Irishman "moved forward on foot, waving his cap; and," he said, "I lost sight of him in the smoke and din of battle." Seconds afterward he was shot down, a bullet just below the heart. Govan said, "[His body] was found within twenty yards of where I last saw him waving his cap and urging his command forward."

By now the thick white smoke of battle had obscured the field, making it virtually impossible to see much more than twenty feet away. About the time Cleburne had gone steaming off into this cauldron of flame-stabbed smoke and dust and racket, Colonel Emerson Opdycke, whom Wagner had disgustedly told to "fight when and where you damn please," was preparing to do exactly that.

As the rest of Wagner's division fled past him up the pike, Opdycke witnessed from his reserve position a hundred yards behind the Carter house the Confederates gaining footholds not only inside the federal fortifications but up to the very yard of the Carter house itself. Without orders, the "stubbed, curley-headed Dutchman," as Wagner had branded him, formed his seven regiments of Illinoians, plus some men of Reilley's reserve, and plunged them headlong into the deadly fracas, which he later characterized as an "indescribable fury."

Coming from the direction of town, General Stanley had nearly been swept off his horse by Wagner's fleeing men. After trying unsuccessfully to stanch the retreat, he gave up and rode to Opdycke's position to get him in the fight, only to find that he was already on his way. A man in one of Opdycke's regiments recalled, "We had our guns stacked and were ready to make coffee when, like a thunderbolt out of a clear sky, on looking up we saw the line breaking in front of us."

Young Union Colonel Arthur MacArthur—who was to live to sire a famous general—was commanding the 12th Wisconsin of Opdycke's brigade. He swung into the saddle shouting, "Up Wisconsin," and sabered his way toward the leading Confederate flag. One of his staff officers recorded that MacArthur's horse was shot down, and he was hit by a bullet in the shoulder. On foot, the colonel fought his way forward until he came to the Confederate major who was holding the flag. The Confederate shot MacArthur in the chest, MacArthur stabbed the major through the stomach, and even as he was falling, the Confederate managed to shoot MacArthur in the knee.

Stanley, who had galloped forward when the uproar began, was horrified to encounter a mass of hundreds of Confederates, "seen dimly through the smoke, jumping over onto our side of the low breastworks." Frightened that his lines were broken, the corps commander rode closer to get a better look. Just then a bullet cut down his horse, while another smashed through the back of his neck, and he was out of the battle. Before going from the field, he learned that the Confederates he saw were not charging but surrendering.

In all its bloody four years, the war had rarely—if ever—seen fighting so ferocious on so large a scale in so confined a space. For nearly an hour, thousands of men within an area no larger than a few acres shot, bayonetted, gouged, and bludgeoned one another to death with rifle butts, axes, picks, guns, knives, and shovels. One Union colonel saw a Confederate run one of his men through with a bayonet, but before he could pull it out, "His brains were scattered on all of us that stood near, by the butt of a musket swung by some big fellow whom I could not recognize in the grim dirt and smoke that enveloped us." Opdycke himself started swinging a gun butt after "firing all the shots in his revolver and then breaking it over the head of a rebel." A captain in Colonel Silas Strickland's brigade testified: "I recollect seeing one man, with blood streaming down his face from a wound in the head, with a pick axe in his hands, rushing into a crowd of the enemy and swinging his pick." At one point, said the captain, "A rebel colonel mounted the breastworks and profanely demanded our surrender." A Union soldier stuck a gun to his stomach and said, "I guess not," and pulled the trigger, which "actually let daylight through the victim."

Slowly, grudgingly, the Confederates gave ground as more and
more federal fugitives were rallied and sent back into the fight, and the
Union line was reinforced from the flanks. As the graycoats were
ejected from the grounds of the Carter house, Union infantrymen threw
up hasty fortifications there and began a galling rifle fire. The Carter
house faced the pike and so was perpendicular to the Confederate advance. Its outbuildings consisted of a wood-frame office and a stone
smokehouse. These and the house itself were filled with Union riflemen
firing from any opening. A low picket fence embraced the south side of
the house from the pike to the smokehouse, and a federal line was
drawn up behind it. The Confederates of Cheatham's corps charged
these structures a dozen times but were repulsed after each charge with
horrible losses.

Now the fighting took on a new dimension. The Confederates of
Brown's and Cleburne's divisions finally retired to the ditch behind the
main federal breastworks and an almost point-blank butchery that lasted
for hours. In many cases, the line was such that the Confederates were
in the trenches on the outside of the works, while the federals were on
the inside, with only a mound of dirt separating them. To make matters
worse for the graycoats, the line was not a smooth curve but was angled at
places to allow Schofield's army a fierce enfilading fire on the attackers.

Here Brigadier General George Washington Gordon, a twenty-
eight-year-old former Tennessee surveyor, huddled helplessly in the
ditch with what was left of his command, exposed to such fire from a
federal salient on his left. Gordon's soldiers, unable to either move forward or retreat because of the deathly fire and with men dropping all
around, began putting their caps on their rifle barrels and waving them
above the works as a signal of surrender. At first the federal shot at
these, but they eventually stopped firing and allowed the Confederates
to give up. Gordon was asked by the only other man who stayed behind
if he was not going to go over. Gordon said No, he would "remain
under cover of the dead in the ditch until night, which was fast approaching." But quickly the storm of fire resumed with even more intensity, and Gordon, remarking, "We shall be killed if we remain
here," handed his subordinate a white handkerchief with which to sur-

render them. As he came inside the federal works, a Union soldier bashed at his head with a gun butt, but another bluecoat intervened, and Gordon was marched off to the rear, a prisoner.

In the brigade to Gordon's immediate left, Brigadier General Otho Strahl was having the fight of his life. Sergeant-major Sumner Cunningham recalled how the men had to plow through a cheval-de-frise of sharpened locust tree branches the federals had thrown up in their front. It was impossible to shoot from the deep ditch outside the breastworks, so the Confederates devised a system by which some men would crawl up on the embankment and fire, while others in the ditch handed them loaded weapons.

By now a murky twilight had settled over the battle area. The sad-faced General Strahl stood on a pile of dead bodies in the ditch, loading and handing up weapons like everybody else. Those riflemen shooting from the embankment had a fearfully short life expectancy. The enfilading fire cut them down with such regularity that the ditch was soon "leveled up" with the dead. Sergeant-major Cunningham, who watched the men around him get hit and slide back into this grizzly mass grave, finally worked up the courage to pose to Strahl a pleading question—on grounds, he said later, that, "I felt there was no rule of warfare whereby all the men should be killed."

"What had we better do?" Cunningham asked.

"Keep firing," was Strahl's stern reply, but those were also his final orders. At that moment the man on Cunningham's right was struck down, and at the same instant Strahl was shot in the neck, and, "throwing his hands over his head, almost to a clasp," the general fell limp on his face. Cunningham at first thought he was dead, but then, calling for Colonel Stafford, his senior regimental commander, Strahl began to crawl away, "his sword dangling against dead soldiers." Several members of his staff tried to carry him off the field, but a simultaneous double death warrant of two bullets killed him on the spot.

The brigade to Strahl's immediate left was commanded by Brigadier General John Carpenter Carter. A tall, lanky, thirty-seven-year-old Memphis lawyer and graduate of the University of Virginia, Carter had distinguished himself in practically all the battles of the Army of Tennes-

see. In his part of the line the men had devised an ingenious, if unpleasant, method of getting at the bluecoats on the opposite side of the
breastworks. They collected the abandoned rifles of the dead and
wounded and pitched them bayonet-first over the pile of dirt that separated the two sides. Carter was directing operations much as Strahl had
been, when a bullet also cut him down with a mortal wound.

By this time Brown's division had been virtually decimated, and,
to make matters worse, Brown himself was shot off his horse by a bullet
that shattered his leg. Thus the division lost not only its commander but
all four of its brigadier generals; Gordon, Strahl, Carter, and Gist were
by now either dead, dying, or captured. Not only that, but by this time
most of the brigade's staff officers and regimental commanders were
killed or wounded, too. With the exception of States Rights Gist's brigade, which consisted of South Carolinians and Georgians, the vast majority of these men were Tennesseans—twenty-five regiments in
all—"the flower of Tennessee youth," one participant noted, "in the
midst of their homes and friends."

Over in Pat Cleburne's division on the eastern side of the pike,
things were no better. Cleburne was lying cold and dead, and not less
than fourteen of his brigade and regimental commanders were killed,
wounded, or missing, including Brigadier General Hiram Granbury,
who had led eight regiments of Texans into the fray. Granbury was a
boyish-looking thirty-three-year-old native Mississippian who before the
war had been a lawyer in Waco, Texas. Like most other general officers
in this army he had fought in almost all the campaigns in the west, from
Fort Donelson to Vicksburg to Chickamauga and the Atlanta battles.
Cleburne's aide, Lieutenant Mangum, who had been told to go with
Granbury by his commanding general just before his death, was within
ten feet of him when Granbury shouted his final words: "Forward men;
never let it be said that Texans lagged in the fight." As he spoke, Mangum recalled, "a ball struck him in the cheek and passed through his
brain. Throwing both hands to his face he sank down on his knees and
remained in that position until his body was taken off the field after the
battle."

Brigadier General Mark Lowrey, whose brigade of Alabamians and

Mississippians was on the right of Govan's, testified that at least half of
his men had been cut down in successive charges against the federal
works near the Carter cotton gin. Like the scene in front of Brown's
division, the ditch along Cleburne's entire front also was heaped with
Confederate dead, and the ground for fifty yards in the rear was strewn
with corpses and mutilated men. In the dim and din of the roaring, flashing twilight, the gray-clads charged a dozen times to force their way
over the Union breastworks. A federal soldier in General James W.
Reilly's brigade recalled, "I saw three Confederates standing within our
lines, as if they had dropped down unseen from the sky. They stood
there for an instant, guns in hand . . . dazed, as in a dream. I raised my
gun, but instinctively I felt as if about to commit murder. When I
looked again, the three were down—apparently dead; whether shot by
their own men or ours, who could tell?''

The battle was now more than an hour old, but Cheatham knew little of
the fate of his corps. Smoke and darkness had obscured the battlefield,
and from his command post about half a mile away on rocky Merrill Hill
all that could be divined even with binoculars or spyglass was a seething,
stinking, flame-stabbed cloud from which the tumult of gunfire and bat-
tle-racket echoed relentlessly across the valley floor. Practically all the
couriers and staff officers that Cheatham had sent riding into this evil
storm had failed to return, and the corps commander was now left to
fret and worry and wonder as the night came down.

Way back in his straw pen near Winstead Hill, John Bell Hood was
even more in the dark. As he looked forward from his blanket on the
ground, the "blue light of battle" might have flickered in his eyes, and
he could certainly see the flashes of guns and hear the ceaseless muttering of gunfire, but the success or failure of the twenty thousand soldiers
he had plunged toward Franklin that afternoon was totally obscured by
the fog of war. The one thing both Cheatham and Hood did know at this
point was that the charge had not been repulsed. What they could not
know was that the Confederates were actually stuck in their exposed
positions outside the Union works like animals in a slaughter pen; to go

forward was to be shot in the face, to retreat meant being shot in the back. One Confederate testified, "Sixteen of our soldiers sprang up and ran out of the ditch . . . a whole volley of musketry killed them to the last man. I raised in a stooping position, thinking I would run also, but they being killed so quickly caused me to abandon the idea of escape."

In the town the terrified civilians huddled in basements and wondered what was to become of them. The schoolgirl Frances McEwen remembered that "the patter of the bullets on the blinds was anything but soothing." Young Harding Figures, who had spent the afternoon on rooftops and trees watching the battle take shape, was now in his house a hundred yards behind the Union lines. "Every minute or two," he said, "a bullet would strike the house above and frequently sizzle in a pile of potato's in the cellar." Harding's mother had hustled her smaller children to a house farther away, and only Harding, his older brother, and a Negro man remained while the tempest raged above them. Something caused Harding to laugh, and the Negro man said, "Marse Hardin, don't you know that we will all be killed if you laugh?" Harding's dog, Fannie, "crouched at [his] feet and moaned piteously."

Finally, when a large cannon shell tore into the house, Harding ran out of the cellar and up the stairs only to find his home filled with wounded Confederate prisoners, guarded by a few bluecoats. "I made up fires, found pillows," he said, "and made them all as comfortable as possible by making pallets on the floor and dressing their wounds as best I could." Soon Figures realized a physician was needed, and he raced down to the Public Square, where he found a doctor. "I shall never forget his reply," Figures wrote afterward: " 'If they are as bad off as you say, I could not do them any good, and it is too dangerous to risk going up there.' I was ashamed of him then, and am ashamed of him now, and will not give his name."

Meantime, Sallie Carter, who that morning had been obliged to purchase a sack of flour for $10 in order to cook two federal officers their breakfast, watched a host of Union wounded coming by her house nearer town. "Some of them asked for water. One was very weak from loss of blood, and I gave him some whisky. Another was badly shot, and I tore one of my lace curtains for a bandage."

Private Bill Keesy had been on a weird kind of odyssey since being routed with Wagner's unfortunate brigades at the beginning of the battle. First he had run with everyone else into the town, looking to get to safety across the Harpeth River. But on reaching the bridge, he found guards posted to prevent anyone from crossing. He wandered around for a while, at one point observing two fugitive Union officers swimming across the river to safety, and finally decided to go back to the front and try to find some part in the battle. Walking down the "fair street, which one hour ago [had been] a thing of beauty," he described it now as "literally covered with wounded, dying and dead men. They are lying with their heads toward the fences and buildings and their feet toward the streets," he said. Their cries and moans, coupled with the brays of mules, the clink of surgeons' tools, orders being shouted by officers galloping past, and the dull racket of the carnage still in progress led him to imagine that he was "just awakening from some horrible nightmare."

Before darkness closed in, General Schofield had been observing the action from his command post a mile behind the lines at Fort Granger on Figures Hill, which, as one participant put it, was "well out of harm's way" on the far side of the Harpeth. A fellow general later charged it was common knowledge in the army that Schofield was personally cautious "to an eminent degree" and reluctant "to expose his carcass to the fire of the rebels." Captain Shellenberger characterized the conduct of his commanding general this way: "When Stanley started for the front, Schofield started for the rear." Whatever the case, from Figures Hill, Schofield had a commanding view of almost the whole battlefield. One of his surgeons, who had joined the general and his staff to observe the scene, remembered following with his eyes the black cabbage-sized shells as they arced out of the artillery at Fort Granger and struck at Hood's advancing lines.

As the Confederate army marched toward him on a two-mile front, Schofield waited impatiently for Wagner's little rear guard to fall back to the Union breastworks, but impatience turned to horror when the vast gray host began to envelop and grind up those helpless men. Furious at Wagner for having left his two brigades exposed to the tender mercies of Cheatham's whole corps, Schofield later suggested that not only Wagner but the individual brigade commanders, Lane and Conrad, as well should "be court martialed and shot. My heart sank withm me," Schofield said, as he witnessed Cheatham's men mauling their way into his lines behind his fleeing federals.

The Union commander's anxiety became indescribable as the Confederates pressed on to the very grounds of the Carter house, threatening to pierce his center irrevocably, but his heavy heart was lifted by the charge of Opdycke's brigade and Reilly's reserve, which he characterized as "magnificent."

Meantime, though Hood's attack on the federal center had stalled, there was still Stewart's entire corps charging down on the right, and, over on the far left, the nearly corps-sized elements under Bate, including his division, plus Johnson's division of Lee's corps, as well as Chalmers's dismounted cavalry—perhaps seven thousand in all—were beginning to make their attack.

Major General Alexander Peter Stewart—"Old Straight" to his soldiers—was a West Point graduate who had resigned from the old army to become a college mathematics and physics teacher before the war. His soft-spoken, studious demeanor could be misleading, for he was also a brazen fighter who had been wounded several times in battle. Just turned forty-three, Stewart led the late Bishop Polk's corps onto the field as the right wing of Hood's advance, with orders from Hood to "drive the enemy into the river at all hazards." However, Stewart— like Bate over on the far left—had a greater distance to travel to reach the Union lines than did Cheatham's corps, which charged straight up the Columbia Pike. From the aspect of the advancing Confederates, the shape of the battlefield was more or less conical, with the width contracting toward the Union fortifications at the bottom of the cone. Thus the march of both Stewart and Bate had to be made en echelon—what the soldiers called "stair-stepping," a kind of crablike sidle left or right, in Stewart's case, left—in order for Hood's whole line to strike the federal position simultaneously. Trouble was, Stewart did not strike the enemy simultaneously with the other corps—or even with his own corps.

Stewart's advance was roughly northwesterly, along the Lewisburg Pike. On the left of his march were the tracks of the Alabama-Nashville railroad, which ran almost due north into the far left of the federal line. His divisions were arranged as follows: French on the left, Walthall in the center, and Loring on the right. Things started out pretty well but quickly began to go wrong. As Stewart's corps neared the Union works, Walthall and Loring encountered obstacles, which left Sam French, alone and unsupported, to slam into the enemy line with his small division of two brigades; his third brigade, General Matthew D. Ector's, was back in the rear, guarding the pontoon train.

French's line of march was toward the Carter family cotton gin, an imposing barnlike structure about a hundred yards across the pike from the Carter home. When they got within shooting distance, the Confederates witnessed an astonishing spectacle. Standing exposed on the parapet of the federal breastworks was a man making a speech. This was Colonel John ("Jack") Casement, commanding the Second Brigade of Cox's division. "Men, do you see those damn rebel sons of bitches coming?" Casement shouted, "Well, I want you to stand here like rocks and whip hell out of them." Having delivered this oratory, Casement then "faced about and fired his revolvers until they were empty, and jumped down with the men."

French hit the Union breastworks at about the same time Cleburne and Brown did, but with even worse success. His regiments had marched right up to the line with bands playing when the first federal volley blasted them full in the face with a terrific sheet of flame. At the same time, artillery in their front and from across the river at Fort Granger let loose a splintering barrage that decimated the leading brigade. These were the Missourians of Brigadier General Francis Marion Cockrell, a dignified-looking thirty-year-old lawyer who had fought in all the bloody early engagements across the Mississippi before joining the Army of Tennessee. Not only did Cockrell's men find no gap in the works to their front as Cleburne and Brown had, but they also drew the bad luck to attack the part of the Union line that was held by infantrymen armed with the revolutionary Spencer repeating rifles. Observers from the Union side reported that the Missourians marched into this deadly cyclone actually "bent over, with their hats pulled down over their eyes and their arms shielding their faces, as though for protection in a hail storm."

Probably a third of Cockrell's brigade were casualties at this point, but the others went on, driving up to the crest of the Union breastworks, where, as instructed, they delivered a massed volley and then pitched down into the mass of bluecoats with bayonets. Some federals were thrown back, but most held firm, and the slaughter continued. Capturing enemy regimental flags was, of course, a matter of great import on both sides. Private J. K. Merrifield, of Opdycke's brigade, noticed a "fine-looking" Confederate officer advancing with the regimental banner of the 1st Missouri Infantry. A Union volley smashed into the gray line, and it went down in a heap—including the fine-looking officer, who was regimental commander Colonel Hugh Garland of St. Louis, Missouri. On some odd impulse, Merrifield scrambled over the works and rushed forward about a hundred feet to where the Confederate colors had gone down. As he picked up the flag, Garland, who had been shot in the knee and was pinned under several dead bodies, asked Merrifield to "pull a dead man off his leg." "He then asked me for a drink of water," Merrifield said. "I leaned over so he could drink out of my canteen without my taking it off my neck." Garland then asked Merrifield to unbuckle his sword belt, which he was in the process of doing when he saw a second line of Confederates coming, and he rushed back to his own lines carrying the flag, the belt, and Garland's sword. Moments later Garland was killed by a second shot.

Some of Cockrell's men managed to push through the federal lines toward the Carter cotton gin, but not Cockrell, who was shot down at the works. Those who got through weren't all men, either. At least one was a drummer boy "of not more than 15 years, with a drum on his back, belonging to one of the Missouri regiments." According to Captain Levi Scofield, this boy "foolishly attempted to force his way through one of the embrasures" surrounding a battery of federal artillery and "thrust a fence rail into the mouth of a cannon thinking, by his brave act, to stop the use of that gun. It was heavily loaded at the time and was fired, tearing the poor boy to shreds, so that nothing was found of him."

Now Walthall's division began to come up on the right of the beleaguered Sam French. They had had a hard time of it even before they reached the Union line, when, about fifty yards from the breastworks, they encountered a "splendid hedge of osage orange" that stopped them in their tracks. "They were bewildered," Scofield testified. "They couldn't get over it; they undertook to pull it away, but the sharp thorns pierced their hands, and they gave that up; then, right in the smoke of our guns they faced to the right and filed through a gap made by a wild charging horse."

They soon must have wished this gap had not appeared and they could have stayed to contend with the thorny hedge, because these men—Tennesseans of General William Quarles's brigade and General Dan Reynolds's Arkansas—were greeted with a gruesome cyclone of artillery fire that literally blew them off their feet.

Captain Aaron Baldwin, commanding the 6th Ohio light artillery, had noticed the Confederates' plight through the Osage orange and decided to take advantage of it. Seeing that the long gray line had broken up and the men were filing in mass through the break in the hedge, Baldwin ordered his men to take off their shoes and socks and stuff the stocks with bullets from the infantry ammunition boxes. These deadly packets of hosiery, called "dummies," he crammed into his guns one after the other until the cannon were loaded with them up to the muzzle.

"At every discharge of my gun there were two distinct sounds," Baldwin reported later, "first the explosion, then the bones." That the captain was able to distinguish between the blast of his cannon and the subsequent crunching of human bones is testimony enough to the fury of the fight on this part of the line. From his vantage point, Levi Scofield recorded that the Confederate dead in front of Baldwin's battery "were piled up like snowdrifts in winter time." John Copley, a private in Quarles's brigade, told of whole platoons of men being killed in this fashion. "In many places they were lying on their faces in almost as good order as if they had lain down on purpose," he said, adding that, "the force and wind of the grape and canister would lift us clear off the ground at every discharge.''

Those of Walthall's men who did reach the ditch found the going there about the same as it was all along the line, and so the work settled down in deadly earnest. The method of choice for both sides was simply to hold up a loaded gun at arm's length above the parapet and fire it down into the opposite side. "Two lines of men fought with but a pile of dirt between them," said D. H. Patterson. "In firing, the muzzles of the guns would pass each other, and nine times out of ten, when a man rose to fire he fell back dead." Another soldier added that "many of the men had both hands shot off." Another resourceful way of dealing with a persistent enemy shooter was to reach out and snatch him by the hair or collar and drag him back over the fortifications, which was done on numerous occasions. As the grim work continued, corpses and the bodies of the wounded piled up in the ditch, the bottom of which "was covered with blood to the depth of the shoe soles."

Walthall was having a rough afternoon; his chain of command was by now almost nonexistent. Quarles's brigade was practically without leadership—Quarles had been shot in the head, his whole staff was killed, and all of his regimental commanders were casualties. Ultimately, the ranking officer in the brigade was a captain. Not only that, but Walthall himself was having impossible trouble coordinating his attack. The thirty-two-year-old former district attorney of Holly Springs, Mississippi, had already had two horses shot from under him that afternoon but still found time for courteous formalities. After the second horse was killed, he looked up to a mounted staff officer and said, "Let me have that horse if you please." According to William M. Pollard, who was there, the staff officer graciously dismounted, and Walthall got on and was about to ride off when the general, suddenly conscious of the fact that Confederate officers owned their own mounts, turned to the officer and asked, "Has this horse been appraised?" When the officer replied that it had not, Walthall called for someone knowledgeable about horses and "then and there they had an appraisal, and the value of the horse was fixed. All this was done in the twinkling of an eye."

Things were going no better on the far right of Stewart's line.

There, Major General William Wing ("Old Blizzards") Loring, who had lost an arm in the war with Mexico, was encountering obstacles just as aggravating as Walthall's. As they approached the federal line, the brigades of the feisty, forty-four-year-old Loring were forced to cross westward over a railroad cut on the Alabama-Nashville tracks, which ran straight into the Union lines. But this crossing point had been enfiladed by the federal artillery, which could shoot straight down the tracks. As Loring's men began to cross, they were mowed down in whole ranks, just as ten pins in a bowling alley. Worse, they also encountered the terrible Osage orange hedge, which curved around very close to the federal works at this point. "A wall of fire rose that swept our ranks like hail," an Alabama soldier from Scott's brigade recorded. "Poor Captain Stewart, the last I saw of him he was trying to cut a path through the hedge with his sword. He fell with four bullets in him."

Some of Loring's two lead brigades—General Thomas M. Scott's and Winfield S. Featherston's—managed to get to the ditch, but most were shot down, and still others fell back from the flaming torrent of lead and iron. Loring himself was hopping mad because in the confusion at the railroad cut and the Osage orange hedge some of Walthall's regiments had become mixed in with his. Finding Walthall directing operations from a small gully, Loring began chastising the Mississippian for allowing this to happen. Walthall listened to all this and then said, "General Loring, this is no time for a personal quarrel. When the battle is over, you will know where to find me."

Disgusted, Loring rode back to his line, only to find that Scott's brigade had fallen back, with Scott himself wounded and out of action. Chaplain James M'Neilly, who was organizing the litter bearers, said Loring tried every ploy to rally the men—"commanding, exhorting, entreating, denouncing . . . to no purpose."

Then, M'Neilly said, as the men streamed past him toward the rear, Loring turned his horse to face the Union lines, to which he must have presented an appalling sight: "He was in full uniform that glittered with golden adornments," M'Neilly remembered. "His sword belt around him and the broad band across his shoulder and breast were gleaming in gold; his spurs were gilt; his sword and scabbard were polished to the utmost brightness; over his hat drooped a great dark plume of ostrich feathers.''

"He sat perfectly motionless," M'Neilly said, "glittering in the light of the sinking sun. As the bullets hissed about him thick as hail, he seemed to court or defy death . . . and he cried out, 'Great God! Do I command cowards?' ''

Loring got Scott's men reformed and sent them tearing back into the smoky maelstrom, only to be repulsed again. Nothing living could stand this for long—but now it was General John Adams's turn to try. His brigade had been in reserve, but now he brought it smashing into the federal position. Early on in the fight the thirty-nine-year-old West Point graduate and career officer in the old army had been severely struck in the shoulder by a bullet, but when urged to leave the field, he replied, "No; I am going to see the men through." Adams then rode his horse from the rear to the front of his men but apparently became separated from most of them in the heavy smoke of battle because he was several hundred yards to the west of his main body—in front of Walthall's division, near the cotton gin—when Private Tillman Stevens, of the 65th Illinois, recorded the following:

> Just then, for the first time, we noticed Gen. Adams conspicuously. He rode along the line urging his men forward. He then rode through the line and placed himself in front and rode straight toward the colors of the Sixty-fifth Illinois. We looked to see him fall every minute, but luck seemed to be with him. We hoped he would not be killed. He was too brave to be killed. He seemed to be in the hands of the Unseen.

Adams dashed up to the federal works, leaped his horse across the ditch, and bolted up the parapet where the colors of the 65th Illinois were planted. As he reached out to grab them, he was shot down, horse and all, by a point-blank volley from the color guard. The Union soldiers were astonished with admiration for this death-defying act, and when the Confederate charge was repulsed, they rushed to the parapet and dragged Adams from beneath his horse.

"He was perfectly conscious and knew his fate," remembered Lieutenant Colonel Edward A. Baker. "He asked for water, as all dying men do in battle. . . . One of my men gave him a canteen of water, while another brought an armload of cotton from an old gin nearby, and made him a pillow. The General gallantly thanked them and, in answer to our expressions of sorrow at his sad fate, he said, 'It is the fate of a soldier to die for his country,' and expired." General John Casement, commanding the Union brigade, took Adams's saddle, watch, ring, and pistol as trophies of war.

Over on the far left of Hood's line, the forces under Bate were also making their fight. Bate had not, for some reason, come into contact with the left of Brown's division so as to make a concerted attack. Some remember that Bate struck the Union line before anybody else; others say he struck it afterwards. Whichever the case, he indeed struck it but with mixed results.

Bate had only two thousand men in his division, but he had the whole six-gun battery of Colonel Steven Presstman to support him, and he was supposed to have an additional two thousand of Forrest's dismounted cavalry fighting with him under General Chalmers on his left. Since he had a longer way to go than the rest of Cheatham's corps, he may have been late launching his assault against the Union right, which was defended by the strong division of General Thomas H. Ruger. The Georgians of Henry R. Jackson's brigade and the Tennesseans of Thomas Benton Smith drove the federals from their breastworks, but—as with Brown and Cleburne—the bluecoats simply retired to the second line of entrenchments around the Carter house, and a merciless exchange of fire began. On his left, Bate was not so lucky—if he called it luck—General Jesse J. Finley's brigade of Floridians, now led by Colonel Robert Bullock, was repulsed as it hit the Union line at the Carter's Creek Turnpike and retired from the battlefield. Worse, Chalmers's two thousand dismounted cavalrymen never appeared, according to Bate, "which exposed [his] flank to a furious fire." At this point, Bate apparently settled down and hoped for the best. Meantime, Jackson's and Smith's brigades were undergoing the same kind of steady slaughter as those in other parts of the line.

Here one of the sad ironies of the campaign occurred. Twenty-year-old Captain Theodoric (Tod) Carter was serving as staff officer to General Smith as Bate's charge led them toward the Union breastworks just a few hundred yards from the Carter house, where young Tod's father, brother, sisters, and their children were huddling in the cellar. As the brigade passed their rallying point, a home called Everbright belonging to a widow named Bostwick, it passed into an open field where they became "terribly exposed." Here, within sight of his own home, which he had not seen for two years, Tod Carter was rallying some troops when he was shot down, a bullet in his brain. Moments before, his fellow captain and close friend, James L. Cooper, had been riding beside him: "I told him not to start the men forward too soon," Cooper remembered, "but his own reckless daring caused his death. His horse, a powerful gray, lay dead a short distance from him. One by one, my true, tried friends were passing away and I felt that unless I received my quietus soon, I would stand alone."

Although Bate sourly denounced the character of Chalmers's cooperation in his after-action report, Chalmers had in fact been on the field—though very ineffectively—and in another bitter twist of irony he alone might have had the best opportunity to stage a convincing breakthrough of the federal position. From Spring Hill, Chalmers had been sent by Hood to march toward Franklin on the westerly Carter's Creek Pike, because Hood simply could not believe that Schofield's whole army had slipped away up the Franklin Pike right under his nose. Chalmers discovered that no federals had used the Carter's Creek Pike and so moved on up to Franklin, where he remained, guarding the Confederate left.

Although Chalmers later testified that he faced an enemy "drawn up in two lines of battle behind a double line of intrenchments," he actually faced no such thing—or at least not anything like the holocaust that the rest of the army was being called upon to deal with. In positioning the Union defenses, Cox had seen that the heavy work of ditching, barricading, constructing abatis, headlogging, and so on extended to the

Carter's Creek Pike. But from the pike westward, as the line curved back to the north near the Harpeth, it was only lightly fortified, and this was the line Chalmers was supposed to assault. It was defended, however, by the three brigades of Stanley's First Division, commanded by General Nathan Kimball, a forty-two-year-old Indiana doctor who had fought his war in both the eastern and western theaters.

Chalmers's dismounted division—actually, it was something less than that in numbers—easily drove in Kimball's skirmishers, but when it had pushed up to the federal line, Chalmers later reported, "My force was too small to justify an attempt to storm them, and I could only hold my position." Had he connected with Bate and told that general what the situation was in his front—or had Bate himself gone over to take a look—it is not inconceivable that between the two of them they could have dislodged Kimball and turned the weaker federal right flank in a rush. In any case, that was not what happened, and, as elsewhere that afternoon, Hood's assault bogged down.

As night enveloped the bloody field, there was one final card left for Hood to play. The army corps of General Stephen Dill Lee had not arrived at the Winstead Hills until 4 P.M., well after the charge by Cheatham's and Stewart's corps had commenced, but Hood immediately ordered Lee to move his leading division, belonging to Major General Edward Johnson, onto the field and into the fight "if necessary" and to personally go find Cheatham and coordinate with him. About dark Lee finally located Cheatham and told him that part about "if necessary," to which the amazed Cheatham responded that not only Johnson but anybody else Lee had on hand was needed "at once."

So Johnson and his men were filed off the pike to the west and groped their way in darkness across the Franklin plain to a position between Bate's and Brown's divisions where finally, around 7 P.M., they were able to form up for an assault. The Mississippi brigades of Generals Jacob Sharp and Arthur Manigault and the Alabamians of General Zachariah Deas were set forward with instructions to forgo the rebel yell and make a silent stealthy rush on the federal works. It almost worked, remembered General Sharp: "We were within thirty paces of the enemy's works when the darkness was lighted up as if by an electric display." Cannon and rifle flashes illuminated the field as the Confederates scrambled up to the ditch and over into the works. This new onslaught caught Ruger's blue-clad division off guard, and for a moment it seemed as though a breakthrough finally was possible. Sharp's Mississippians managed to capture several stands of Union colors, and the fighting along this front was hand to hand and as savage as anything else that had been seen that day—which is saying a lot—but in the end it too stalled as Ruger's men poured volley after volley into the Confederates, including General Manigault, who was shot in the head.

Soon a big autumn moon rose up and loomed low over the Winstead Hills, bathing the Golgothan scene with an eerie silver glow. Men were still firing, but the intensity of the battle began to slacken under its sheer weight. The Union soldiers had had virtually no sleep or rest since the long retreat from Columbia began two days before, and the Confederates were not much better off. Now between the diminishing cracks of rifle shots, a horrible and uncanny sound rose off the smoky floor of the Harpeth valley—the pathetic pleadings and cries from thousands of mangled men.

14

All Those Dead Heroes ★

Late that night as the fighting finally died away and quiet settled over the valley, behind the Union lines there was a kind of collective disbelief at what had happened. The analogy the soldiers most commonly used to describe the Confederate charge was an ocean—a "living sea" or "cresting wave." One soldier colorfully compared the charging and receding Confederate lines with "the brown seaweed carried by the white-capped waves" from the point of view of someone looking down on the ocean from the Cliff Road at Newport. Most were filled with admiration and awe. A colonel on Thomas's staff who had been sent to Franklin as liaison said it was "impossible to exaggerate the fierce energy" of the Confederates, who he said fought "with what seemed the very madness of despair." Another federal said, "I never saw men put in such a terrible position as Cleburne's division was for a few minutes. The wonder is that any of them escaped death or capture."

For many soldiers in Hood's army, however, there were no such words. "To describe truly that which followed is beyond the power of tongue or pen," one officer said. A private later wrote, "I cannot describe it. It beggars description. I will not describe it." A colonel on Stewart's staff wrote his wife, "I am tired of the sickening details. You can see our dreadful loss from published accounts." Another said, "The scene that met my gaze baffles description." And these were men who had seen much during four years of war.

As the battle died away, Frank Cheatham came forward from his headquarters on Merrill's Hill and began to traverse the battlefield, looking into the faces of the dead by lantern light. Seeing firsthand the carnage that had befallen his "boys," as he called them, "great big tears ran down his cheeks and he began to sob like a child." Later Cheatham was to say, "You could have walked all over the field upon dead bodies without stepping upon the ground. I never saw anything like that field, and I never want to again."

Around midnight, Colonel W. D. Gale, A. P. Stewart's adjutant, rode with his general to Hood's headquarters, where the commanding general was holding a council of war. When Hood asked for a report from his three corps commanders, Stewart told him his corps was "all cut to pieces; that there was no organization left except with the artillery." Cheatham's report "was even more despondent and gloomy." Finally, Hood "looked fiercely" at Lee, and asked, "Are you, too, going back on me?" Lee replied that one of his divisions was "badly cut up," but that he still had two left. There and then Hood announced to his astonished lieutenants that he planned to continue the attack in the morning, now that Lee had brought all the artillery onto the field. The plan was to open up on the federals with a daybreak barrage from one hundred guns, after which the whole army would charge the breastworks again at 9 A.M.

Leaving Stewart and the other corps commanders to sort out the details with Hood, Gale rode back across the Franklin plain toward the scene of slaughter, shaking his head at the idea of a renewed assault, which he called "a bitter prospect for our poor fellows." As he neared the breastworks just to the left of the pike, the spot where Strahl and his men had been cut down so savagely that afternoon, he was "struck by the stillness in the enemy's works, and asked the officer nearest [him] if the enemy had not gone." The officer said they had; that he had just a party to investigate, and they had "found no one there."

*　*　*

Schofield had indeed pulled out. In fact, he had all his wagons across the Harpeth even before the attack began, but he was afraid to withdraw the army with Hood's legions about to bear down on him, for fear of being overtaken in the rear. But now that the Confederate assault had failed, Schofield was on the move, in spite of Cox's strenuous pleadings that they should stay and grind up the rest of the Army of Tennessee at sunrise. Schofield gave as his reason for retreating a telegram he had received from Thomas at 3:30 that afternoon, before the Confederate ranks even hit his line, telling him to move back to Nashville. Thomas's wire had been in response to an earlier message from Schofield saying, "I do not think I can hold [Hood]," but that, of course, was before he had done exactly that. In any event, shortly before 9:00 Schofield began quietly to move his brigades across the river, so that by midnight the only Union soldiers left to occupy Franklin were the dead and wounded he left behind.

As it became apparent that Schofield had abandoned the field, the Confederates slowly began to approach the town. Chalmers went in on the left, up the Carter's Creek Pike, while others picked their way through the gap where the breastworks intersected the Columbia Pike, the scene of so much bloodshed—probably half the dead on both sides lay within a few hundred yards on either side of this grim landmark. Meantime, the citizens of Franklin began to emerge from their cellar holes. A few buildings in town, including the stables and the Odd Fellows Hall, had been set afire, and some people were worried that the whole town might be burned. Soon, however, the flames were extinguished, and people began to wander about or open their doors to the arriving Confederate soldiers. Frances McEwen, the schoolgirl, remembered that the first to arrive at her house was General Bate, a family friend, "all bespattered with mud and blackened with powder, but a grand and glorious soldier under it all."

Over at the Carter house, the "seventeen souls" came out of their hole to find the house filled with Confederate soldiers and the parlor carpet "wet with blood." Alice McPhail Nichol remembered "seeing a lot of soldiers in Yankee uniform coming down the stairs with a Confederate officer. He had captured them in an upstairs room. There were thirty of them, and they had never fired a gun." Not long afterward, as she was standing on the porch, General Thomas Benton Smith rode up and, saluting, asked, "Missie, is this where Squire Carter lives?" When she said it was, Smith told her, "Tell him Captain Carter is severely wounded and I will show him where to find him."

At this dire news, a search party of family members, including old Fountain Branch Carter, trudged out across the grisly fields, their lamplights reflecting on the faces of the dead and dying. Presently, the older Carter found his son, barely alive and delirious, and with the help of some soldiers brought him to the house. "I can see his limp legs and arms now, with his captain's uniform and cavalry boots and spurs. He had a black hat with a plume in it," wrote Alice Nichol. A surgeon cut the bullet out from over his eye, but Tod Carter died, at home, in his bed.

Houses and mansions not only in Franklin but all over the valley of the Harpeth began to fill up with a seemingly endless stream of wounded. At Carnton, the elegant brick estate of Colonel Randall McGavock, which lay in the rear of Stewart's line, in "every room, every spare space, niche, and corner under the stairs, in the hall, everywhere" lay the bleeding and dying survivors of the charge. Throughout the night, Mrs. McGavock supervised her home as a hospital as the surgeons' saws and probes did their grim work. When the doctors ran out of bandages, she gave them linen, "then her towels and napkins, then her sheets and tablecloths, then her husband's shirts and her own undergarments." But they still came on, until not only the house but the porches and all the outbuildings and even the massive lawns were completely occupied by the wounded and the dead.

Uncle Wiley Howard, General States Rights Gist's loyal servant, received news from one of the wounded that Gist was shot somewhere on the battlefield, and determined to go and find him. "It tuck me er long time ter make my way. De ground wuz piled wid wounded men an wid dead men. Sometimes I stopped en done what I could. I wuz halted four time. 'Who goes dar?' dey wud say. I sez, 'I'm Wiley, en I want Marse States.' After a while I got ter de hospital. At de hospital I find Dr. Wright, er friend of Marse States. He sez, 'What does yer want, Wiley?' I sez, 'I come ter see about de General.' Dr. Wright says, 'I done all I could, Wiley, but he died at half past eight. He suffered very much et fust, but towards de end, de pain wuz but little. Once or twice he sez, "Take me ter my wife." ' "

A chill mist settled over the valley during the night, and by sunrise a drenching dew had blanketed the field almost as if it had rained. Rising over the trees east of the Harpeth, the sunlight of this first day of December revealed a tableau as chilling as any devised in Dante's worst nightmare—or, for that matter, the Book of Revelations. More than two thousand dead men lay in inconceivably grotesque positions; at places in the ditch the bodies were stacked seven deep. Some dead men were actually standing, propped up by other fallen comrades. Some were frozen in the act of loading or firing their weapons. Others, blue and gray, were fixed in the act of bayonetting each other. Regimental and company commanders lay with hat in one hand and sword in the other. In front of the federal batteries there were not so much men but parts of men: limbs, trunks, and heads. Not a few of the dead were found with their thumbs gnawed to a pulp, as they chewed them in agony before they died. So many bullets had been fired from the federal works that the torn-up ground, where it was not covered by bodies or the carcasses of horses, for acres all along the line "resembled fields recently raked or harrowed." West of the pike at the locust grove through which Bate's and Johnson's men had passed, the trees that had not been shot down outright were stripped of all their leaves and limbs and bark.

It almost defied reason that anything human could have lived through this, but many did. Six or seven thousand men lay wounded, moaning and begging for water while squads of infirmary corps troops wandered about, hauling them away on litters. As the residents of Franklin began to come onto the field to look for relatives or friends or just to lend assistance, young Harding Figures came upon an old Confederate who was sitting up. His jaw had been torn off by a grape shot, and his tongue and lip were hanging down on his breast. "I knelt down and asked him if I could do anything for him," Figures said. "He had a little piece of pencil and an envelope, and I shall never forget the impression made by what he wrote: 'No; John B. Hood will be in New York before three weeks.' "

Soon the Franklin citizens were joined by people from other towns in the surrounding countryside who had heard the battle in progress and now came to pick sadly across the battlefield. So many of Hood's army—more than half—were from Tennessee that the entire state was "plunged into mourning." More than one Confederate soldier remembered with grim irony the sign they had passed when they crossed the state line from Alabama: TENNESSEE—A FREE HOME OR A GRAVE."

By midmorning details were busy collecting the bodies of enlisted men—what a Confederate soldier called "all those dead heros"—and burying them in mass graves for more than a mile and a half on both sides of the Columbia Pike. They dug the trenches two and a half feet deep and laid the Confederate men out two to a grave, covering their faces with pieces of oilcloth or blankets. At the head of everyone who could be identified, they put small wooden name markers. The federal dead received somewhat rougher care. They were simply piled pell-mell into the ditch by the breastworks—most after being stripped of their clothes—and a foot or two of dirt shoveled on top of them.

The dead Confederate generals and other officers were treated with a reverence believed due their rank. Most were removed to Carnton, the McGavock mansion, and laid out side by side on the wide back gallery. At dawn, a Mississippi officer who had been positioning artillery for Hood's now canceled barrage came across the body of Pat Cleburne, about fifty yards from the breastworks, "lying flat upon his back, as if asleep, his military cap partly over his eyes. He had on a new gray uniform . . . unbuttoned and open. He had on a white linen shirt, which was stained with blood on the front part of the left side. This was the only sign of a wound I saw on him. He was in his sock feet, his boots having been stolen. His watch, sword belt and other valuables all gone, his body having been robbed during the night."

The officer, John McQuaide, saw an ambulance up at the breastworks that was in the charge of Reverend Thomas Markham, the Presbyterian chaplain of Featherstone's brigade. Markham was at that time loading the body of General John Adams into the ambulance; when told that Cleburne had been found, he went and got him, too. Markham

What the Confederates Saw

*The Columbia Turnpike, looking north from the base of the Winstead Hills
(courtesy of the U.S. Army Military History Institute)*

What the Federals Saw

*The view from Carter's cotton gin, looking south toward the Winstead Hills
(courtesy of the U.S. Army Military History Institute)*

From the Columbia Turnpike, a view of Carter's cotton gin house, where some of the most severe fighting took place (courtesy of the U.S. Army Military History Institute)

The Columbia Turnpike, looking north toward the Carter House, where General Opdycke launched his last-ditch attack (photograph taken ca. 1900; printed courtesy of the U.S. Army Military History Institute)

The McGavock House (Carnton), where the bodies of the dead Confederate generals were placed (courtesy of the Carter House, Franklin, Tennessee)

Confederate Cavalry Commander General Nathan Bedford Forrest

General James Chalmers, who bore the brunt of the Confederate cavalry fighting at Franklin

The Tennessee state capitol at Nashville, the main objective of the Nashville campaign

The Federal gun emplacements on the capitol's veranda

The outer line at Nashville, December 16, 1864, beyond which Thomas has just advanced his army

Rear-guard Union troops watching the action during the battle, December 16, 1864

The Battle of Nashville, observed from the grounds of the Military Institute

A Nashville hillside where local citizens turned out to watch the final battle

*General John Bell Hood, as he appeared during the Nashville campaign
(courtesy of the Chicago Historical Society)*

drove the bodies of Cleburne and Adams over to Carnton, where they were laid out on the McGavock veranda beside the body of Otho Strahl, who had been brought there earlier. Shortly afterward, soldiers discovered the body of Hiram Granbury, and it was placed alongside the rest of the generals on the McGavock porch, "perfectly protected and cared for until their friends removed them."

Cleburne's devoted aide, Lieutenant Mangum, arranged for coffins, and as he stood sadly on the porch during the death watch, he removed a "lady's finely embroidered handkerchief" that someone had placed over Cleburne's face, substituting another, saying, "This handkerchief was sent to him from Mobile, and I think he was engaged to the young lady."

Later that morning, a tearful Uncle Wiley Howard removed States Rights Gist's remains from the field hospital. "Dr. Wright holped me ter git er cedar box. We couldn't git a coffin. We got er ambulance." Howard took Gist's body to the William White home, a brick mansion on the far right of the battle area, where he was met at the door by Mrs. White. "I told her General Gist had been killed, en axed her if we could bury him in her graveyard. She made us drive de ambulance up de walk ter her front door. She had him tuck out en laid on de sofa in her parlor. She sont fer er preacher ter hab de burial service. We buried him in her yard, under er big cedar tree."

General John Carter, mortally wounded with a bullet in the abdomen, was taken to the Harrison home, on the far side of the Winstead Hills. He lingered for a few days, begging for chloroform and ministered to occasionally by Chaplain Quintard, who said that Carter "could not be convinced he was going to die." Finally, Quintard posed the question that if he *should* die, what was his message to his wife? "Tell her that I have always loved her devotedly and regret leaving her more than I can express," was Carter's reply. He was buried in Columbia not long afterward.

The body of General Adams was taken down to Pulaski, where Schofield and his army had started out a long week before, and buried by his family. The other three generals, Strahl, Granbury, and Cleburne, were carried to Columbia and buried in St. John's churchyard at Ashwood, in the spot that Cleburne had remarked was so beautiful a few days earlier.

Meantime, every available house, church, school, and public building in Franklin was being turned into a hospital—forty-four in all, three for wounded federals, the rest for Confederates, each marked with a red flag—but these were not enough, and many of the wounded had to stay in cloth tents. The Confederate surgeons corps had not prepared to deal with a disaster of this magnitude, and there were critical shortages of everything from medicines to food and shelter. Dr. Deering Roberts, chief surgeon of the 20th Tennessee, described one of the "hospitals" he created. "I found an old carriage-and-wagon shop, two stories high. It had a good roof, plenty of windows above and below . . . and a good well. This I immediately placarded as 'Bate's Division hospital,' and put part of the detail to work cleaning out the work-benches, old lumber and other debris." Farther up the same street Roberts also commandeered an unoccupied brick store and the chancery court building on the square and sent his wagons to scour the countryside for fresh straw. By midday he had the floors scrubbed and covered "with clean wheat straw, ten or twelve inches thick," and the wounded were ready to be brought in.

There were four principal types of dangerous wounds in that era. Head wounds, if not superficial, were almost always fatal. So were wounds to the abdomen because, as Dr. Roberts explained, "the intestines were perforated." Wounds to the upper chest, however—unless to the heart—were frequently curable because "the swiftly moving conical ball often produced a clean-cut wound." The last, and perhaps most common potentially fatal, wound was "the shattering, splintering and splitting of a long bone." Experience during the war had taught surgeons that amputation of those injuries was the preferred way to save the patient because otherwise gangrene typically set in, and the victim died in a matter of days. Accordingly, one Franklin civilian reported, "When I went past one of their hospitals there were several wagon loads of limbs that had been amputated." It is an interesting fact that in the year following the war the single largest item in the Mississippi state budget was for artificial limbs.

Antibiotics were unknown, and infections in an unclean wound regularly spread. Pain killers, if they could be had, were highly addictive derivatives of opium, and for years after the war tens of thousands of veterans were hopelessly hooked on these drugs. Chloroform was the anesthetic commonly used to sedate men before their limbs were sawed off or probes tore through their flesh searching for a bullet, but little of it was available to the Confederates at this stage of the war. Most of the time, a sort of unwritten rule stated that the wounded man either got better or he didn't.

The women of Franklin quickly rallied to the crisis. They cut up their bedding, linen, and even their clothing for bandages and worked tirelessly in the hospitals night and day. They baked cakes, pies, cornbread, and contributed what little meat, tea and coffee, and other things they could spare. One woman and her mother took charge of a hospital for Union wounded in the Presbyterian Church and were dismayed to find that "they drew scanty rations from the rebels—flour the color of ashes, and a little poor beef not suitable for well men, much less for wounded. We furnished them every little luxury we could prepare, for several days." Even young Harding Figures got in on the act. "Many a day," he reported, "I went out through the country in an old dump cart hunting for food. We would take a large wash kettle, holding about twenty gallons, and make it full of soup, with plenty of red pepper. For this soup I brought in from the country Irish potato's, cabbage, dried beans, and turnip, and in making it we used any kind of meat obtainable. The soldiers thought this was a great diet; in fact, the best they had had for more than a year."

Sometime that morning, John Bell Hood and his staff rode into Franklin. Pausing at the nauseating sight around the breastworks, an artilleryman recalled that the commanding general sat on his horse and "wept like a child." Hood took up headquarters in the yard of a Mrs. Sykes of Franklin. Alice McPhail Nichol remembered seeing the sling-armed, one-legged officer sitting there in a chair, surrounded by his staff. "He looked so sad," she said, "and grandpa told me it was Gen. Hood."

Frances McEwen was there, too, but later said she didn't look on Hood as a hero, "because nothing had been accomplished that could benefit us."

This was another of the understatements commonly associated with Hood's campaign. Hood had not only accomplished "nothing," he had in fact wrecked his army.

Like the Spring Hill affair, from the moment the fighting died down at Franklin, the finger pointing began and never let up. Many thought Hood should not have attacked at all, that he should have moved off to the right across the Harpeth and flanked Schofield out of his breastworks. Others believed he should have waited for Stephen Lee's whole corps to come up—especially since it had the army's artillery— and launched a vast bombardment before the first attack was made. Still others believed he failed to reconnoiter properly, and that his main strike should have been against the federal right instead of the stronger left and center. Some suggested that he was in tantrum over his failure to bag Schofield at Spring Hill and ordered the charge only out of spite. Others claimed he attacked vindictively because he wanted to teach his army to assault breastworks.

Each position has its supporters and detractors, and the arguments will continue so long as the history of the Civil War is studied. In Hood's defense, however, are these observations: First, any flanking movement across the Harpeth was certain to be observed by Schofield, who had been tricked by Hood once at Columbia and was not about to be tricked again. Furthermore, the Franklin plain was open to view, and any Confederate advance could be plainly seen from the Union positions. By the time Hood might have initiated such a turning movement, Schofield would probably have been on the move. He already had his supply wagons and one of his five divisions across the river by the time of Hood's attack and would have had a head start of at least two miles along a good macadamized road, while Hood would first have had to ford a high river, then negotiate fields, woods, and back roads in the chase.

Forrest's assertion that with the help of an infantry division he could have "flanked Schofield out of his position" may or may not have been true. After all, Wilson's cavalry outnumbered Forrest's at that point, and Schofield had already moved a division of bluecoats to the other side of the Harpeth in anticipation of just that sort of maneuver. Furthermore, it was getting late in an already short day, and would be even later before Hood could swing any sizable part of his army around to attack Schofield in flank. And the one thing he did *not* want to do was spook Schofield out of Franklin only to have him flee up the pike and join with Thomas's other forces behind the formidable Nashville defenses. This argument was clear in Hood's mind when he told Cheatham he would rather fight the enemy where they had been fortifying for eight hours, instead of Nashville, where they had been fortifying for years.

That Hood's attack might have benefited from the addition of Stephen Lee's corps is debatable. Had Hood postponed his movement until 4 P.M., when the head of Lee's column finally arrived at the Winstead Hills, he would have had only about forty-five minutes left till sundown to get that ten-thousand-man element into formation and moving toward the federal breastworks. Considering that it took nearly two hours to get Cheatham's and Stewart's corps onto the field and ready for action, it would have been well after sundown before Lee could have been effectively positioned. Even if Lee could have joined the charge, the question arises of whether he would have just added to the Confederate casualty lists. There is a possibility that Hood could have deliberately launched a night attack with all three of his corps up, but night attacks were extremely rare and often failed because command coordination was practically impossible; furthermore, Schofield had already given orders for his army to withdraw across the Harpeth to Nashville at 6 P.M.

Moreover, the notion that all the Confederate artillery—somewhere far back in Lee's column—could somehow have been hauled out on the field and positioned before nightfall to deliver a sizable barrage is unsound. Even if it were possible, Robert E. Lee's experience with his huge two-hundred-gun artillery bombardment of the Union center at Gettysburg certainly demonstrated that it was no guarantee that Pickett's charge would have succeeded. Also, Schofield's men were safely behind breastworks five to ten feet high and five feet wide, against which artillery would have little effect. From Hood's point of view, Schofield was there, at Franklin, where he could actually see him, and he wanted to get at him before nightfall gave him a chance to slip away, which was exactly what Schofield planned to do.

Perhaps Hood could have let Cheatham's and Stewart's corps stage a strong and lengthy demonstration in hopes of keeping Schofield pinned to his works, while Lee's corps tried to ford the river and march around the federal right. Certainly, though, Schofield would have detected this and probably been off like a shot—burning his bridges behind him— before Lee could get on his flank.

Another possibility is that Hood could have directed his main assault against the federal right, which was defended by a full Union division but apparently not behind such formidable breastworks as what Cheatham and Stewart encountered. What Hood knew about that part of the line is unclear, but if a division had been pulled away from Cheatham or Stewart to assault that part of the line along with Chalmers's dismounted cavalry, it might have met with some success. Again, however, Schofield surely would have noticed any such movement and taken measures to counter it.

The battle of Franklin is filled with what-ifs, might-have-dones, could-have-dones, should-have-dones—each with its advocates. But from Hood's perspective, right or wrong—and he was the general on the ground—the elusive Schofield was there in plain sight, and there Hood intended to fight him—a desperate plan for desperate times. It should also be considered that in some Civil War battles the mighty impetus of a massed charge—if the attackers could get close enough to a defensive position—often tended to dislodge the defenders. This seems to have been on Hood's mind, and if it had worked, he would have become a hero. Instead, many in his army agreed with Texas Captain Sam Foster that this wasn't war: "It can't be called anything else but cold blooded murder."

In any event, on this first day of the last month of 1864, John Bell Hood sat in his chair in the sunlit yard of Mrs. Sykes trying to digest the ration of bad news that was served to him in a steady diet by his commanders and staff. Nobody knew any exact figures, but it was clear that he had lost nearly one-third of his army. In Cleburne's and Brown's divisions, his largest and best, casualties were nearly 50 percent. In all, about seven thousand men were killed, wounded, or missing. How many were actually dead no one would know. The official records say that 1,750 were buried on the battlefield, while hundreds of others were carried away by friends and family, some dead, some dying. Nevertheless, Hood sought to put the best possible face on it, there in Mrs. Sykes's yard, issuing a General Field Order to be read to each regiment:

GENERAL FIELD ORDERS, HDQRS. ARMY OF TENNESSEE

No. 38
Near Franklin, December 1, 1864

The commanding general congratulates the army upon the success achieved yesterday over our enemy by their heroic and determined courage. The enemy have been sent in disorder and confusion to Nashville, and while we lament the fall of many gallant officers and brave men, we have shown to our countrymen that we can carry any position occupied by the enemy.

By command of General Hood:
A.P. MASON, Assistant Adjutant-General.

Hood fired off other orders that morning amid the Franklin carnage. First, he told his corps commanders to have the field scoured for loose weapons—of which there were thousands—which were to be stacked for collection by the quartermaster. Next, he ordered them to prepare at once a list of all the dead and wounded field-grade officers. Finally, he issued his marching orders. Stewart, whose cut-up corps had occupied the Confederate right, was to cross the Harpeth skirting Franklin, march toward Nashville, and bivouac north of the town. Lee and Cheatham were to march their divisions straight up the Columbia-Franklin Pike, right past the scene of the crime, and cross the river at the bridges on the other side of town.

This last order had such a dampening effect on the morale of the Army of Tennessee that Captain Robert Banks, an adjutant in Walthall's division, was inspired to say, "Nothing better calculated to affright and demoralize an army could have been devised than the exhibition of the dead, as they appeared to those who viewed them there in marching by the gin-house that morning." Wondering why the men of Cheatham and Lee were not detoured around the "sickening, blood-curdling, fear-kindling sight," Banks described the scene as a living hell.

It was in this putrid and ghastly atmosphere that Hood had to make yet another decision—what to do next? There were not many options. He could admit he was beaten and turn around and march out of Tennessee. But he feared if he did, his army would disintegrate; and it probably would have. He could bypass Nashville and move up through Kentucky toward the Ohio, but, by leaving Thomas and the ever strengthening federal army behind him, he knew he would find few recruits in either Kentucky or Tennessee, and those were what he now needed most. He had to have a decisive victory, and soon, if more men were to be rallied to the cause. So Hood, ever the fighter, scorner of defeat, determined to fight it out once more. He would bring the army to Nashville, he told his generals, and whip George Thomas to a pulp.

15

Nashville, Tennessee ★

The men John Bell Hood left buried on the plain before Franklin signified another kind of grim statistic. Never in any single-day battle during the entire war had that many Confederate soldiers been slain. The number of Hood's dead was greater than the number of Confederates killed at First and Second Bull Run or at Fredericksburg, Antietam, Chancellorsville, Shiloh, Vicksburg, Chattanooga, Spottsylvania, or Cold Harbor. Only during the prolonged two-day slaughter at Chickamauga, the bloody Seven Days battles around Richmond in 1862, Hood's various sorties at Atlanta, the entire Wilderness Campaign, and the three-day holocaust at Gettysburg did the number of Confederate killed exceed that of the Army of Tennessee that short afternoon at Franklin. In fact, Hood's losses were double those of George Pickett's famed charge at the height of the Gettysburg campaign. To add to the misery quotient, on no single-day battlefield of the war had so many generals been killed.

Just how much of this Hood absorbed as he rode the long dusty road up to Nashville is hard to assess from his initial report to Confederate Secretary of War James A. Seddon:

HEADQUARTERS ARMY OF TENNESSEE

six miles from Nashville, on the Franklin Pike
December 3, 1864

Hon. J.A. Seddon:

About 4 P.M. November 30 we attacked the enemy at Franklin and drove them from their center lines of temporary works into their inner lines, which they evacuated during the night, leaving their dead and wounded in our possession, and retired to Nashville, closely pursued by our cavalry. We captured several stand of colors and about 1,000 prisoners. Our troops fought with great gallantry. We have to lament the loss of many gallant officers and brave men. Major-General Cleburne, Brig. Gens. John Adams, Gist, Strahl and Granbury were killed. Maj. Gen. John C. Brown, Brigadier-Generals Carter, Manigault, Quarles, Cockrell and Scott were wounded. Brigadier-General Gordon was captured.

J.B. Hood
general

In a campaign filled with understatement, this dispatch augurs with the best, prompting one sour historian to brand Hood as a "pathological liar." While that would seem excessive, there is no doubt he was seeking to put the best possible face on what had happened to his army at Franklin. His lack of mention of overall casualty figures could have been that, because there were so many, he actually did not yet know them. Seddon and the Confederate officials in Richmond were alarmed and appalled at what Hood did report, however, and apparently wired him back for more information because two days later, on December 5, he sent another dispatch to the secretary of war, which stated: "Our loss of officers in the battle of Franklin, on the 30th, was excessively large in proportion to the loss of men." Furthermore, he issued a directive to all his commanders to immediately report to him how many stands of colors had been lost during the battle and which regiments they were from; armed with that information, he wired Richmond: "The enemy claim that we lost thirty colors in the fight at Franklin. We lost thirteen, capturing nearly the same number. The men who bore ours were killed on and within the enemy's interior line of works." Again, he was trying to put a good face on bad news. In fact, the infantry had captured only a handful of federal colors, but Forrest's cavalry, in the course of its running battles, acquired a larger number of Union cavalry colors, and Hood disingenuously decided to include those in his report to his superiors.

Hood had other business to attend to as well, foremost being to deal with whoever was responsible for foiling his cherished plans to capture Schofield back at Spring Hill. Hood finally settled on Cheatham as the culprit—apparently for not following his midnight order to have someone close up the Franklin Pike. On December 7 Hood wired Seddon to "withdraw" his previous recommendation for Cheatham's promotion to corps commander, "for reasons which I will write more fully." He followed this up next day with a request that Richmond send "a good major-general at once" to command Cheatham's corps. But in an extraordinary turnaround that same day, he reversed himself and wired Seddon again: "Major-General Cheatham made a failure on the 30th of November which will be a lesson to him. I think it best he should remain in his position for the present. I withdraw my telegrams of yesterday and today on this subject."

What had caused this strange change of mind? The answer turned out to be as intriguing as the question, and many years later the exiled Tennessee Governor Isham Harris, who had been traveling with Hood's army, provided the explanation. On the night of the misfortune at Spring Hill, Harris and Hood were sharing a room in the Absalom Thompson mansion when they were awakened by the private soldier who told Hood of seeing vast columns of Union troops and trains marching northward along the Franklin Pike. Without getting out of bed, Hood, according to Harris, told his adjutant, Major Pen Mason, to send an order to Cheatham "to move down the road immediately and attack the enemy." Having done that, Hood and Harris both went back to sleep, secure in the notion that the pike would be sealed off by Cheatham and next morning they would only have to accept the surrender of Schofield and his flanked and cut-off army.

Of course, it did not turn out like that; Cheatham did not manage to seal off the Pike and Schofield escaped the trap, paving the way for the tragedy at Franklin, and Hood was out for blood. But Harris provided an answer for Cheatham's odd failure. According to the governor, the day after the Spring Hill disaster, as the Army of Tennessee was marching toward Franklin, Hood, Major Pen Mason, and Harris were riding together, and Hood was fulminating over Cheatham's disobedience of orders. When Hood rode off to attend to something, Mason, according to Harris, confessed to him, "General Cheatham was not to blame about the matter last night. I did not send him the order." Mason, it seems, exhausted by twenty-four hours without rest, had fallen asleep before finishing the order for Cheatham to attack the pike, and thus Cheatham never got it.

Harris claimed that he told Mason that in fairness to Cheatham, he must report this matter to Hood, and that Mason did in fact tell the commanding general, who, according to Harris, admitted to him later that he had "done an injustice" to Cheatham and "did not censure or charge him" with failure to make the attack. Later, according to both Harris and Cheatham, Hood even wrote Cheatham a note saying he "held him blameless."

But all this, of course, only deepened the riddle of the Spring Hill failure when Cheatham later claimed that he did receive Mason's never-sent order and did in fact move a division to the pike, only to find it empty. Whatever the truth, Hood's army, only about twenty-five thousand strong, with Cheatham still in command of his corps, now stood before Nashville, where George Thomas and some seventy-seven thousand federal troops awaited him.

If any place was home to the Army of Tennessee, it was Nashville, which every soldier could now plainly see from the Confederate positions along the hills south of the city. The enormous white granite portals of the new state capitol building, the Stars and Stripes waving over it, gleamed in the winter sun. The federals had captured Nashville three years earlier, turning it into not only the largest supply center for the Union army but also perhaps the most heavily fortified city on the American continent.

Before the war, Nashville had flourished as the Tennessee heartland's premier city, occupied by about thirty-five thousand souls. Tucked into a bend in the Cumberland River, Nashvilleans considered their home a cosmopolitan "Athens of the South"—and, for its day, perhaps it was. There were several colleges, a medical school, five daily newspapers, a seven-hundred-foot-long suspension bridge, theaters, and an opera. Gas lights lit the streets at night, the city sidewalks were paved with brick, and telegraph lines and steamboat services linked it with the other important cities of the South. By the outbreak of the war, Nashville boasted foundries, machine shops, mills, and dry goods stores. Down by the river, the docks teemed with steamboats loaded with cotton, vegetables, grains, and tobacco from the fertile farms in outlying areas. But now, after four years of conflict, Nashville seethed.

Most of the original citizens considered themselves subjugated to a "reign of terror" by the Union occupation. Newspapers thought to print disloyal items were shut down and their editors thrown into jail, as were many prominent ministers. Residents were required to take a loyalty oath and post cash bonds to insure their allegiance to the federal government. Many were either arrested or expelled from the city and their property confiscated. Mail was censored, elections were rigged, passes were required to move around the city, and any talk thought favorable to the Confederacy brought swift punishment. All of this was presided over by a corrupt military secret police commanded by one William Truesdail.

Moveover, by this stage of the war, Nashville was bulging with over one hundred thousand people—soldiers, refugees from the fighting in the countryside, homeless Negroes, peddlers, speculators, carpetbaggers, and an enormous flock of prostitutes. The prostitutes became such a problem that somebody decided to round them up and ship them north. Several hundred females—including a few respectable Nashville ladies swept up by mistake—were herded aboard a steamer, which tried unsuccessfully to offload this offensive cargo in several cities, including Louisville and Cincinnati, but in the end was forced to return it to Nashville, where it was again set loose on the community. Other vices infested the city, too; drinking became such a problem that the military instituted prohibition, but so much bootleg whisky was available, the policy had no effect. Drunken soldiers preyed upon the Nashville citizenry, stealing, insulting, and performing all kinds of depredations and illegal acts. One newspaper complained that the city "swarms with a host of burglars, brass-knuck and slingshot ruffians, pickpockets and highwaymen who have flocked hither from all parts of the country."

By the same token, federal authorities—namely, the ubiquitous Truesdail and his secret police—viewed all Nashville residents as a menace and described the city as "swarming with traitors, smugglers and spies . . . whose sole aim is to plot secret treason and furnish information to the rebel leaders." In this they were at least partly correct. Nashville contained a web of Confederate spies and saboteurs, including a Doctor Hudson and his wife, who smuggled saws and chisels in cakes to the Confederate prisoners in Nashville camps. In fact, some of Nashville's most prominent Confederate spies were women, who, according to a staff member of Stewart's corps, "would go into Nashville, get what information was needed, and place it in a designated tree, stump or log to be conveyed to [them by their] secret scouts." This officer, Bromfield Ridley, believed that two women, Kate Patterson and Robbie Woodruff, were responsible for delivery to the Confederate command of a complete diagram of the federal fortifications around Nashville, apparently stolen from the table of the Union general Grenville Dodge.

Of course, not all citizens of Nashville were Confederate sympathizers. At the beginning of the war there were a considerable number of loyal Unionists living in the city, but most of those were soon hounded out of town and their property confiscated, or forced to swear allegiance to the Confederacy by a series of persecutions by Confederate authorities. Confederate laws allowed the setting of high cash bonds against suspected Unionists and in other cases citizens who expressed Union sympathy were formally banished northward, out of the Confederate states. However, all that changed in February 1862, when the federal army marched into town. With Nashville occupied by Union troops, President Lincoln appointed Andrew Johnson as governor of Tennessee to replace the banished Confederate governor Isham Harris. Johnson was a former tailor who had managed to become a U.S. senator and spoke vehemently against secession. He soon became immensely unpopular with the people of the state and in particular with the people of Nashville. Johnson evicted the state officials and legislators who had supported secession—and that was virtually all of them—and installed a Union-loyal government, which began enacting such laws as to suppress Confederate sympathy or assistance.

These measures were even more stringent than the Confederate attempts to purge Unionist support; newspaper editors were arrested and replaced by imported Northerners who wrote what they were told. Nashville's jails began to bulge with "old gray haired men" who made the mistake of criticizing the federal government or uttering pro-Confederate statements. A loyalty oath to the Union was required, with the penalty for failing to take it ranging from jail to banishment to confiscation of property, which converted most of the city's population into jailbirds, paupers, or, most commonly, liars. Confiscation of property probably had the most profound effect and led to the most egregious abuses. One edict demanded that if secessionists harassed a Unionist, authorities would arrest five suspected Confederate sympathizers and confiscate their property. The confiscated property—mostly houses and land—was often sold off to Northern carpetbaggers or Union sympathizers in the area for a fraction of its value. The newly formed seven-hundred-member Nashville branch of the Union League, a social arm of the Republican party, adopted a declaration advocating that foreigners immigrating into northern ports be encouraged to come to Tennessee and take up residence, presumably on the lands of displaced secessionists.

So the people of the city lived in turbulent and uneasy times, the grand balls of earlier days replaced by smaller parties in private homes with much whispering and vindictive talk. The sons of most Nashville families were away fighting with the Confederate army, while the hated Union sympathizers were holding all the political offices and enjoying carte blanche under blue-clad military occupation. After nearly three years of this, as John Bell Hood's army marched relentlessly toward Nashville in December of 1864, Southern sympathizers felt their hearts leap with joy at the prospect of deliverance, while the Unionists began to have grave second thoughts as to what would happen to them if Hood succeeded in retaking the city.

Hood's besieging army, still shocked and shattered by the experience at Franklin, was making the most of it outside Nashville. Dr. Quintard recorded that he performed marriages between Confederate officers and Nashville belles and ate "sumptuous" dinners, particularly at the Overton residence, which had become Hood's headquarters on the Nashville-Franklin Pike. There were more parties, dances, music, and serenading for officers, but somehow it was without the luster they had enjoyed a few weeks before at Columbia. Too much had happened since then, reflected poignantly in the absence of missing friends.

On paper, Hood's army still seemed formidable—three corps, nine divisions, twenty-seven brigades of infantry. In better times this might have signified an army of seventy-five or eighty thousand men. But now in the cold hills around Nashville in the closing month of 1864, regiments that once held eight hundred men had less than one hundred. Divisions were scarcely the size of brigades. Fifty-two of Hood's field-grade officers had been left on the bloody ground at Franklin, and regiments were commanded by captains instead of colonels, who were now commanding brigades; enlisted men often commanded companies. The condition of the army was also reflected in the gaunt, hunger-glistening eyes of the ragged soldiers. Shoes had a predictable life span, and after the 250-mile march from Atlanta, that span had long ago run out. Clothing was torn or rotten, and many men had no overcoats or blankets. To make matters worse, the balmy weather had given way to a freezing blizzard, the coldest on record, with much snow, sleet, and ice, and the men shivered on the frozen ground and cursed the weather and the army, and in many cases they cursed General Hood. Frequent cases of severe eye problems were reported, due to the men getting so close to their campfires trying to keep warm that they suffered smoke irritation.

Hood tried to alleviate these conditions by firing off a barrage of telegrams to Beauregard and other authorities in Mississippi and Alabama, urgently demanding shipments of shoes, clothing, and, most of all, more men. But the replacements were not to be had. Some few trickled up the line, and a few men who had been on detail were sent back to the army, but it was barely a drop in the bucket. Hood ordered that the countryside all the way down to the Gulf of Mexico be dragooned for "units belonging to this Army."

The lone hope Hood held out was that heavy reinforcements would arrive from General Kirby Smith in Shreveport, on the Texas border. Hood seems to have held on to this expectation to the bitter end, but when Beauregard—acting on Hood's request—wired Secretary of War Seddon for permission to have the brigades of Kirby Smith brought across the Mississippi, he received a reply that even the adjutant general's office in Richmond branded as "strange." Beauregard, Seddon said, was free to order the Texans to Hood's relief, but he noted that Kirby Smith had "failed heretofore to respond to like emergencies, and no plans should be based on his compliance." This unusual revelation by no less than the secretary of war speaks for itself as to the condition of the Confederacy at this stage of the game. In his pleading letter to Kirby Smith, Beauregard stated, "The fate of the country may depend upon the result of Hood's campaign in Tennessee." He asked that two of Smith's divisions be sent to the Army of Tennessee immediately. When Smith finally got around to replying, the answer was No—the river was too high; he had no way to get his men across; and even if he did, Union gunboats and land forces would prevent a crossing. At one point the frustrated Beauregard even suggested that Smith might try to send his army across the Mississippi in canoes.

And so Hood waited in vain and prayed and planned for Thomas's undoing. To accomplish that, he positioned his army in a convex semicircle facing Nashville from the south. Initially, he designed his lines to stretch around the city with both ends anchored on the Cumberland River, but, with the paucity of troops, that proved impossible, so the semicircle was shortened by several miles. Cheatham's corps was posted on the far right down to a natural barrier called Brown's Creek; Lee was in the center and Stewart on the left with his own left thrown back in a series of five little forts to refuse a flanking movement. To Stewart's left, stretching down to the river, was Chalmers's cavalry. All this was about two miles south of the federal fortifications around the city. In fact, the battle area at Nashville was eerily reminiscent of that at Franklin (except that it was on a much larger scale), the city tucked into the bend of a river with a series of roads and pikes converging on it from the south in a sort of triangle. It was Hood's hope at this point that Thomas would come out and attack him, as he had so disastrously attacked Schofield at Franklin. And Hood's men, whether by orders, or on their own, began to build the breastworks their commander so despised.

The right flank of this line would normally have been held all the way to the Cumberland by Forrest's cavalry, except that Forrest was not present. He and Bate's division of Cheatham's corps had been dispatched by Hood to Murfreesboro, scene of the bloody battle two years earlier, to capture a detachment of federal troops there and tear up railroad tracks that ran from Nashville to Chattanooga. Unfortunately, Hood was misinformed about what kind of forces Forrest could expect to find at Murfreesboro, and in fact Forrest was unpleasantly surprised to discover that the place was formidably defended by more than eight thousand bluecoats under General Lovell H. Rousseau, a forty-six-year-old Kentuckian who had his own ideas about being captured by anybody.

The Confederate commander wasn't the only one to have administrative problems. Over in the Union lines there was the question of what to do about George Day Wagner, who had disobeyed orders at Franklin by leaving two of his brigades too long exposed in front of the breastworks and nearly costing the federals the battle. Following its withdrawal from Franklin, Schofield's army had plodded up the Nashville Pike, arriving in the city a little before noon. Not long after that, an anxious Wagner appeared in the quarters of General Cox. Already Wagner had heard of "severe criticism" against him by his brigade commanders, Lane, Conrad, and Opdycke, which he realized "was likely to lead to an official inquiry, if not a court martial." To soften the penalty he feared was about to drop on him, Wagner tried to persuade Cox that he had not ordered the two brigades to fight the whole Confederate army, but had instead told them to fall back if things got too hot, and unfortunately somebody waited too long—and so on. This, of course, was a lie, but Cox did not know it at the time and told Wagner that he would give him a favorable report. Colonel Conrad, however, who had commanded one of the sacrificial brigades Wagner left in the lurch, took the extraordinary step of dashing off his own official after-action report the moment he got to Nashville—not even stopping to rest from the twenty-mile march—and this bitter document became, as Cox said, "the equivalent to preferring charges against the division commander." Thomas then held an inquiry. Whether Wagner's alleged drunkenness became part of it is not known, but within two days Wagner was relieved of his command and, at his own chagrined request, was allowed to resign from the army.

As if that weren't enough, Thomas soon became embroiled in a great controversy with Grant, Halleck, and Lincoln himself that very nearly cost him his job.

Hood, of course, was crippled by the losses at Franklin but was still dangerous, like a wounded beast. Since Sherman and his sixty-thousand-man army had completely vanished from the map and the public eye, all attention in the North was now focused on Thomas at Nashville. The newspaper reports ranged from the merely frightening to the hysterical. A huge Confederate army, it was written, was advancing—perhaps to Chicago, or Cleveland, or who knew where—and the only thing standing in its way was George Thomas at Nashville. Thomas himself was not frightened, but he was prudent, which others nervously translated into "slow."

On the day of the battle of Franklin, however, Thomas had been frightened. He knew Schofield was going to have a tough time of it with Hood, and the only word he had of the fifteen thousand reinforcements under A. J. Smith was that they were delayed at Paducah, Kentucky. All he commanded otherwise were smatterings of units that had been called in from outposts, raw recruits, supply garrisons, convalescents from Sherman's army, and eight regiments of untried U.S. Colored Troops—none of which constituted a combat army. But Thomas's assistant quartermaster later remembered that about nine o'clock on the night of the Franklin fight, Thomas received a telegram from Schofield saying Hood was defeated, to which Thomas reacted thusly: "His broad brow cleared up and his strong and massive face began to shine with the fierce light of impending battle." Two hours later steamboat whistles from Smith's fifty-nine-boat river armada began tooting along the Cumberland levee, followed by Smith himself, whom Thomas greeted with a wild bear hug.

At this point, Thomas was confident of being able to successfully fight a defensive battle, but he still did not feel strong enough to go on the offense against Hood. His reasoning was that a sizable part of his cavalry was still in Kentucky dragooning citizens' horses in an attempt to remount themselves. Thomas wanted them back and in good order before launching an attack. Further, he wanted time to organize all his various units into a cohesive fighting force. Also, he was operating under the misinformation received from Schofield that Hood's army was far larger than it was and that Forrest's cavalry numbered twelve thousand, which was ridiculous.

Thus, the day Hood arrived before Nashville, Thomas telegraphed Halleck in Washington that he wished to delay an attack on the Confederates for a few days, but the very notion of that sent Grant and everybody in Washington into an uproar.

Secretary of War Edwin Stanton opened the furor as soon as he got into his office next morning by immediately wiring Grant, who was down by Richmond, that Lincoln was particularly worried by Thomas's telegram and wanted Grant to order an attack. "This looks like the McClellan and Rosecrans strategy of do nothing, and let the enemy raid the country," Stanton fumed.

The same day he received this dispatch, Grant wired Thomas with dire predictions that by not attacking Hood forthwith he might "have to abandon the line of the Tennessee River, and lose all the roads back to Chattanooga." Furthermore, Grant told Thomas to arm private citizens and civilians working for him and put them in the trenches to hold the city while he moved out with his forces to fight the Confederates.

Evidently not satisfied with that, two hours later Grant telegraphed Thomas again, warning of "incalculable injury upon your railroads" and further complaining that Thomas should have ordered Schofield to attack Hood immediately after the battle of Franklin, instead of retreating to Nashville.

Thomas answered this rebuke with a long and painful explanation, detailing all his woes over supplies, the weaknesses of his army, lack of cavalry, and so forth. He closed with a promise to try to fight Hood "in a few more days."

Grant let the matter rest for "a few more days" but then resumed his haranguing. On December 5 he wired Thomas, "Hood should be attacked where he is. Time strengthens him, in all probability, as much as it does you." Next day, his patience sorely tried, Grant telegraphed, "Attack Hood at once. . . . There is great danger of delay resulting in a campaign back to the Ohio River." Next morning, Secretary of War Stanton wired Grant in a dither, "Thomas seems unwilling to attack because it is hazardous, as if all war is anything but hazardous. If he waits for Wilson to get ready, Gabriel will be blowing his last horn." Grant replied that if Thomas dallied any longer, he should be replaced by Schofield. "There is no better man to repel an attack than Thomas," Grant said, "but I fear he is too cautious to ever take the initiative." Then Grant wired Thomas again, "Why not attack at once. By all means, avoid the contingency of a footrace to see which, you or Hood, can beat to the Ohio."

Meantime, the authorities back in Washington were getting panicky. Halleck was gravely telegraphing all western commands to send reinforcements to Thomas, and it was even suggested that governors of northern states be called on to raise sixty thousand troops in case Hood started for the Ohio River. Finally, on December 9, Grant blew his fuse.

Schofield, or so it was alleged, had been undermining Thomas by sending secret and uncomplimentary telegrams about him to Grant. It was misinformation in such a telegram—though it has never been positively laid at Schofield's door—that caused Grant to decide to fire Thomas. The previous night someone had erroneously wired Grant that Hood's army was "scattered for seventy miles down the River," and he fumed that Thomas had still not attacked. Of course, the information was absurd, since Hood's army was concentrated directly in front of Nashville at the time.

Thomas's chief of staff, General William D. Whipple, began to smell a rat, and he prevailed on General James B. Steedman, fresh in from Chattanooga, to investigate. Steedman got one of his aides to snoop around and see what he could find out, and sure enough, the aide discovered a copy of a telegram in the wire office from Schofield to Grant that said, "Many officers here are of the opinion that General Thomas is certainly too slow in his movements." That assertion appears to be a bald-faced lie. Only a day or so earlier, at the height of an ice storm, when the telegrams were flying thick and fast between Washington and Nashville, Thomas had called a council of war in his room at the St. Cloud Hotel. There, he laid out for all his senior generals what was going on between him and Washington and wanted to know what they thought. Wilson, the cavalry commander, first stated his case, which was that Thomas should wait until the ground thawed before attacking. Otherwise, horses, men, and equipment would dangerously slip and slide on the frozen ground. One by one the other corps commanders agreed—all, that is, except Schofield, who, Wilson said, "upon this notable occasion sat silent." As the officers were leaving the room, Wilson said, Thomas asked him to stay for a moment, and when they were alone, Thomas said painfully, "Wilson, the Washington authorities treat me as if I were a boy." What Thomas sorely wanted to do at that moment was find out why Grant was so adamant about him attacking Hood immediately, when, for the past six months, Grant himself had been sitting outside Petersburg, Virginia with one hundred thousand troops mostly just looking at Robert E. Lee's fifty thousand inside the city. But it was a question that never got asked.

In any case, Grant had by now made up his mind to relieve Thomas and drew up orders to that effect. A presidential directive was simultaneously written handing over command of the Army of the Tennessee to Schofield. But then another strange turn of events intervened. A few hours later, Grant changed his mind and decided to "suspend the order relieving him," he said, "until it is seen whether he will do anything." At the same time, something apparently changed Grant's mind about Schofield, too, because he dispatched General John Logan, who was visiting his headquarters, to hurry on the train to Nashville and be prepared to assume command of the army if necessary.

Meantime, Steedman had shown Thomas Schofield's telegram to Grant, and the imperturbable "Rock of Chickamauga" stared at it in disbelief. "Can it be possible that Schofield would send such a tele-gram?" he wondered, and when Steedman pointed out Schofield's sig-nature on the document, Thomas asked, "Why does he send such telegrams?" Steedman, the politician, smiled at "the noble old soldier's simplicity" and replied, "General Thomas, who is next in command to you and who would succeed you?" Thomas sadly shook his head as it dawned on him. "Oh, I see," he said.

That Schofield was ambitious was no secret, but there might have been an even darker motive for his behavior. Way back when he was a cadet at West Point, he had gotten himself into some trouble that had to do with breaking regulations and might have involved lying. He was sen-tenced to be dismissed from the academy, but the members of the court-martial voted to remit the sentence—with two exceptions, and one of them was George H. Thomas. Schofield said that at the battle of Franklin he had repaid Thomas's "stern denial of clemency to a youth" by saving Thomas's army from disaster and Thomas himself "from the humiliation of dismissal from command."

In any case, just because Grant had decided for the moment not to relieve Thomas was no reason to stop nagging him, and the wires sang daily with his pestering impatience. As the ice storm continued to rage outside, Thomas wired both Grant and Halleck that he had done all he could until the weather broke, adding, "If you should deem it necessary to relieve me, I shall submit without a murmur." But Grant railed on, unconvinced, "If you delay attack longer the mortifying spectacle will be witnessed of a rebel army moving for the Ohio River, and you will be forced to act, accepting such weather as you find. Let there be no fur-ther delay."

16

★ Like a Lot of Beasts

Down at Murfreesboro, about twenty-five miles from Nashville, Forrest and his people had been having a hard time of it. When Bate had marched off toward the town the day after the battle of Franklin, he expected little or no trouble in his mission of ruining the railroad from Nashville south to Chattanooga, but that expectation was rudely dispelled by the presence of General Rousseau and his eight thousand bluecoats at Murfreesboro itself. Forrest and two of his cavalry divisions arrived to Bate's assistance shortly afterward, as did two small infantry brigades from Lee's and Stewart's corps, but even then the Confederate force numbered only about six thousand, and Rousseau was strongly entrenched in the town.

Bate had been successfully performing his mission of tearing up rails and destroying bridges and federal strongpoints along the track, when along came Forrest to assume command with the surprising orders that they were now to attack the federals at Murfreesboro. Not liking what he saw there, Forrest baited Rousseau to come out of his stronghold and fight, which he did, sending more than half his force under General Robert H. Milroy, a forty-eight-year-old Indiana lawyer who until recently had been under disgrace for letting his command get "gobbled up" by Lee on the way to Gettysburg. Seeing a chance to exonerate himself, Milroy boldly marched his brigades into Forrest's left flank and routed the startled Confederates, causing losses of two hundred men and two guns.

Forrest reported, "From some cause which I cannot explain, [the infantry] made a shameful retreat," while Bate counter-complained, "If the cavalry on either flank were engaged, I was not aware of it." It was not a particularly important engagement strategically, tactically, or otherwise, except to produce a gloomy omen regarding the state of mind of Hood's army.

Next day, Milroy marched his men back to Murfreesboro, and Bate and his people were sent back to Hood at Nashville. Forrest, meantime, resumed destruction of the railroad, burning blockhouses and capturing supplies and hundreds of prisoners—including an entire federal regiment from Chattanooga and the thirteen-car train it rode in on.

By mid-December, Hood's army was as strong as it was going to be. Most of those soldiers who after Franklin had taken "French leave" (later called awol) to visit the families and homes they had not seen in two years had returned to their units. Bate was back with Cheatham, and the Confederate soldiers huddled in their trenches and fortifications while bitter winds howled around them and the ground remained covered with "a perfect sheet of ice."

They had been there for two weeks, and as in any army that has a chance to sit still for a length of time, things began to assume some appearance of wistful normalcy. They could hear the town clock striking in Nashville and the whistles of steamboats and locomotives and the Union bands playing. "Very tantalizing indeed," said James Cooper of the 20th Tennessee, "to be in sight of home and not allowed to be there." Captain Thomas Key, the artillerist in Lee's corps who had mercifully missed the carnage at Franklin, devoted at least some of his time to sparking local girls. Key entertained them, he reported, by "giving them some interesting particulars of a flower called the 'carnation,' which was examined with the help of the microscope of Sir John Hill."

Others plied more utilitarian pursuits. Captain Sam Foster, of Cleburne's old division, described the establishment of a shoe shop, "not to make new shoes, for there was no leather, but," he went on, "they take an old worn out pair of shoes and sew moccasins over them of green cow hide with the hair side in. The shoe is put on and kept there and as the hide dries, it draws closer and closer to the old shoe." Meantime, several grain mills that had been liberated by Bate in his Murfreesboro expedition, were put to work grinding out flour for biscuits and bread, and numerous hogs were rounded up for bacon. Beef was not so plentiful. Thomas B. Wilson, one of the cavalrymen assigned to drive the herd behind the army, reported that the cattle had mostly been fed on dried corn stalks, and that they only butchered the ones that had died or were dying. These were so dry and devoid of fat, Wilson said, "that the boys would amuse themselves by throwing thin stakes of it against trees to see it stick in the bark." This pastime did not last long, however. The freezing weather necessitated such a clamor for firewood by the hundred thousand men of both armies that by mid-December the once lovely and forested hills around Nashville were completely denuded of trees, and they would remain that way for decades to come.

All was not tranquil on the lines, either, where there was vicious skirmishing and sharpshooting day and night. Sam Foster reported several federals killed so close to Confederate lines they could not be carried back, "So they remain where they fell, froze as hard as a log." Federal batteries regularly shelled the southern trenches, but the graycoats had to take it without reply because Hood had ordered no return of fire to save ammunition. At one point, Chalmers's cavalry captured two Union gunboats about twelve miles below Nashville, and brought off fifty-six prisoners and nearly two hundred mules and horses "belonging to the United States Government." And despite a few rawhide shoe shops like Sam Foster's, as much as half of the Confederate army hobbled around unshod. "Their bloody tracks could be plainly seen on the ice and snow," wrote James Cooper. "I had read of such things occurring during the Revolutionary War, but here were scenes eclipsing in suffering all that I had ever imagined." Furthermore, the immoderate winter weather not only continued, but got worse, according to a private in Bate's division, who said, "We had to take the weather like a lot of beasts."

Daybreak on December 14 brought a warm sun and clear skies, and the ice and snow began to melt. That afternoon, Thomas called a meeting of his corps commanders to issue final orders for the attack against Hood, only to be interrupted by yet another needling telegram from Washington. This time Halleck tried a new tack. After going on about Grant's "great dissatisfaction" over Thomas's handling of matters, Halleck proceeded to inform Thomas that his lack of action was disturbing the overall policy for the conduct of the war across a five-hundred-mile front from Savannah to Vicksburg, even jeopardizing Sherman's expedition to the sea. Thomas responded with the simplest of replies: "The ice having melted away today, the enemy will be attacked tomorrow morning."

In ten short paragraphs of Special Field Order 342, Thomas outlined his plans for the destruction of the Army of Tennessee, which for two weeks had defiantly reposed in the Nashville outskirts, daring him to come out and fight. The strategy was to be a feint at Hood's far right by Steedman's corps and the pinning down of his center by Schofield's and T. J. Wood's corps, with the major blow to come as a classic turning movement against Hood's left flank by the newly arrived Sixteenth Corps of A. J. Smith. All this was to be encased by a wide sweep around Hood's far left by Wilson's cavalry corps, now about twelve thousand strong. It was the same strategy Sherman had used to break Hood's final grasp on Atlanta and similar to the one Grant had employed to drive Lee back into the Petersburg defenses. In fact, it was the same strategy the Union had employed since 1861 in its grand design for winning the war in the west, from western Kentucky to western Tennessee to western Mississippi at Vicksburg: to turn the Confederate left flank.

In essence, what Thomas was preparing to spring on Hood was a great right wheel that would hook around his line to the west and crowd him back on himself. Schofield was the only one to raise an objection. Being assigned to hold Hood's center, along with Wood (who now commanded Stanley's corps, after Stanley's wounding at Franklin),

Schofield argued that his men would be too cramped to be of any use and recommended that they be placed along with Smith's corps in the right wheel movement. Thomas readily acceded to this. The agreed-upon time of the attack was to be 6 A.M. Just before daylight, Thomas packed his suitcase, paid his bill at the desk, "as any ordinary traveler," and checked out of the St. Cloud Hotel an hour before the movement was to commence.

To demonstrate something of Thomas's confidence and stability at this point, even though he would shortly be fighting the biggest battle of his career—which was very much on the line—as he rode with his staff through the foggy Nashville streets, he saw standing on the sidewalk a Major Mills, the quartermaster officer assigned to the fuel depot. Thomas halted his entourage and beckoned Mills over, asking him, "Have I drawn all my allowance for coal for this month?" When Mills replied that he had not, Thomas said, "Will you please send fourteen bushels of coal to Mr. Harris, my neighbor? I was out of coal and borrowed that number of bushels from him the other day." That important business out of the way, the commanding general of the Army of the Tennessee then rode off into the fog toward his field headquarters to fight the battle of Nashville.

Just how much Hood knew of Thomas's intentions is not clear, but apparently there wasn't much early warning. Undoubtedly, Hood was receiving information from spies in Nashville, but even on December 10—five days back—he had issued a circular to his corps commanders saying, "[It is] highly probable that we will fight a battle before the close of the present year." Two days later it still seemed that Hood expected to stay at Nashville unmolested for a while, because he telegraphed the War Department that Wheeler's cavalry should be sent back to him "when Sherman completes his raid." On the afternoon of the 13th, Hood informed Stewart that Thomas's cavalry had been crossing the Cumberland all day and going into Nashville and told Stewart to send one of his infantry brigades to cover the Harding Pike on the far left. Around midnight on the 14th, Hood got some kind of information that

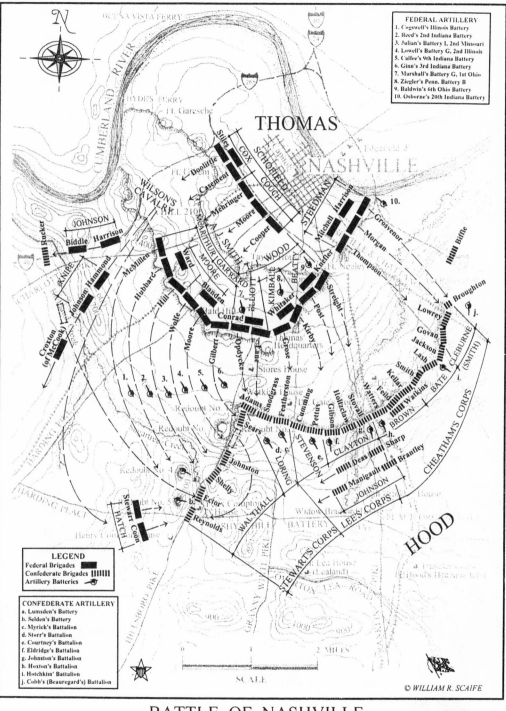

FEDERAL ARTILLERY
1. Cogswell's Illinois Battery
2. Reed's 2nd Indiana Battery
3. Julian's Battery I, 2nd Missouri
4. Lowell's Battery G, 2nd Illinois
5. Calfee's 9th Indiana Battery
6. Ginn's 3rd Indiana Battery
7. Marshall's Battery G, 1st Ohio
8. Ziegler's Penn. Battery B
9. Baldwin's 6th Ohio Battery
10. Osborne's 20th Indiana Battery

LEGEND
Federal Brigades
Confederate Brigades
Artillery Batteries

CONFEDERATE ARTILLERY
a. Lumsden's Battery
b. Selden's Battery
c. Myrick's Battalion
d. Storr's Battalion
e. Courtney's Battalion
f. Eldridge's Battalion
g. Johnston's Battalion
h. Hoxton's Battalion
i. Hotchkiss' Battalion
j. Cobb's (Beauregard's) Battalion

© WILLIAM R. SCAIFE

BATTLE OF NASHVILLE
December 15, 1864

provoked him into sending a warning that Chalmers's position was going to be attacked by cavalry next day. But as late as the morning of Thomas's main assault, Hood was still cranking out telegrams to various authorities in the rear, trying to reclaim detached troops and other things for his army. He even sent an order to his inspector general back at Corinth, Mississippi, saying, "The officers of the military courts must come forward at once."

One of Hood's problems that day—and he had many—was that a pea-soup fog had blanketed the whole area, easily masking Thomas's movements. In fact, the fog was so thick that Thomas was unable to get his corps in place for the anticipated dawn attack, and it was past 8 A.M. when Steedman, on the federal left, was finally able to open the battle with his "feint" against Cheatham's entrenched divisions.

Steedman's corps was truly a grab-bag arrangement. It wasn't exactly a corps that Steedman commanded but something called the Provisional Detachment of the District of the Etowah. This was a collection of garrison soldiers, stragglers, invalids, deserters, quartermaster troops, detached and unattached units, and eight regiments of U.S. Colored Troops. It also contained a brigade commander by the name of Benjamin Harrison, who would one day become the twenty-third president of the United States. Steedman himself was a character of some controversy. He was a forty-seven-year-old failed politician who, with no formal education, had managed to become a newspaper owner back in Ohio before the war. When the Fourth Army Corps under David Stanley returned from Georgia to Chattanooga before Hood launched his campaign, Stanley encountered Steedman as the commander there, in the company of Prince Felix Salm Salm, a thirty-year-old soldier of fortune cavalry officer who had served in the Prussian army, spoke no English, and wore a monocle. Stanley gave the following description:

> [Steedman] was the most thorough specimen of a political general I met during the war. He always managed to hold commands where there were emoluments. At this time he was living in very high style, holding a gay court. The Princess Salm Salm was his guest, and occasionally the Prince, who was the colonel of a New York regiment

stationed twenty miles from headquarters, dropped in. The Princess was a very beautiful woman, afterwards mixed up with the tragedy of Maximilian. Steedman was dead in love with the woman, and such an idiot that I could not get any work out of him. In fact, he was so taken up with making love to the Princess and drinking champagne that it was difficult to see this great potentate of Chattanooga.

It was the Colored Troops under Steedman who bore the brunt of battle on that section of the line. Steedman's regiments, black and white, seventy-five hundred strong, came marching out of the mist "as if on dress parade" where Cheatham's men were waiting for them. The federal force consisted of two brigades of the Colored Troops under Colonels Thomas J. Morgan and Charles R. Thompson and one brigade of white "convalescents, conscripts and bounty-jumpers" under Colonel Charles H. Grosvenor.

Grosvenor's men were to support the main attack by Morgan, but in this they failed miserably. The Confederates of Granbury's old brigade had formed in a little lunette near the main line, and when Grosvenor's men got within good range, Cheatham's artillery opened up on them in full force, causing the line to hesitate, then waver. At that point, Granbury's men and others rose and delivered a devastating volley into the already shaken ranks, which, Grosvenor reported, "stampeded the whole line," and his brigade of bluecoats fled from the field in five minutes. Next, Thompson's Colored Troops came up, only to receive the same treatment, and no further assault was attempted by them, either.

That was bad enough, but compared to what Cheatham's men had in store for Morgan's Colored Troops, it was child's play. Cheatham's right curved around to rest on a cut along the Alabama-Nashville railroad, and Morgan's direction of march would apparently have taken him not only across the exposed cut but actually into Cheatham's rear. As the amazed Confederates watched, Morgan's men came steadily forward, and it was immediately determined "to make a trap for them"— just as the men of Stewart's corps had been trapped and slaughtered in the railroad cut at Franklin.

The Confederates stealthily held their fire as Morgan's men advanced unmolested up to the railroad cut; then, suddenly, two brigades made an about-face, with one wheeling left, and the trap was sprung. Morgan's men walked straight into a slaughter. As the graycoats opened up on the surprised blacks along the exposed cut, many jumped into the cut itself and were shot down. Others jumped into a small pond that was made from the embankment of the cut and "were killed until the pond was black." Morgan and what was left of his brigade quickly fled the scene. Some 630 blueclad bodies were later counted on the scene, the vast majority from the U.S. Colored Troops.

In their after-action reports, the three Union commanders had various things to say about their performances. Grosvenor admitted that his men, "with a few honorable exceptions, behaved in the most cowardly and disgraceful manner." Thompson indicated that his brigade "took the works in [their] front"; however, since those were obviously not near the main Confederate battle line, they must have been old skirmishers' outposts. Morgan forthrightly stated that he had walked into a trap but claimed he could not have known that Granbury's men were in such strength in their lunette. Morgan also insisted that even though his men had retired from the field, they had nonetheless accomplished their main purpose of keeping Cheatham's corps pinned in position on the right while the main attack was being launched against Hood's left. In this the Union colonel was wrong, because Hood was not deceived—at least not for long—and just as soon as it became apparent that the heavy blow was going to fall four miles to the west, Hood ordered Cheatham to rush most of his men over to support Stewart's flank.

First to feel the brunt of Thomas's attack on Hood's left was the emaciated brigade of General Matthew Ector, now commanded by Colonel David Coleman. These seven hundred survivors of the fight at Franklin had been posted about two miles to the northwest of Hood's main battle line near the Harding Pike. What they felt as fog lifted to reveal twenty thousand bluecoats from Smith's and Wilson's corps bearing down on them must have been similar to what the men of Wagner's unfortunate brigades experienced back at Franklin. Providentially, the Confederate's instructions—unlike those of Wagner—were not to stand and fight the whole Union army but to "hold the line until forced to retire, then fall back over the ridge in order, and make a run of about two miles to the Hillsboro Pike." Lieutenant J. J. Tunnell, a Texan, recorded that the federal lines moved slowly but steadily forward into "a warm reception," but, he added, "When they got uncomfortably near, we hastily fell back."

What Ector's brigade fell back on was a fairly formidable line of defense that Hood had been fortifying for about a week. While Cheatham's and Lee's corps were positioned in a long crescent facing Nashville to the north, Stewart's corps joined them facing westward for a mile on a series of hills along the Hillsboro Pike. Not only was Stewart dug in, but also for most of the length of his line a stone wall ran along the road, providing excellent protection. In addition, Hood had ordered the hills in front of this line to be crowned with a series of redoubts, numbered 1 to 5, small, mutually supporting earth-and-timber forts, each containing a battery of artillery and manned by 150 infantry. These were supposed to represent an impregnable barrier to anything that attacked from the west, but construction on them was still unfinished when the full fury of Thomas's assault came wheeling across the fields.

As Ector's exhausted men came panting into the main Confederate positions, Stewart recorded that his line "was stretched to its utmost tension" but still could not reach far enough to support the number 4 and 5 redoubts at the southernmost end of it. Notified of this, Hood reinforced him with two brigades—Manigault's and Deas's—from Lee's corps in the center, but it was too late. A flurry of increasingly nervous correspondence was dashed between brigade, division, and corps commands, commencing about 10 A.M., when Brigadier General Claudius W. Sears reported to General Loring, "A heavy column of infantry is moving to our left." A few minutes later, Colonel Robert Lowry, now leading the late John Adams's brigade of Mississippians, wrote Loring, "There seems to be a movement of some magnitude on our left." Shortly afterward, Stewart received word from Sears's adjutant, "Brigadier General Sears requests me to inform you that the demonstration of the enemy on the left is increasing."

Stewart knew too well what that meant; any large federal move-ment against his left meant he was being outflanked. Stewart's line, from right to left, was composed of Loring, French, and Walthall, ex-cept that French had gone on sick leave that morning, and his men were put under Walthall's command. Stewart again applied to Hood for rein-forcements, and he was told that two of Cheatham's divisions would be coming up, but they were nearly five miles away on the other end of the line.

Slowly and deliberately, the blue juggernaught advanced on the lit-tle redoubts in Stewart's front. Number 5, at the far south end of the line, was the first to be struck. A Union brigade from General John McArthur's division of A. J. Smith's corps advanced on it from the west, while a brigade of cavalry under Colonel Datus E. Coon had sidled around southeast and was now approaching from the flank. Coon's men, dismounted, were equipped with the new Spencer repeating rifle, an in-timidating weapon that gave a single soldier more than five times the firepower of his enemy. Also, Union artillery had been pounding re-doubt 5 for about an hour. When the combined cavalry and infantry fi-nally charged the isolated little outpost, it was quickly overwhelmed with the loss of its four guns.

Redoubt 4 was next. Smith had massed four batteries half a mile across the way and had been blasting at the wood and dirt fort all the time Coon and McArthur were wrapping around number 5. Now the Confederate guns they had captured there were also turned on number 4. It seemed as though number 4 would come to a quick end, but this was not the case, for it was commanded by Virginia Military Institute graduate Charles L. Lumsden, who had no intention of giving up with-out a fight. For three hours, beginning at 11 A.M., Lumsden and his gun-ners gave as good as they got, while overhead flew what one man remembered as a veritable "network of shrieking shells." At one point the federals sneaked a battery into some haystacks behind number 4 and opened up on the exposed rear of the fort, but the Confederates hauled their guns out of their embrasures and turned them on the bluecoat ar-tillery, which "soon got away from that position and troubled [them] no more."

Meantime, the dismounted cavalry and second brigade of McArthur's division had begun creeping nearer, and shortly after 2 P.M. it rose and made a charge. Lumsden and his cannoneers loaded up with double cannister and blew many of the bluecoats to kingdom come, but they were only a hundred or so against thousands. As the federals raced to and past number 4, Sergeant James Maxwell heard someone shout, "Look out, Jim!" He dropped to his hands and knees just in time to escape being decapitated by a double-shot cannister blast that sailed over his head from one of the other guns and tore into the advancing enemy. Maxwell, Lumsden, and some of the other gunners still stayed at their posts, firing as fast as they could, until Lumsden gave the order "Fire" and nothing happened—the man holding the friction primers had run away. Maxwell shouted, "Captain, he's gone with the friction primers," whereupon a federal soldier leaped over the fort wall and landed almost in Maxwell's lap. Lumsden cried out, "Take care of yourselves, boys," and that, finally, was the end of number 4.

The remnants of number 4 raced back as best they could to the stone wall, behind which was the main Confederate battle line. A little later, after Lumsden had received personal congratulations from Stewart for holding the fort so long, Lumsden and Maxwell were still trying to catch their breath and clean up, and Lumsden kept picking at something in his beard. During the battle one of their gunners had gotten part of his head blown off, and finally Lumsden said in disgust, "Maxwell, that is part of Rosser's brains."

The fall of number 4 signified far more than the loss of its guns and garrison. With that obstacle out of the way, the massed federal batteries now turned their attention to the Confederate line behind the stone wall, now occupied by the two brigades from Lee's corps—Manigault's and Deas's—that had been rushed over as reinforcements in the early afternoon. Under cover of the bombardment, McArthur's men steadily advanced on the stone wall, finally charging with a cheer that broke the line. Later, in his report, Stewart unhappily described how the two brigades, "making but feeble resistance, fled, and the enemy crossed the pike, passing Walthall's left.'' Meantime, Stewart had ordered a battery of artillery brought from a redoubt in Loring's front, which was not yet under attack, and put east of the pike, telling Deas's and Manigault's men to reform there. ''They again fled, however,'' Stewart wrote, ''on the approach of the enemy, abandoning the battery, which was captured.'' By now, two additional brigades from Lee's corps had been rushed to the scene, but even they, Stewart recalled, ''were unable to check the progress of the enemy, who had passed the Hillsborough pike a full half mile, completely turning our flank, and gaining the rear of both Walthall and Loring, whose situation was becoming perilous in the extreme.''

Meantime, General Wood, commanding the wounded Stanley's Fourth Army Corps, had been massing in front of Loring's section of the line, exchanging heavy fire with the Confederates. About 4 P.M., an order was given to charge redoubt number 3—in conjunction with a brigade from McArthur's division—which they did, clomping across a muddy corn field and capturing the fort and its guns. But once inside the fort they suddenly came under a galling crossfire from the Confederate guns in numbers 1 and 2. Realizing the peril, the federal brigade commander gave the order to storm number 2, but he ''was shot through the head the next moment.'' The executive officer, who had heard the order, repeated it, and the men leaped out of number 3 toward number 2, which, like number 1, was being hastily abandoned by the Confederates. Seeing the collapse of their flanks, the rest of Walthall's men began to run, and Stewart quickly issued an order for both Loring and Walthall to immediately retreat eastward and reform on the Granny White Pike about a mile away. But this was not before Brigadier General Claudius Sears, a forty-seven-year-old West Point graduate and former mathematics instructor at Tulane, had his leg blown off by a cannon shot and was ultimately made a prisoner.

Just how perilous Stewart's position was at that point is illustrated in a letter written by his adjutant, W. D. Gale, to his wife, shortly after the battle. Gale had set up a headquarters office and signal station in a house near the Hillsboro Pike and was sending and receiving dispatches to and from Hood and the other corps commanders until late in the afternoon when the lines broke. "I remained in my office until the Yankees advanced to within three hundred yards," he wrote. "I then mounted and made my escape through the back yard, with my clerks. As our men fell back before the advancing Yankees, Mary Bradford [a neighborhood girl] ran out under heavy fire and did all she could to induce the men to stop and fight, appealing to them and begging them, but in vain. General Hood told me yesterday that he intended to mention her courageous conduct in his report, which will immortalize her. I never witnessed such want of enthusiasm and began to fear for to-morrow."

Meantime, Wilson's cavalry had been doing yeoman's duty for Thomas. Assigned to protect the federal right and sweep wide to get into Hood's flank and rear, Wilson and his twelve thousand men had opened the battle that morning with a spirited attack on Chalmers's thin line of twelve hundred. These outnumbered graycoats put up a stubborn but futile resistance. Time and again they either dismounted and tried to check Wilson's advance from behind such fortifications as they found, or pitched directly into him on horseback. Chalmers himself, along with his personal escort, led several of these charges, one of them accompanied by a cripple-armed seventy-five-year-old civilian resident named Cockrill, who charged along with the rest, holding the reins in his teeth and waving his hat with his one good arm.

Late in the afternoon, just as the main Confederate lines were crumbling under Thomas's assault, Chalmers's escort, much depleted and now under command of Lieutenant James Dinkins, reached the Belle Meade mansion, a Nashville landmark even then, with orders to secure Chalmers's wagon train. Finding the train burned and the lawn of Belle Meade swarming with hundreds of federal soldiers, Dinkins sneaked his little entourage behind a barn and formed up for a charge. The Confederates swooped down, hollering and firing, but no sooner had Dinkins's mad dash cut through the totally surprised bluecoats, when they encountered a line of Union infantry and were forced to withdraw. As they returned to Belle Meade, where "bullets were clipping the shrubbery and striking the house," an astonishing apparition

appeared on the mansion's front steps. This turned out to be Miss Selene Harding, who, oblivious to the danger around her, was waving her
handkerchief and exhorting the Southerners to fight. "She looked like a
goddess," Dinkins said, adding, "She was the gamest little human being
in all the crowd."

Chalmers's outmanned cavalry was gradually cut off and pushed
back more or less out of the battle picture, with Chalmers losing all his
wagon train, records, and personal belongings. When redoubt number
5 collapsed and the bluecoats of McArthur's division began swarming
across the Hillsboro Pike, Ector's men were effectively cut off from the
rest of Walthall's men and had to beat a hasty retreat south and east to
keep from being annihilated. As darkness fell on the short December
day, these forlorn men were making their way back to whatever now
constituted the Confederate line, when they encountered General
Hood, who had come forward in the afternoon to get a better look at
things. Hood had ridden to the top of an eminence that would presently
become known as Shy's Hill, near the Granny White Pike, about a mile
east and two miles south of his original line of battle. When Ector's men
came dragging along, Hood stopped them and led them personally to
the top of Shy's Hill. "Texans," he said, "I want you to hold this hill
regardless of what transpires around you." Already twice overwhelmed
and routed that day, the bedraggled Texans replied, "We'll do it,
General."

So far, Thomas's plan was moving along pretty much on schedule. He
had not quite succeeded in hooking all the way around Hood and
clamping him in a hopeless vice, but he had managed to pry the
Confederates out of their strong fortifications on the left and shove the
west wing back more than two miles to the south. This precipitated a
total realignment by Hood of all his forces and the abandonment of his
original positions.

As darkness ended the fighting, Thomas sent a telegram to Halleck
in Washington:

Nashville Tenn., December 15, 1864—9 P.M.

Maj. Gen. H. W. Halleck, Washington, D.C.:

I attacked the enemy's left this morning and drove it from the
river, below the city, very nearly to the Franklin Pike, a distance
about eight miles. Have captured General Chalmers' headquarters
and train, and a second train of about 20 wagons, with between 800
and 1000 prisoners and 16 pieces of artillery. The troops behaved
splendidly, all taking their share in assaulting and carrying the
enemy's breast-works. I shall attack the enemy again to-morrow, if
he stands to fight, and, if he retreats during the night, will pursue
him, throwing a heavy cavalry force in his rear, to destroy his trains,
if possible.

GEO. H. THOMAS
Major-general, U.S. Volunteers, Commanding.

This good news at last from Nashville aroused fierce rejoicing in
the capital. Secretary of War Stanton immediately telegraphed Thomas
a congratulatory message and told him they would fire a hundred-gun
salute to him in Washington next morning. Grant, however, was more
reserved. In fact Grant had actually been en route to Nashville to see
about the situation and take personal command when the news of
Thomas's attack reached him. Wiring Thomas just before midnight, he
said, "I will go no farther. Push the enemy now, and give him no rest
until he is entirely destroyed." Then, from hundreds of miles away, he
went on to gratuitously lecture Thomas on how he should conduct the
next attack on Hood, closing with the admonition, "Much is now expected." Fifteen minutes after he sent that telegram, however, he apparently realized that he had not even congratulated Thomas and
rectified the omission in a new wire, lauding Thomas and his army.

For his part, Thomas simply remarked to one of his staff, "I think
we have done pretty well today" and set about making plans to undo
Hood entirely next morning. Steedman would renew the attack against
Hood's right, Wood would continue to hold the center in place, while

Smith and Schofield and Wilson would hammer away at the left and rear. Before he went to bed, Thomas sent a brief telegram to his wife in New York: ''We have whipped the enemy, taken many prisoners and considerable artillery.''

17

Didn't I Tell You ★ We Could Lick 'Em?

The next morning, December 16, dawned gray and somber, and before long it began to rain. Back around Nashville, the hills were dotted black with civilian spectators who had come—as they had the previous day—to watch the impending battle. This was a dour and sullen crowd, occupying rooftops, balconies, upper-floor windows, and practically every rise of ground where a vantage point might be had. Being for the most part in sympathy with the South, it was not a happy occasion for these Nashvilleans, who were fully aware of the federal successes the day before. To some it was as though they were witnessing firsthand the demise of the Confederacy, and in this they were all too correct.

During the night, Hood had drawn his army into a contracted line shaped like a shallow U, in the Brentwood Hills, about two miles south of his previous position. He had moved Cheatham's corps from the far right of the line to the far left, so that now Lee, who had held the center, was on the far right, and Stewart, who had been on the left, was holding the center. The commanding position on the left, where Thomas again intended to make his strike, was Shy's Hill, occupied now only by Ector's depleted little brigade. Here Hood ordered that Cheatham should place Bate's division, and in the darkness Cheatham personally led Bate to his assigned lines on the hill. Not satisfied with his position,

Bate complained to Cheatham, but the corps commander replied that he was "not authorized to change it," so all through the dark of night Bate's men worked feverishly to fortify themselves against the onslaught they knew would come next day. Because of the wet and marshy ground, Bate had been unable to bring up any of his artillery, but at dawn he discovered a road that allowed him to field a section of howitzers on a small plateau from which they could sweep the approaches to the field. These guns were under the direction of Captain R. T. Beauregard, son of the former commanding general of the Army of Tennessee.

As the sky lightened and the chilling drizzle continued to pester the men in both armies, Hood had a prescient thought. At 8 A.M. he issued contingency orders to his corps commanders giving their routes of retreat "should any disaster happen to us to-day."

Over in the Union lines, the mood did not match the weather. Pap Thomas knew he had Hood on the run; the question now was whether or not he could catch him. He had just received another of those schizoid telegrams from Washington, this one from Lincoln himself, in which the president first extended the nation's thanks to Thomas for his "good work of yesterday" and then snatched the bloom off the rose by tacking on this patronizing admonition: "A grand consummation is within your reach. Do not let it slip."

If Thomas was rankled by this, he said nothing of it. So far, his battle plan had worked almost perfectly—possibly more than any other major battle plan of the Civil War. Not only had he hammered Hood out of his positions, but he had done so without running any substantial risk to himself. Even if he had been repulsed, Hood's plan of "following the defeated enemy into Nashville" would never have succeeded because, with his superiority of numbers, Thomas was able to maneuver the bulk of his army—fifty-five thousand men—against Hood and at the same time leave the Nashville defenses thoroughly manned and fortified.

As he rode through the city that morning, a window from a nearby home slammed down in Thomas's face, and when he looked up, he saw a young woman scowling down at him. He rode on "with an amused smile,'' unaware that the lady in question would soon become the wife of one of his officers.

The first order of business that morning was to get Wilson's cavalrymen moving again against Hood's far left. That done, the next step was to figure out precisely where Hood's new line was. This was accomplished by a general movement of skirmishers from each corps, who quickly developed Hood's position, followed by the alignment of Union divisions and establishment of a horrific artillery bombardment against the thin gray line.

As it had the day before, Thomas's initial assault fell on Hood's right, in hopes of causing the Confederate commander to draw troops off from his left to reinforce it. Shortly before noon, the corps of Steedman and T. J. Wood assaulted a hill defended by the division of General Henry D. Clayton and were nearly cut to pieces. The Alabama, Georgia, and Louisiana brigades poured a steady stream of lead into the advancing blue line, while Confederate artillery pounded it with shot and shell. A Union officer in this advance was hit by an artillery round that literally tore out his heart and left it dangling on his stomach, where it was said to have beat for fifteen minutes. By midafternoon, after several charges, the federals were no closer to dislodging Lee's men than they were on the first try.

It was here that the U.S. Colored Troops gained their measure of glory but at a terrific cost. Clayton reported: ''Five color-bearers with their colors were shot down in a few steps of the works, one of which, having inscribed on its folds, 'Eighteenth Regiment, U.S. Colored Infantry; presented by the colored ladies of Murfreesborough,' was brought in.'' And General James T. Holtzclaw wrote: ''At 12 P.M. the enemy made a most determined charge on my right. Placing a negro brigade in front they gallantly dashed up to the abatis, forty feet in front, and were killed by hundreds. Pressed on by their white brethren in the rear they continued to come up in masses to the abatis, but they came only to die. I have seen most of the battle-fields of the West, but never saw dead men thicker than in front of my two right regiments.''

Meantime, over on Hood's far left, Wilson and his horsemen were having a rough time of it. The ground was slippery, the woods dense,

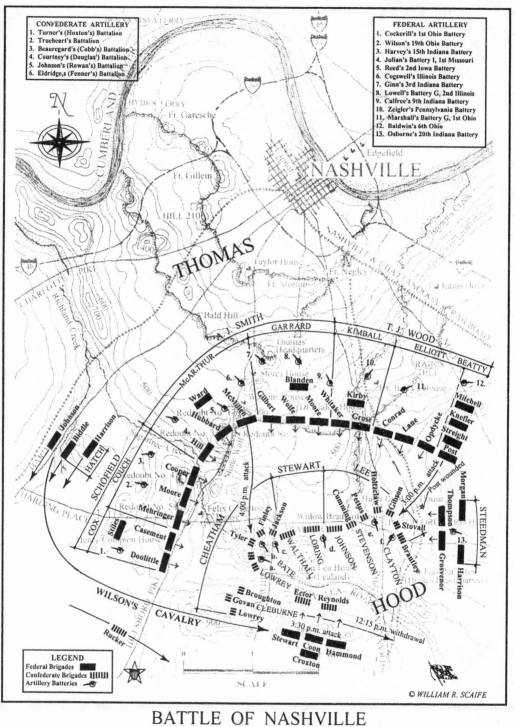

BATTLE OF NASHVILLE
December 16, 1864

and Wilson wasn't making much progress getting in Hood's rear. About 10 A.M. he sent a message to Thomas asking if it might not be better for him to take his cavalry around to the opposite side of Hood's line and see what they could do from there. Thomas declined, telling Wilson to keep at it where he was. About noon, more than four thousand of Wilson's dismounted men, with their fast-firing repeaters, finally managed to get around Cheatham's flank and began moving in behind him. It was about then that some of Wilson's troopers captured a courier Hood had sent to Chalmers, and on him they found this desperate message from the Confederate commander: "For God's sake [drive] the Yankee cavalry from our left and rear or all is lost."

At this point, Wilson knew—or thought he did—that victory was at hand. The overall battle plan for that day called for him, once in position on Hood's flank, to join with Schofield in launching the general attack, which would be the signal for the other corps to assault all down the Union line. Realizing that the time had come, Wilson forwarded Hood's captured message directly to Thomas and then "sent three staff officers, one after the other, urging Schofield to attack the enemy in front and finish up the day's work with victory." Schofield, however, was unmoved by Wilson's pleas. In fact, not only did he not think Hood was beaten, he actually was scared that Hood was going to attack *him*. During the night he had requested and received from Thomas a full division of reinforcements from the corps of A. J. Smith, and now, even more nervous, he was calling for additional fresh troops.

"Fearing that nothing would be done," Wilson said, "I rode around the enemy's left flank to Thomas' headquarters, which I found on the turnpike, about two miles from my own." By then, he recalled, it was nearly 4 P.M., and the short day was already growing dark from the clouds and rain. Arriving on the scene "with ill-concealed impatience," he found Thomas and Schofield standing together on a hill from which the whole panorama of the battlefield was plainly visible in the dim, smoky light. They could see the entire Confederate left flank, marked by flashes of cannon and rifle fire, spread across the hills to the east, and also Wilson's own dismounted men, who "were in plain sight, moving against the left and rear of the enemy's line."

Thomas at this point was not as happy with the progress of things as he had been the day before—and particularly not with Schofield's performance. Here it was nearly dark and nothing much had been accomplished except the futile bloodshed during the abortive attacks on Hood's right. A little while earlier, Thomas had received a request from A. J. Smith saying that General McArthur wanted to immediately attack the Confederate salient in his front, but Thomas demurred, proclaiming: "The prescribed order of attack gives the initiative to General Schofield." But now Thomas was discovering that Schofield was reluctant to move. When he told the Twenty-third Corps commander to assault the positions to his front, Schofield complained that it would cause a great loss of life, prompting Thomas to respond disgustedly: "The battle must be fought, [even] if men are killed."

Now, with Wilson at his side, Thomas calmly raised his field glasses to scan the area where Wilson earlier claimed his cavalry could be seen, and asked him again if he was sure those were *his* men. Just then a mass of bluecoats moved out from the trees on the left and started toward the Confederate line. It was McArthur, who, even more impatient than Wilson, was defying orders from both Thomas and Smith and launching his assault anyway. Thomas turned to Schofield: "General Smith [meaning McArthur's division] is attacking without waiting for you," he said. "Please advance your entire line."

It had not been such a good afternoon over in the Confederate lines, but neither did the army exude the kind of gloom that hung over the misty Tennessee landscape. Hood had moved his headquarters to the Lea House near the Franklin Pike and was feeling more confident now that darkness was closing in and all federal assaults so far had been handsomely repulsed. By this point, he later recalled, he had "matured the movement for the next morning." He postulated that Thomas's left flank—which had suffered so much that day at the hands of Lee's men— "stood in air some six miles from Nashville." In what indeed would have been a bold move, he said he had now decided "to withdraw [his] entire force during the night and attack this exposed flank in rear [the next day]," adding that he could have done so safely because, "I still had open a line of retreat." Earlier that day he had had the following order read to the troops: "The commanding General takes pleasure in announcing to his troops that victory and success are now within their grasp; and the commanding general feels proud and gratified that in every attack and assault the enemy have been repulsed; and the commanding general will further say to his noble and gallant troops, 'Be of good cheer—all is well.'"

Hood was not alone in his confidence. Brigade and division commanders over in Lee's corps reported that they actually had to restrain their men from counterattacking against the failed bluecoat assaults, and Hood himself reported that men were "waving their colors in defiance, crying out to the enemy, 'come on, come on.'" Thus it must have come as a sour surprise for the Confederate commander when the unmistakable sounds of a major battle on his left began to waft back to him across the darkening hills.

For Cheatham's corps—and for the men of Bate's division in particular—things had not appeared so rosy. Atop Shy's Hill, a node-like lump that constituted the left salient of Hood's defenses, there was a crawling uneasiness over the positioning of the line that Bate had unsuccessfully tried to correct. Thomas's attack on the Confederate right had caused Hood to withdraw vital units from his left to reinforce Lee, and this had spread Cheatham's line to the snapping point. They had worked all night to throw up some kind of breastworks, but, as one man explained, "Tools were very scarce, about one to every ten men." When morning came, "We had very poor works—at some places only old logs and rocks piled together and a few shovels of dirt thrown on them." Hood's own engineer had laid out this line, it seems, and no one—not even Cheatham—was authorized to change it. Problem was, the line was a defensive disaster waiting to happen. The position had been drawn so far back from the "military crest" of the hill that one officer complained, "A six foot man could not be seen twenty yards from the front, thus rendering it possible [for the federals] to mass an attacking party within a few yards of the position and be perfectly sheltered from our fire."

This was precisely what the bluecoats did. In positioning their lines, they massed a full division under the shelter at the bottom of Shy's Hill, perfectly impervious to any fire the Confederates could bring to bear, and when the time came, they were ready. The exposed Confederate positions came under fire in midmorning, but about 2 P.M. the Union batteries began to open up on them in earnest. General Bate explained in his report, "[The federal artillery] threw shells directly in the back of my left brigade, and placed a battery on a hill diagonally to my left, which took my first brigade in reverse."

So now Bate's men were getting it front, sides, and rear. An officer in the line commented, "If a man raised his head over the slight works he was very apt to lose it." Another staff officer noted later that "the men seemed utterly lethargic and without interest in battle." Private Sam Watkins, who was on that line, wrote later, "[The army was] somewhat like a flock of geese that have lost their leader. I have never seen an army so confused and demoralized. I remember when passing by Hood, how feeble and decrepit he looked, with an arm in a sling, and a crutch in the other hand, and trying to guide and control his horse."

Meantime, Chalmers's cavalry was involved in a heroic but futile struggle against Wilson's overbearing forces. Some twelve hundred men under command of Colonel D. C. Kelly were pitched against perhaps eight thousand of Wilson's ferociously armed troopers who were moving up the Granny White Pike to gain Cheatham's flank and rear. With Kelly riding up and down the lines crying, "Pour it into them boys, pour it into them," the little band of cavalry held up Wilson's advancing megalith much of the day but finally caved in to superior numbers about 4 P.M.

Private Sam Watkins was on the far Confederate left as Wilson's men poured in on them. He recalled the bluecoats rising out of some bushes and calling for their surrender, at which point he and his men threw down their rifles. But then, Watkins said, the federals raised up and "deliberately took aim," killing two of his surrendered companions. Watkins recounts how he snatched up his own gun and "killed the Yankee who killed Billy Carr," then ran into the woods with "a hail storm of bullets" behind him.

Colonel Gale, Stewart's adjutant, had a commanding view of the Union advance as it "poured over in clouds" into Bate's division. "We could see his whole line in our front," Gale wrote his wife, "every move, attack or retreat. It was magnificent; what a grand sight it was. We could see the capitol all day, and the churches."

As the divisions of Smith's and Schofield's corps bore down on the hill occupied by Bate's men, they struck first a position occupied by the 20th Tennessee, a regiment commanded by Colonel Bill Shy, a likable twenty-five-year-old Franklin farmer. Fighting soon became hand to hand as federals warmed into the Confederate lines, and Shy, like the rest, leaped into the melee. He had just fired a rifle into the line of blue when he was struck dead by a bullet to the head. After the battle federal troops named the hill he died on after him.

Captain James Cooper, formerly of Shy's regiment, was now adjutant of a brigade commanded by twenty-six-year-old Thomas Benton Smith, known as "the Boy General." McArthur's lead brigade, led by Colonel W. L. McMillen, slammed into Shy's Hill, having been ordered "not to cheer or fire a shot until the works should be gained." They cheered anyway, however; Cooper, who was just below the crest of the hill, remembered it. "I heard someone say, 'look up yonder,' " he said, "and on looking I saw the Yankees and our men so mixed that it was scarcely possible to tell one party from the other." Benton Smith's graycoats were soon overwhelmed and came dashing down the far side of the slope with the federals in hot pursuit. "Our men had to cross a ploughed field where the mud was knee deep, and the vile Yankees were right after them," Cooper said, "shooting as fast as the Devil would let them, and he seemed to have very little objection to their shooting as fast as possible. I now felt that the Confederacy was indeed gone up, and that we were a ruined people."

General Benton Smith, a product of the Nashville Military Institute, was holding the line at all hazards when he realized that most of his men had melted away, and he was surrounded. "Drawing his handkerchief from his pocket and waving it above his head, he commanded the little squad near him to 'cease firing,' " according to Dr. Deering Roberts, the surgeon of Bate's division. Disarmed, Smith was marched north toward Nashville, guarded by three federal soldiers, when the party came upon Colonel McMillen, whose brigade had led the Union charge. For no apparent reason, McMillen suddenly attacked Smith with his saber, wantonly striking him three blows that split open his skull and exposed his brain. When they got him to a hospital, the Union surgeon, seeing Smith's brain oozing from a crack in the skull, remarked, "Well, you are near the end of your battles." But that was not to be. Somehow Smith survived, but he was confined for most of his remaining sixty years of life in the Tennessee State Hospital for the Insane.

Another of Bate's brigade commanders, General Henry R. Jackson, had been watching the federal assault on his right when suddenly a host of blue-clad soldiers appeared in his rear. As Jackson tried to make his escape across the marshy fields, his knee-high boots became so loaded with mud he found it impossible to run. An aide persuaded him to remove the boots, but just as he had got one off and was trying to remove the other, they heard somebody shout, "Surrender, damn you!" They looked up to see four federals on a fence row not far away with guns leveled at them. The aide said, "They have got us, General," and cried out, "We surrender." As Jackson tried to pull his boot back on, the aide slyly turned down the collar on his uniform to disguise the general's three-star insigne. But when the Union soldiers arrived on the scene, Jackson stood up and turned his collar back up, whereupon one of the bluecoats walked around him a couple of times, then said, "You are a general!" When Jackson replied, "That is my rank," the soldier began to whoop and wave his hat and holler, "Captured a general, by God! I will carry you to Nashville myself!"

The break of Bate's division at Shy's Hill was the catalyst that sent Hood's whole line crumbling like a row of dominoes. Stewart's corps, suddenly realizing the enemy was in their rear, quickly joined the flight. Stewart's adjutant, Colonel Gale, wrote to his wife, who was the daughter of Bishop-General Polk, "It is impossible to give you any idea of an army frightened and routed. Every man fled for himself." Seeing that the rout was unstoppable, Gale sent a courier to his boss, Stewart, who was at Hood's headquarters "to inform him of the fact that he might save himself.'' But the courier was killed. Gale then rounded up his clerks and rode to where he thought Hood would be, but all he found were bluecoats, who immediately opened fire on him. Gale dashed away but found the hill in front too steep for his horse to climb, so he galloped on, skirting the hills until he found a spot to go up. ''All along,'' Gale wrote, ''frightened fellows were crying out to me, 'Let me hold on to your stirrup, for God's sake. Give me your hand and help me, if you please.' '' At some point his saddle got shot off, and he was dismounted, but, he said, ''I twisted my hands in my horse's mane and was borne to the top of the hill by the noble animal, more dead than alive.''

As the blue line swept along, shooting men in the back, brigade after brigade of Confederates streamed eastward and south, across the woods and fields to Granny White Pike and then to the Franklin Pike, their only route of escape. The break was so sudden that practically all the artillery in the main line had to be abandoned because the horses could not be gotten forward in time to save it. In all, fifty-four guns— more than half the army's artillery—were lost.

Cheatham and other officers—including Hood himself—tried to rally the routed soldiers but with little success. Sam Watkins reported, ''It was like trying to stop the current of the Duck river with a fish net. The army was panic-stricken. The woods everywhere were full of running soldiers. Wagon wheels interlocking each other, soon clogged the road, and wagons, horses and provisions were left indiscriminately.'' Cheatham managed to stop one soldier with his horse, but as Cheatham started yelling at another fleeing bunch, the soldier ducked under the general's horse and continued running. At one point a young staff officer who had not been in the battle but had just come up from some point south started riding among the confused mob, shouting, ''Stop. Stop. There is no danger there.'' A grizzled old soldier looked up at him and said, ''You go to hell—I was there.''

By now the entire Union army was in motion. The pouring rain became mixed with snow as the Confederates ran from one hill to the next ''as if the devil himself was after them.'' Watching the action through his field glasses, Thomas was elated by the cheering of his soldiers as they swept into Hood's breastworks. "The voice of the American people," he called it. An officer on Thomas's staff gave this colorful description:

> It was more like a scene in a spectacular drama than a real incident in war. The hillside in front, still green, dotted with the boys in blue swarming up the slope; the dark background of high hills beyond; the lowering clouds, the waving flags; the smoke slowly rising through the leafless treetops and drifting across the valleys; the wonderful outburst of musketry; the ecstatic cheers. . . .

As his army streamed past him, Hood was fit to be tied. "I beheld for the first and only time a Confederate army abandon the field in confusion," he said later. With his army in full and uncontrollable retreat his only job was to save as much of it as possible from capture. He frantically dispatched a courier ordering Chalmers to "hold the Granny White Pike at all hazards." Chalmers gathered up his worried little two-brigade command and began piling up fence rails, trees, and anything else he could find to build a barrier on the newly threatened section of the pike. Presently, Wilson's cavalry—all four divisions of it—began arriving on the scene, anxious to seize the pike as a route to smash into Hood's army, which was headed south on the parallel Franklin Pike three miles to the east. It was now so dark Wilson's men "could scarcely see their horses' ears," but a savage battle broke out anyway, with rifle flashes the only light to discern friend from foe. In the melee there was a strange and brutal hand-to-hand clash between two brigade commands, Union Colonel George Spalding's and Confederate Colonel E. W. Rucker's.

Spalding and his men had been trying to cut through Chalmers's barricade when out of the darkness came a voice, "Who are you, anyhow?" When Spalding said who he was, a rider rushed out of the gloom and grabbed his reins, saying, "I am Colonel Ed Rucker commanding the Twelfth Tennessee Rebel Cavalry. You are my prisoner." Spurring his horse to a leap, Spalding replied, "Not by a damned sight," and moved out of reach. At this point Union Captain Joseph Boyer joined in the fray, snatching Rucker's saber from his hand, but Rucker returned the favor by grabbing Boyer's saber, and the two commenced a sword-fight using each other's swords. Presently, a pistol shot rang out of the darkness and tore through Rucker's shoulder, putting him out of the fight. He was taken prisoner by Spalding, and later that night, Union doctors sawed off his arm.

As the corps of Cheatham and Stewart streamed down the Franklin Pike, it fell on Stephen Lee and his men to protect the rear of the army. Lee's corps had suffered little and inflicted great damage on their enemy that day and thus were in high spirits when they received the shock that the other wings of the army had broken and federals were moving on their flanks. Seeing the collapse, Lee dashed on horseback to the Franklin Pike, where he found a few artillery pieces and a stand of colors. Seizing the colors, Lee rode among the fleeing men of Cheatham and Stewart and roared at them, "Rally, men, for God's sake. This is the place for brave men to die!" A drummer boy took up the challenge and began to beat the long roll, and slowly men began to stop and try to organize themselves into some sort of unit. Some of Lee's corps had also begun to retreat in disorder, but Lee shrewdly rounded up General Dan Reynolds's brigade and General Henry Clayton's division to hold up the federals at points along the Franklin Pike so the rest of Hood's army could escape. This they accomplished perfectly, under a cold sky that cleared momentarily, bathing the landscape in the glow of a silver winter moon.

Meantime, Thomas and his staff had ridden in the dark out to where Wilson and his cavalry were still embroiled in a running fight with Chalmers. Coming up beside Wilson with a broad grin, the usually taciturn Thomas was clearly beside himself over the day's events and "shouted so that he might have been heard a quarter mile: 'Dang it to hell, Wilson, didn't I tell you we could lick 'em, didn't I tell you we could lick 'em if they [Washington] would only let us alone!' "

18

★ A River of Fire

As midnight tolled the gloomy Sunday, arguably the darkest day in the Southern Confederacy, Private Sam Watkins unhitched a horse from an abandoned team and rode down toward Franklin until he found a hospital where a doctor sewed up several bullet wounds he had received trying to flee the federals. When he realized the hospital was near Hood's new headquarters, he went personally into Hood's tent to ask for a "wounded furlough," to visit his nearby home. Inside, Watkins claimed, he found Hood "much agitated and affected, pulling his hair with one hand and crying like his heart would break."

All along the pike from Nashville to Franklin, Confederate soldiers were either walking south or had collapsed from exhaustion by the roadside. Wilson's cavalry corps and Wood's Fourth Infantry Corps were pursuing and harassing them, but after the initial break few prisoners were taken. Hood's first hurdle was to get the Army of Tennessee safely across the Harpeth River at Franklin, and this he did, though not without some trouble. As the troops crossed through the town, they had the dispiriting experience of marching past the grizzly killing field of two weeks before, where the rains had washed away some of the graves and decaying arms, legs, and even heads protruded from the ground. To add to this, a putrefying stench hung over the ground, emanating from dozens of unburied horses, including the mount of General Adams, which remained where it and its owner had died, halfway across the old Union parapet. Meantime, a division of Wilson's cavalry had crossed below Franklin and immediately began attacking Lee's rear guard, which still consisted mainly of Clayton's division.

One of the officers of that outfit, Colonel Robert Lindsay, was commanding a regiment of Louisianans in the brigade of General Randall Gibson. Lindsay recalled that the bullets were flying thick and fast as he, Gibson, and a surgeon rode down the pike accompanying Lee. "As General Lee sat facing the enemy," Lindsay said, "I heard the ball strike the parlon of his foot. I said, 'General Lee is wounded' and about this time Dr. Stewart was wounded, and I said to General Gibson, the next is for him, then mine. But General Gibson and myself got off scot free." Lee's wound was painful but not fatal, and he stayed in command for several hours before turning things over to his senior division commander and retiring to an ambulance.

Meantime, the rest of Thomas's army came lumbering southward after Hood, rebuilding as they went the railroads and bridges the Confederates were destroying behind them. As Hood's men retraced their own bloody footprints from Franklin to Spring Hill, then to Columbia, they traveled exceedingly light, having lost much equipment during the Nashville disaster. Thomas, however, was finding the going tough. The countryside was virtually stripped of forage, streams were swollen by the rains, and the troops often were held up to wait for the ration trains. This, of course, caused the carping from Washington to begin anew, the subject again being Thomas's alleged sluggishness. Grant started it earlier when he urged Thomas to give Hood "no rest," adding, "Much is now expected." Halleck soon got in on the act, telegraphing, "Permit me General, to urge the vast importance of a hot pursuit of Hood's Army. Every possible sacrifice should be made . . ." and so on.

Thomas, probably feeling his oats from the spectacular success at Nashville, finally sat down and gave Washington a dose of its own medicine. Insisting that he was doing all he could to capture Hood, Thomas pointed out, "We cannot control the elements . . . pursuing an enemy through an exhausted country, over mud roads completely sogged with heavy rains, is no child's play,'' and went on to complain that Sherman had taken with him the best divisions of the army, leaving for Thomas only a "disorganized" force. The effect of this wintry blast on the secretary of war was to produce what amounted to an apology, with Stanton replying that the government "has the most unbounded confidence in your skill, vigor and determination." This seemed to end the matter, at least for a while.

When Hood's lines around Nashville began to collapse, Forrest had been sent an urgent message warning him to leave Murfreesboro and get back to the army as soon as possible. This he did, heading southwestward and driving with him a large store of beef and hogs and captured prisoners and rejoining the army near Columbia. By now the strain of the campaign was wearing on everybody—even Forrest—and for a terrible moment it appeared that one or both of Hood's two best corps commanders would kill the other.

Frank Cheatham was about to cross his corps over the Duck River when Forrest and his cavalrymen appeared and insisted that they were to cross first. "I think not, Sir. You are mistaken. I intend to cross first and will thank you to move out of the way of my troops," responded Cheatham. Forrest, who had personally done his share of killing during the past four years, drew his pistol and growled, "If you are a better man than I am, General Cheatham, your troops can cross ahead of mine." As the standoff grew, "with much tall cursing"—Cheatham and Forrest being among the best cursers in the army—tension mounted in the ranks. Some of Cheatham's men cocked their rifles, vowing to shoot Forrest or anybody else who did harm to their commander. Finally, Stephen Lee emerged from his ambulance and succeeded in separating the two red-faced generals.

It was obvious to everyone, Hood included, that his army was in terrible shape. In addition to the terrific losses at Franklin, more than four thousand of his men had been captured at Nashville, and the condition of those who were left was deplorable. Many did not even have their weapons. As the ragtag soldiers plodded through Columbia, a resident wrote in his diary, "They are passing all night, going south. They are the worst looking, and most broken down looking set I ever laid eyes on." And young Isaac Rainey, a cavalryman with Forrest, said: "Not half have blankets, half are without shoes; their feet are tied up in old cloth or gunny sacks." One of these soldiers was a Tennessean named Carrol Clark who had received a disabling gunshot to the arm way back at the end of the Atlanta campaign and was declared unfit for further service. Nevertheless, he followed the army all the way up to Nashville for no reason other than he "wanted to be with the boys," and with them now on the long, doleful retreat, all he had for shelter was "a little dog fly, no bigger than a table cloth." And even this, he said, "I had to slowly tear up, to wrap around my feet."

It had been Hood's intention to stop at Columbia and face Thomas on the line of the Duck River. But now he had to reconsider. The one thing evident was that the army had to do something—it couldn't just run forever. And there was a real prospect that if Hood moved out of Tennessee, there might be mass desertions by the Tennessee troops. Yet the condition of the army was such that Hood was fearful it would be completely destroyed in another major clash with Thomas. "I am afraid that I have been more wicked since I began this retreat than for a long time past," Hood confided to his friend Chaplain Quintard at Columbia. "I had my heart so set on success—had prayed so earnestly for it—that my heart has been very rebellious."

By this time, Forrest had appeared on the scene, as well as the exiled Tennessee governor Isham Harris, and with his characteristic bluntness Forrest put the case to Hood this way: "If we are unable to hold the state, we should at once evacuate it." Harris concurred, and Hood agreed and immediately told Forrest to take charge of the rear-guard operation, placing Walthall's division under Forrest's command, and the Army of Tennessee began to move southward again.

About this time, William Tecumseh Sherman and his sixty thousand men emerged from the wilds of Georgia, appearing at the sea outside Savannah. In the course of his operations from Atlanta, Sherman had left a trail of blackened chimneys and rubble and ruined fields and factories along a path of destruction sixty miles wide and three hundred miles long. Now he was scouring newspapers for news of what had happened between Thomas and Hood. Sherman had only "piecemeal rumors" until two days after Thomas's victory at Nashville, when a full report finally reached him. He immediately sent Thomas a congratulatory message, but within days he too had joined the column of carpers to complain about Thomas's "slowness." Sherman did not spend much time on the matter, however, having other business to attend, such as the destruction of South Carolina, now that Georgia was disposed of. On Christmas eve, he resumed his relished practice of handing out Jupiter-sized threats against the South. Writing to Halleck about his contemplated move to Charleston, Sherman said, "The truth is, the whole army is burning with an insatiable desire to wreak vengeance upon South Carolina. I almost tremble at her fate, but feel that she deserves all that is in store for her." Almost as an afterthought he added, "I look upon Columbia as quite as bad as Charleston, and I doubt if we shall spare the public buildings there as we did at Milledgeville."

One of Thomas's problems in the pursuit of Hood was that a pontoon train needed to cross the federals over the Duck River had taken the wrong road and gone astray. It was not Thomas's fault—except under the concept that as commander in chief, everything was his fault—but he got blamed for it anyway. Nevertheless, on December 24 he received a message from Washington that he was being promoted to the permanent rank of major general in the regular army.

Jefferson Davis had correctly predicted back in September that there was to be a Moscow-style retreat in the west, but now it was being undertaken by *his* army, not the federals. For more than one hundred miles, through ice and snow and bitter cold that lasted up to Christmas day, the Army of Tennessee trudged toward Alabama and the Tennessee River. Most of the fighting was between Forrest's and Wilson's cavalries as Wilson pressed hard to harass and cut off Hood's men in flank and rear. It was the only such pursuit of such distance by either side during the war. For ten days the two groups of horsemen fought a series of running battles that left both practically used up. Wilson reported losing five thousand horses to disablement or death. "Hundreds lost their hoofs entirely. I have never seen so much suffering," he said. Forrest's plight was even worse. In order to save the army, he reported shortly afterward, "I was almost compelled to sacrifice my command."

It was so unlike the gaiety and lightheartedness of the march up into Tennessee the month before, when pretty girls and children gathered along roadsides to cheer them and wave handkerchiefs. This time, according to Private Sam Watkins, "The citizens seemed to shrink and hide from us as we approached them." Just south of Pulaski, Hood and his staff were riding along the pike, and were about to crowd an old soldier off the road, when the man began to sing this song, to the tune of "The Yellow Rose of Texas":

> So now I'm going Southward,
> My heart is full of woe.
> I'm going down to Georgia
> To see my Uncle Joe.
> You can talk about your Clementine
> And sing of Rosalie
> But the Gallant Hood of Texas
> Played hell in Tennessee

How Hood reacted to this is not recorded, and if he caught the old soldier's reference to Joe Johnston, he apparently didn't let on.

Colonel Gale wrote to his wife: "When we left the pike at Pulaski we had an awful road, strewn with dead horses and mules, broken wagons and, worse, broken pontoons." As the army neared the Tennessee River, Gale said, "Every man was haunted by the apprehension that we did not have boats enough to make a bridge."

But this time the Army of Tennessee was in luck. Without pontoons and with their backs to the river, they would have been sitting ducks for Thomas's army, which would have surely bagged the bunch and shipped them off to northern prison camps. But General Phillip D. Roddy, a thirty-nine-year-old Alabamian who was serving under Forrest, but whose brigade had been kept south of the Tennessee on other duties, saved the day. Seeing the problem, Roddy and his men captured the federal pontoon bridge at Decatur and floated it some miles downstream, where it was reassembled for Hood's men to use. Captain James Cooper described the crossing:

> Christmas day dawned bright and beautiful but upon what a scene did that morning's sun arise. A poor half starved, half clad band of ragamuffins fleeing in disgrace from their last chance for freedom and independence. We thought the Yankees would catch us at last. The gunboats—they had several little ones—came up in our rear and threw a few shells over, but did no harm. After waiting here until some of us were almost frightened to death, our brigade was sent across the river.

The gunboats of the Union navy had indeed presented Thomas with his final opportunity to bring Hood's army to bay. The boats had been ordered several days earlier to steam upriver and destroy the Confederate pontoon bridge by cannon fire, but, according to Wilson, they "let it slip by." Wilson complained that even though the navy got within a mile of the bridge, they did not reach it because the commander had no bar pilot he could trust. "This was indubitably our last and best chance," Wilson wrote, "but the independence of the navy and the natural timidity of a deep-water sailor in a shoal-water draft river defeated it."

At this point Thomas gave up the chase. When Hood's men began to cross the river, the three infantry corps of the Army of the Tennessee were spread out between Columbia and Pulaski, and Wilson's cavalry corps was still nipping at Hood's heels. But here Thomas finally put his army into winter quarters. It was his opinion that the difficulties of supply and the terrible weather were simply too much for his men. This, of course, brought another outcry from Washington, and Grant finally took action. Writing to Sherman that Thomas, "in his pursuit of Hood indicated a sluggishness that satisfied me he would never do to conduct one of your campaigns," Grant delivered the coup de grâce by breaking up Thomas's command. He ordered Schofield and the Twenty-third Corps cavalry east to fight Robert E. Lee and sent A. J. Smith's corps down to the gulf to take Mobile. Thus it was with this stain against him that Thomas ended his significant role in the war.

Through the ever present rain and knee-deep mud what was left of the Confederate army trudged across Alabama to Corinth, Mississippi. The day after the rout at Nashville, Hood sent a short telegram to Richmond in which—after describing his success for nearly two days in fending off Thomas's assaults—he admitted his army had been routed and was "retreating rapidly down the Franklin Pike." Doubtless it was hard for Hood to swallow making such an announcement. After correctly stating, "Our loss in killed and wounded is very small," he went on to tell the secretary of war, "Our loss in prisoners is not yet fully ascertained, but I think it is comparatively small," which—if Hood had any inkling what it really was—was not the truth at all, since nearly 20 percent of his army was now behind Union stockades. When six months earlier he had taken over the Army of Tennessee at Atlanta, he commanded a formidable army of fifty thousand. After Atlanta was lost, the strength was close to forty thousand of all arms. When he entered Tennessee in November, it was estimated he had—including Forrest's cavalry—more than thirty thousand. But recrossing the river on that cold Christmas day were barely eighteen thousand men, beaten and despairing—the remnants of the mighty Army of Tennessee.

That the campaign was a disaster there was no denying, and the last two days at Nashville had been catastrophic. Soon the criticisms began pouring in: Hood's decision to send Forrest to Murfreesboro was branded as "foolish," a "colossal blunder," even "suicidal." There is some truth in this—certainly Forrest was an extraordinary cavalry commander who, with his whole corps of horsemen on hand, might have kept Wilson at bay for a while. But to what purpose? Thomas's army was simply too strong for Hood to have won a clear victory, and sooner or later the three-to-one odds would have been too much, even for Hood, who was said to have once bet $2,000 in a card game on a bluff.

Hood's decision to send Forrest and Bate to Murfreesboro was not with-out reason. After all, what kind of commander would leave a force of enemy nearly a third his size in his rear where they could have easily been ordered to come up and attack him from behind? Perhaps he should have retreated after the first day at Nashville—or even after his experience at Franklin. But he was determined to give the Union one more fight, and that he did.

When word of Hood's loss of Tennessee reached the Southern public back east, it caused an extraordinary uproar. Jefferson Davis, in-creasingly unpopular with the Richmond press, came under blame for a "disgraceful panic" in Hood's lines. Some Confederate brigades were accused of fleeing "before the *skirmish line* of the enemy" and retreating "almost without firing a gun." Hood and Davis were denounced to-gether, and there was a hue and cry to reinstate Joe Johnston to com-mand the army. The Charleston *Mercury* even republished, "with bitter comments," Davis's Macon speech containing his "Moscow retreat" prediction.

Mary Chesnut, now living at her South Carolina plantation, got the first whiff of Hood's defeat through reports in Northern newspapers a few days after the battle, but merely sniffed, "Yankees claim another victory for Thomas. Hope it may prove like most of their victories— brag and bluster." Soon, however, the true magnitude of Hood's loss became known. Confederate senator Louis Wigfall, Hood's old friend from Texas days, but now one of his bitterest critics, stopped by the Chesnut home to heap abuse on his former associate. "Hood is dead," Wigfall proclaimed, "smashed, gone up, finished." It was a sentiment that grew as the days went by, and it was not lost on Hood's lovely young fiancée, Buck Preston, who was living near the Chesnuts. Wed-ding plans were still in the making as far as she was concerned, but her parents, armed now with a growing condemnation of the general, were well situated to present a strong intervention.

On Friday the 13th, a little short of a month after the debacle at Nashville, Hood resigned command of the Army of Tennessee. Two days later the resignation was accepted, and he headed east again, his last trip. The army was not yet finished with John Bell Hood, nor he with it.

But, he had an important stop to make in South Carolina and, he believed, a date at the altar.

If the Tennessee campaign of 1864 had taken its toll on both armies, it had brought no less grief to the citizens of that beleaguered state. Thousands of homes were in mourning for their dead sons, and a good many more had been reduced to ashes or abject poverty by the fighting.

One of these belonged to seventy-three-year-old Nimrod Porter, who was born during the presidency of George Washington, and who, purportedly, had killed the last bear in Maury County. Over the years his plantation near Columbia had suffered greatly at the hands of both armies but never more than during the recent campaign. Porter kept a diary in which he wrote that the Confederate army on its way to Nashville "stole hogs, food, and burned [his] fence rails for firewood. But the Federals stole worse." During Hood's retreat, Porter complained:

> Croxton's Yankees came through and stole everything. They cooked the last old gobbler and all the chickens, over a fire. They even took the boots off the blacks. Last night they took all of black Sukey's money, all my corn and what little oats I have left. Tomorrow is Christmas day, a bitter one for us, black or white. A gray fox ran under the kitchen walk. I shot it for dinner. We have a little parched corn.

And then, in a final entry dated "Christmas Eve," Porter, who had actually tried to remain neutral over the war, penned this dark sentiment, which probably said it for a lot of them:

> I wish there were a river of fire a mile wide between the North and South, that would burn with unquenchable fury forevermore and that it could never be passable to the endless ages of eternity by any living creature.

19

★ Black Care Was the Outrider

By late winter it was apparent that the Confederacy was on its last legs. Robert E. Lee was hopelessly bottled up by Grant near Richmond, and Sherman was conducting a slash-and-burn operation through the Carolinas toward Virginia, where his sixty-thousand-man army would combine with Grant's to finish off Lee for good. As one of its last-ditch measures, the Richmond government finally named Lee as commander in chief of all Confederate armies, and Lee ordered Beauregard to hurry east to see what could be done to keep Sherman from tearing the country apart. It was decided to bring most of what was left of the Army of Tennessee eastward, too, and by the end of January the army was cooking rations and packing its belongings for the long and circuitous journey by rail, steamboat, and foot march. But by then Sherman, reinforced by Schofield, was wielding an eighty-five-thousand-man steamroller across the Carolinas, which the naked little force assembled under Beauregard—and later old Joe Johnston, who replaced Hood—could do little else but annoy.

Hood's dream of marching north to the Ohio River and then on to Richmond to defeat Grant—or, for that matter, taking and holding the state of Tennessee—was, of course, a blurred reverie, a ghostly figment. The soldiers of the army knew it, and many of them—especially the Tennessee troops—deserted to their homes instead of going east. It didn't matter; even the bitter-enders saw the futility in the fight. On the 9th of April, 1865, Lee surrendered to Grant at Appomattox Court House, after being driven from his defenses at Petersburg. Eighteen days later, on the 27th of April, Special Order Number 18—the last order— was issued to the Army of Tennessee, announcing its surrender to Sherman at Greensboro, North Carolina. Thus ended, for all intents and purposes, the bloodiest war Americans have ever fought: ten thousand military engagements, a million casualties, more than six hundred thousand of them dead. In return, three and a half million slaves were free, and the Union was preserved.

Could Hood have done anything to change the result? Probably not, even if he had defeated Thomas and gone north to attack Grant at Petersburg. By then the numerical odds favored the Union by ten to one, and by far more than that in equipment and manufacturing capacity. And yet there was the *possibility,* as Grant and the Washington government certainly realized. The United States Treasury was virtually broke. The relatively new income tax had nowhere near paid for the war, and the government's proclivity then for borrowing was not so great as it would become in future years. In the end, Washington was reduced to raising revenues by selling bales of Southern cotton that were taken by the various Union armies, among other measures. The nation was sick of war—sick to death—and the prospect of a prolongation, even with Lincoln returned to the helm, was something that frightened everyone. While a military solution for the South had faded rapidly in the last year of the war, a political victory might conceivably have been achieved if the Confederacy could have given the impression that there was no end in sight. Hood was meant to be a part of that strategy, though, in retrospect, it seems the South might have achieved better results by leaving Joe Johnston to doggedly contest Sherman's activities in Georgia and the Carolinas, instead of launching Hood in an all-out, last-ditch offensive effort.

Over the years the question of where Hood went wrong has been rolled around and shaped by countless ex-soldiers, politicians, and historians: He should not have launched the costly attacks around Atlanta. He should have turned and faced Sherman's divided army just across the Alabama line. He should have crossed the Tennessee River earlier, before Thomas had a chance to combine his forces. He should have destroyed Schofield at Spring Hill. He should not have attacked Schofield at Franklin. He should not even have gone to Nashville, but once there, he should have retreated his army after the first day's battle . . .

All these contentions have their merit. But not only Hood saw himself as the instrument of an aggressive military policy fighting for a just cause; he was in fact nominated by the Richmond government especially for that purpose. "It was more judicious," Hood said, "that the men should face a decisive issue, rather than retreat—in other words, rather than renounce the honor of their cause, without having made a last and manful effort to lift up the sinking fortunes of the Confederacy." It is almost a forgone fact of personality and human nature that John Bell Hood could no more have pursued the Fabian policy of Joe Johnston than Johnston could have played Scipio to Sherman's host. In the end, said one veteran, "There was nothing *left,* save honor."

After the surrender, the old soldiers of both sides went home—most of them, anyway—either to glory and reward or to pick up the pieces of their shattered dreams and fortunes. But the Civil War did not end there, of course. The last shot of consequence was fired at Abraham Lincoln by the assassin John Wilkes Booth, but there were other shots as well, fired on paper—tons of it—a virtual war of words that began soon after the military conflict ended and did not cease until the last veteran died, well into the next century. Privates, generals, and politicians blamed and condemned each other for whatever failures had occurred, prompting one old widow to call it "another Hundred Years' War."

Schofield, after the battle of Nashville, wrote Grant asking that he be allowed to come east to join him and get away from Thomas, which he in fact did, being present at the final surrender between Sherman and Johnston. Afterward, Schofield was handed an interesting job. While the Americans had been occupied with four years of civil war, the French emperor Napoleon III had taken the opportunity to seize Mexico and set up rule there, and it was now determined by Washington that the French would have to be kicked out. Schofield was given the assignment of organizing an army for this purpose, but before that happened, it was learned that the French wanted to negotiate, and he was shipped off to Paris, where he effectively suggested to Napoleon that his intentions in Mexico were inadvisable. Next, Schofield was made secretary of war, and in a prescient mood he managed to procure Pearl Harbor in the Hawaiian Islands as a U.S. naval base. After serving as the superintendent of West Point, he became commanding general of the army in 1888.

During some of this time, however, Schofield was preoccupied with removing from his name the stain of accusations not only that he had betrayed Thomas at Nashville, but also that his performance there had been below par. In 1870, an anonymous newspaper article—widely believed to have been authored by Schofield—appeared in the New York *Tribune,* arguing among other things that actually Schofield had won the battle of Nashville at Franklin and criticizing and belittling Thomas's role. This set off a years-long firestorm in Thomas's defense, culminating in 1881 with an article in the New York *Times* by General James Steedman, accusing Schofield of "intriguing" against Thomas at Nashville to get his command. Finally, Schofield published his autobiography, using the occasion to deny everything yet still blame Thomas for slighting his role in the Nashville campaign. At age sixty-four, Schofield retired from the army and went to St. Augustine, Florida, where he died in 1906.

George ("Pap") Thomas after the war remained as administrator of a new department, the Military Division of Tennessee, where he contended with the problems of reconstruction, the Ku Klux Klan, and other tribulations. In 1866 the federal-installed Tennessee legislature commissioned a full-length oil portrait of Thomas to hang in the state library. In 1869 he was assigned by Grant to command the Military District of the Pacific, headquartered in San Francisco, where he received news that a new, southern-sympathizing legislature in Tennessee proposed to get rid of the portrait of him. Later explaining, "Self respect required that I should relieve the members of the legislature of seeing a

disagreeable picture every time they went into the state library,''
Thomas offered to buy the painting himself for $1,000, but nothing
came of it, and the portrait hangs today in the Civil War exhibit of the
Tennessee State Museum in Nashville.

On March 28, 1870, Thomas received a copy of Schofield's article
against him in the *Tribune* and was in the actual act of rebutting it on
paper when he collapsed of a stroke and died. He was fifty-four years old
and at the time of his death had bulked up to more than three hundred
pounds. Congress declared a national bereavement. Flags on military
posts were flown at half mast throughout the country, and a mile-long
funeral parade in New York was attended by a host of dignitaries, including the president of the United States, Ulysses S. Grant. Eight
Union generals served as pallbearers, including John Schofield. The funeral cortege did not, however, include any member of Thomas's family in Virginia. To their dying days they never forgave him for siding
with the North and never spoke his name.

Of the other Union generals who fought the last Tennessee campaign, perhaps the most colorful career was enjoyed by the cavalryman
James H. Wilson. For twenty-five years after the war, he engaged in the
railroad business and other enterprises, but when, in 1898, the Spanish
American War broke out, he volunteered for duty at the youthful age of
sixty-one. Recommissioned as a major general of volunteers, he took
part in the American capture and occupation of Cuba and Puerto Rico.
Not content with this, at the outbreak of the Boxer Rebellion in China
in 1900, he volunteered again and led U.S. and British troops against the
gates of the Forbidden City.

In the years following the war, Wilson became a great defender of
Thomas and a detractor of Schofield, Secretary of War Stanton, and
Halleck. In 1912 he published an autobiography in which he made his
likes and prejudices known. His last official duty for the United States
government came in 1901, when he was the U.S. representative at the
coronation of King Edward VII of England, but he lived on until 1925,
when he died in Wilmington, Delaware, at the age of eighty-eight.

David Stanley, who commanded the Fourth Corps until he was
wounded at Franklin, went on to fight the Indians out west and ulti-

mately was put in charge of the Department of Texas. He also penned an autobiography full of venom for his fellow generals at Franklin and Nashville. In particular he objected to Cox's saying in his own book on Franklin that he (Cox) "commanded the line," which Stanley blasted as a "false pretension." Stanley also took harsh exception to the actions of General Thomas J. Wood, who succeeded to the command of the Fourth Corps when Stanley was wounded. Wood, he charged, "was a very selfish and mean man, deceitful and unreliable." Stanley's argument with Wood was that after the battle of Franklin it fell on Wood to prepare the after-action report, and, Stanley fumed, "My name was never mentioned in it. . . . I had always treated him with much consideration and he paid me off with the basest ingratitude in this report." Next on Stanley's Queeglike list was Emerson Opdycke, who, according to him, "proved an ingrate and turned against me. . . . I never saw a more daring man, but he had an ugly disposition that repelled all friendship and he was full of envy and utterly untruthful." But Stanley saved his last blast for Schofield, whom he characterized this way: "Whilst Schofield is a pretty fair man, his fear of politics has made him play a very low, mean part in many things." Having gotten all that off his chest, Stanley lived on until 1902, when, at the age of seventy-four, he died in Washington, D.C., and was buried there at the Soldier's Home.

General Jacob Cox found himself elected to the governorship of Ohio in 1866, even before leaving the army. Next, Grant named him interior secretary, but the corruption of the Grant regime so disenchanted him that he resigned. Returning to Cincinnati, he was elected to Congress and later served as a law professor and a university president. He died at the turn of the century, at the age of seventy-two.

As for Colonel Emerson Opdycke, whom Stanley had branded as "utterly untruthful," he was promoted to major general after saving the federal line at Franklin. After the war, he operated a dry goods store in New York until 1884, when he either committed suicide or accidentally shot himself while cleaning his pistol.

Of the two conspicuous cavalry commanders under Wilson, General Edward Hatch went west to fight Indians after the war, while General J. T. Croxton became U.S. ambassador to Bolivia. General Thomas

H. Ruger, who commanded part of the Union line at Franklin, became superintendent of West Point, while General T. J. Wood became embroiled in some kind of scandal involving the Atlantic-Pacific Telegraph Company. General John McArthur, who had impatiently attacked the Confederate lines at Nashville without orders, was later involved in a federal bank-fraud scheme while serving as postmaster of Chicago. General James Steedman went on to become a tax collector for the Internal Revenue office and later police chief of Toledo, Ohio, where he also edited a newspaper.

William Tecumseh Sherman succeeded to commander in chief of the U.S. Army when Grant became president. For many years, he was reviled in the South for his pyrotechnical brand of warfare, but he always professed a love of the Southern people. In the North he was, of course, a hero and was solicited to run for president, but, having a deep-seated distrust of politics, he declined. Ten years after the war, he published his memoirs, which quickly became a best seller and made him a wealthy man. In a nation filled with heroes, Sherman was among the most revered until his death in New York City, February 14, 1891.

Jefferson Davis, only months before the war's end, finally embraced Pat Cleburne's despised theory of freeing slaves and enlisting them in the Confederate army. This created a new starburst of vituperation in Richmond. The bombastic old General Howell Cobb roared, "If slaves will make good soldiers, our whole *theory* of slavery is wrong." Davis rebuked him this way: "If the Confederacy falls, there should be written on its tombstone, 'Died of a Theory.' " In the end, four months after Cleburne's death, and less than a month before Lee's surrender at Appomattox, the Confederate Congress approved a bill providing for the partial emancipation and enlistment of slaves in the Confederate armies.

As Grant closed in around Richmond, Davis fled on a train south with his cabinet and, presumably, whatever gold was left in the Confederate treasury. His flight carried him through Virginia, the Carolinas, and finally to Georgia, where he was captured. He was confined in prison at Fort Monroe, Virginia, for two years. After he was released from jail, he spent the remainder of his years in farming and business enterprises. Toward the end of his life, which came in his eighty-first year, he published a two-volume work called *The Rise and Fall of the Confederate Government.*

Joe Johnston, after surrendering the remnants of his beloved Army of Tennessee to Sherman, went on to become a U.S. congressman from Virginia and later the United States commissioner of railroads. He also wrote his memoirs of the war, in which he severely criticized Hood for what he called the "useless sacrifice" of his army in the Nashville campaign—touching off an acrimonious dispute between the two men. Johnston further alienated Jefferson Davis and his supporters by letting himself get reported in the newspapers as wondering where the more than $2 million in gold from the Confederate treasury had gone after it was loaded on Davis's escape train out of Richmond. On a cold and rainy February day in 1891, Johnston took the train to New York City, where he attended the funeral of his old friend William Tecumseh Sherman. As he stood bareheaded in the freezing rain, someone told him he should put on his hat, lest he catch pneumonia. Johnston respectfully refused, saying that Sherman would have done the same for him. A few weeks afterward, he was dead, of pneumonia, at the age of eighty-four.

Nathan Bedford Forrest was finally brought to bay by Wilson's men in southern Alabama, one of the last commands to surrender. Afterward, he made a speech to his men. "You have been good soldiers, you can be good citizens." Some years later Jefferson Davis wrote that he regretted not being aware of just how great a general Forrest was until near the end of the war. The "wizard of the saddle" went home to Memphis and rejuvenated his farming and timber operations along the Mississippi. In 1866 he went into partnership with half a dozen former Union and Confederate officers and became the very model of national reconciliation. But he was still so fearsome a figure in the North that rumors began to circulate that he had gone to Mexico to reorganize and continue the fight against the Union.

Forrest had been home only a year when the government indicted him for treason for his participation in the war, but two years later, before a trial could be held, he received a presidential pardon. Meantime, his farming and business enterprises had failed, and he declared bankruptcy. He joined the newly organized Ku Klux Klan in 1866, rising to its leadership until the Klan's activities became so distasteful to him that in 1869 he issued an order for the society to disband itself. That same year Forrest led an adventure to build a railroad from Montgomery to Memphis, but that failed, too. In the last years of his life he returned to planting on an island in the Mississippi, using leased convict labor. He also turned to the church, becoming a Presbyterian. By the mid 1870s his health began to fail, and in 1877, at the age of fifty-six, he died peacefully in bed, in Memphis. His last words were, "Call my wife."

Of the Confederate infantry corps commanders under Hood, Frank Cheatham returned to Tennessee, where at the age of forty-seven he married a woman in her twenties and began operating a livestock farm near Nashville. It was said he delighted in raising fine hogs. He ran unsuccessfully for Congress but in the late 1870s was appointed by the state governor—who was, incidentally, his old chief of staff, James D. Porter—as superintendent of the prison system. Cheatham instituted considerable prison reform but later returned to farming. In 1885 he was nominated by President Grover Cleveland as postmaster of Nashville, but soon afterward he was struck ill with a hardening of the arteries. He died peacefully at home, September 4, 1886, his last words reportedly: "There go the troops. Bring me my horse. I am going to the front." He was buried wrapped in a Confederate battle flag, at the age of sixty-six.

A. P. Stewart—"Old Straight"—went back to teaching mathematics but later got into the cotton brokerage business along the Mississippi River. In 1874 he became chancellor of the University of Mississippi, a post he held for twelve years. He died in 1908, at the age of eighty-seven. Stephen Dill Lee, a native of Charleston, moved to Mississippi after the war, where he served as a state senator, as well as president of what is now Mississippi State University. He died in 1908, three months before Stewart, at the age of seventy-five.

Generals Edward Johnson, Sam French, and Henry Clayton, whose efforts saved Hood's retreat at Nashville, all became planters

after the war. W. H. ("Red") Jackson, who commanded a division of
Forrest's cavalry, married Selene Harding, the mistress of Belle Meade
mansion who tried to rally the troops during the first day at Nashville.
He went on to become a famous breeder of thoroughbred horses. General Daniel Govan became an Indian agent in Washington state. General
James Chalmers, who led Forrest's beleaguered cavalry on Hood's left
at Nashville, returned to Tennessee and threw in his lot with the Reconstruction Republicans, becoming a three-term U.S. congressman.

Bate and Brown, the two lawyer-generals who figured so prominently in the infamous Spring Hill affair, were both elected governor of
Tennessee, following the Reconstruction era, and both later ran for the
U.S. Senate. Brown was defeated by former president Andrew Johnson
and successively became president of two large corporations, but Bate
was elected and served in Washington nearly twenty years. Bate died in
office, at the age of seventy-nine, while Brown passed away at sixty-two
in 1889. At the time of his death, Brown had written some sort of personal memorandum on his role in the Spring Hill affair, but his family
never permitted it to be made public, possibly because by then his wife
had become the head of the United Daughters of the Confederacy and
did not want any hint of stain on her dead husband's record.

As for the Spring Hill affair itself, the controversy has never been
fully resolved. For decades after the war there were charges and countercharges. After exonerating Cheatham shortly after the battle, Hood,
in his posthumous memoirs published fifteen years later, again laid the
blame on him for failing to capture Schofield's army, a charge that Cheatham bitterly denied till the end of his days. What actually occurred
there became the subject of many a treatise, scholarly and otherwise,
until finally—some fifty years after the fact—a man named Remington
appeared in 1913 claiming to have solved the mystery.

Remington, a former Union soldier then living in Florida, asserted
it was *he* who was responsible for the Confederate disaster at Spring
Hill. In a letter published in the *Confederate Veteran* magazine, he maintained that while he was nominally a lowly cook-baker in the brigade of
Emerson Opdycke, he was actually a Union spy who dressed up as a
Confederate captain and went behind Confederate lines to mislead the

enemy. Remington alleged that late in the day as Hood's army was moving on Spring Hill, he rode into a group of Confederate officers—including General Pat Cleburne—and represented himself as an aide to General Hood. Hood, Remington told these people, wished Cleburne to get no closer than four hundred yards from the Columbia-Franklin Pike at Spring Hill and "under no circumstances to fire at anyone unless attacked."

If Remington's story was true, it could in some ways explain why no one in the Confederate force blocked the pike below Spring Hill as Schofield's army marched by unmolested on their way to the killing ground at Franklin. However, publication of his letter produced such a hailstorm of malediction from former Confederates—who by that time had dissected the Spring Hill business from top to bottom—that he was branded a fraud and a charlatan. He even offered to serve up character references and documents from the by then deceased Opdycke proving his case, but the debunking continued, and in the end Remington was dismissed as a crank.

As for John Bell Hood, upon his resignation as commander of the Army of Tennessee, he wired Jefferson Davis that he thought he could still be useful to the Confederacy. His plan was to go to the trans-Mississippi—where Kirby Smith had so ungraciously failed to provide him with reinforcements for his late Tennessee campaign—and personally bring back those twenty-five thousand troops for service in the east. First, however, he planned to go to Richmond to make his official report of the Army of Tennessee. On the way, of course, he stopped off in South Carolina to see Buck Preston.

In December, before the disaster at Nashville, two letters from Hood had arrived for Buck saying he was coming in January to get married. "Buck is happy," Mary Chesnut told her diary, "and says, 'fancy my raptures.' " Now that Hood had finally arrived, Mrs. Chesnut noted the frame of mind of her old friend "Sam," who she said seemed to talk only of defeat and sadness. "He says he only has himself to blame."

Hood was staying with Buck and her family, and soon after he arrived the Chesnuts were invited over for dinner. Hood was going on about his losses when someone quipped, "Maybe you attempted the impossible," then launched into a funny story. "Sam did not listen," Mary Chesnut said. "He did not hear a word she was saying. He had forgotten us all." Jack Preston tugged at Mary Chesnut's sleeve, and they slipped unobserved outside into the courtyard, leaving Hood to stare into the fire with "huge drops of perspiration that stood out on his forehead."

"He is going over some bitter hour," Mary Chesnut said. "He sees Willie Preston with his head shot away. He feels the panic at Nashville and its shame."

"And the dead on the battlefield at Franklin," Jack Preston added. "And that agony in his face comes again and again. I can't keep him out of those absent fits. When he looks in the fire and forgets me and seems going through in his own mind the torture of the damned—I get up and come out, as I did just now."

Next day somebody's carriage was put at Hood's disposal, and he took Mary Chesnut for a ride, telling her he wanted to marry Buck, but, she said, "dreads opposition." That opposition was formidable, in the form of Buck's mother and others in her family, who were still staunchly opposed to him. "He blushes like a girl," Mary Chesnut said. "Sam, the simplest, most transparent soul I have ever met in this great revolution."

Hood's wedding clothes had been left in a trunk at the Chesnuts for six months. Young Captain John Chesnut, Mary's son, had these observations: "Then why don't he put them on his back and go and be married? There will be no wedding, you see. He lost his chance last winter. He made his siege too long. He grows tedious."

In this, Johnny Chesnut was correct. There was to be no wedding.

Meantime, Hood continued on up to Richmond, where army business awaited. A few days earlier, en route to his visit with Buck, he had stopped over at Augusta, Georgia, where he met with his relative, Confederate General Gustavus Woodson Smith, and a few days later an article was published in the Augusta newspaper that sharply criticized Joe Johnston's handling of the Army of Tennessee and praised Hood's performance during the Nashville campaign. The author of the article was identified only as "G.W.S."

The article, which also dealt harshly with General William J. Hardee, who was fired by Hood as a corps commander after the fall of Atlanta, was reprinted in Richmond a few days after Hood got there. Hardee responded by challenging Hood to what essentially would have been a duel, but nothing ever came of it. Hood then made his report, which was remarkably similar to the newspaper article, and this caused another explosion. He blamed Johnston for the condition of the Army of Tennessee—for, among other things, continually retreating and letting the men fight behind breastworks for so long that they were not of a mind to attack. When the report was published, Johnston announced he was pressing charges against Hood, but nothing ever came of that, either. Many people thought Hood had been duped into denouncing Johnston by Jefferson Davis, who hated Johnston and was afraid public clamor would force him to restore him to the army. In any case, publication of the document caused such an outcry from all quarters that Hood was glad to get out of Richmond and be on his way to the trans-Mississippi and Texas.

Naturally, he stopped over in Carolina again to settle things with Buck, but in this, he was bitterly disappointed. By this time, the fat was in the fire, and everybody knew it. Buck's parents apparently laid down the law, and Hood, who had faced everything a dozen bloody battlefields could offer, for once in his life backed away.

"If he had just been more persistent," Buck wailed to Mary Chesnut, sounding very much like a character out of a melodrama. "If he had just not given way under Mamie's violent refusal to listen to us, if he had asked *me.* When you refuse to let anybody be married in your house—well, I would have gone down on the sidewalk. I would have married him on the pavement, if the parson could be found to do it. I was ready to leave all the world for him, to tie my clothes in a bundle and, like a soldier's wife, trudge after him to the ends of the earth."

In any event, she did not, and by the middle of April Hood was on his way west, having held his hat in his hand until he was out of sight of the Preston house. Seeing this, someone remarked, "Black care was Hood's outrider this morning."

A month later, after the surrender, Mary Chesnut reversed her silent opposition to the idea of Buck marrying Hood, saying Buck's parents had done the girl a "cruel wrong." She described Hood as a "poor wounded hero and patriot" and called him "the only true man I have seen in your train yet." By the time another month had passed, Mrs. Chesnut was able to record in her diary that Buck was happily flirting with a twenty-five-year-old captain of the late Confederate army, but a few weeks later the Preston family, Buck included, were on a steamer headed for Paris, where they spent the next two years waiting to see what was going to happen politically back home.

Hood made his way westward across the South, dodging Wilson's cavalrymen, who by now had pretty much a free run of things. While he was still in South Carolina, he had "received the painful intelligence of Lee's surrender," but he continued with his staff and escort to Natchez on the Mississippi. Actually, he wasn't in Natchez, but in the thick woods and canebreaks outside it, waiting for the river to drop and dodging federal patrols night and day. It was well into June before he learned of Kirby Smith's surrender in Texas, and, with little else to do, he calmly rode in to the headquarters of Major General John W. Davidson, chief of cavalry for the Union Department of West Mississippi, and handed over his sword. Davidson told him to keep it and wrote out a parole for Hood and all his men. At last it was over.

Hood wound up settling in New Orleans, where he became a cotton merchant and head of an insurance company. A year after the war, he went to Louisville on business and learned that George Thomas was also in town. Hood arranged for a meeting with his old friend from the Second Cavalry and foe in the Atlanta and Nashville campaigns. As Hood hobbled on his crutches down the hotel corridor, Thomas threw open the door to his room and embraced the former Confederate commander warmly, helping him inside, where they spoke for more than an hour. Afterward, Hood would say of the Virginia Unionist, "Thomas is a grand man. He should have remained with us, where he would have been appreciated and loved."

In 1867 Sally Buck Preston returned from Europe and married Rollins Lowndes, who had been a young colonel in the late Confederate army. Lowndes's wealthy Charleston family had put their money in England at the beginning of the war and thus were not bankrupted like so many Southerners were. Whether Hood learned of the marriage is not known; he apparently did not speak of Buck after he last saw her. And the following year, 1868, he fell in love again and married the daughter of a prominent family of Louisiana lawyers. The Hoods settled down to a reasonably comfortable life, having children and dividing their time between their home in the fashionable Garden District of New Orleans and their plantation manor outside town. All the while, Hood was determined to write the memoirs of his career—especially when he learned that Johnston was publishing his, which were decidedly uncomplimentary of Hood. He began them around 1875 and by 1879 had finished the book that would be known as *Advance and Retreat*.

In the summer of that same year, a yellow fever epidemic broke out in New Orleans, and, because of a quarantine, many businesses went under, including Hood's. In August, his wife was taken with yellow fever and died in two days. Two days after her funeral, their oldest child was stricken and died the same day. The following morning, Hood himself contracted the illness. He lasted two days, in and out of delirium. Once he rose up with the old blue light of battle again in his eyes and asked that his remaining children be taken care of by his old outfit, the Texas brigade. He died early next morning, a week after his wife, and was buried that same afternoon from Trinity Episcopal Church, with only a small contingent of mourners to lead him to the grave. He was forty-eight years old, vanquished, as it were, by a mosquito.

As the war came to a close, the United States Treasury was not only broke but so deep in debt many wondered if it could ever be recouped. The human toll, of course, could not be measured in dollars and cents but was pitifully reflected in the homes of more than a million dead and maimed men on both sides. Lincoln had favored a policy of reconciliation, but following his assassination there was much serious talk in the federal Congress of hanging and imprisoning Confederate leaders—military and political—confiscating their property, and other dire retributions. But in fact, Jefferson Davis was the longest held Confederate official; a handful of governors and cabinet members were arrested, and a few others, like Forrest, were indicted, but they, like virtually all the military men, were granted clemency by Lincoln's successor, President Andrew Johnson, a policy that became a factor in impeachment proceedings against him in 1868. Only one Confederate was tried and convicted, Captain Henry Wirtz, commandant of the infamous Andersonville prison camp; a drumhead court sentenced him to be hanged, which he was on November 10, 1865. Nevertheless, some Confederates, especially officers, fled to Mexico, South America, or Europe, but most of those returned to America when the scare was over. A few settled for good in foreign lands and took permanent jobs abroad. One such was William Wing ("Old Blizzards") Loring, who had sat on his horse at Franklin facing the federal firestorm and roared, "Great God! Do I command cowards?" After the war he accepted an offer to command a division in the army of the khedive of Egypt, which he did for ten years.

The years immediately after the war produced an uncertainty for both sections of the country, but the North recovered far more quickly than the South, spawning the great westward expansion, as well as a riotous binge of unrestrained capitalism that culminated with the age of the robber barons. Eventually, the mutual animosities began to break down. The Reconstruction measures imposed on the South disenfranchised many ex-Confederates well into the 1870s and—if this legislation did not call for their hanging—at best it put them under stern military rule, which led to unfortunate abuses. But by the Spanish American War and the turn of the century, the great conflict of the mid 1800s was for most only a dimming memory. A friend likes to tell the story of the time when as a small boy he was walking over one of the battlefields with his great aunts and grandmother, whose father had fought in the war. Standing at the edge of a huge cemetery with white marble tombstones stretching as far as the eye could see, the boy asked one of the women, "But why did they do it? Why did they die?" to which the old lady replied wearily, "Oh, I don't know, son. I guess they'd all be dead by now anyhow."

Grant, Sherman, Thomas, Lee, Johnston, Jackson, Hood, and all the rest gradually vanished like the dinosaurs, but for a while they were giants that ruled the earth. In their prime, probably no armies as yet assembled could have matched them. Some lived on to see the age of airplanes, radios, skyscrapers, moving pictures, and world wars on an unimaginable scale, and when they were gone, their dust enriched the national trust. For the footsoldiers, black and white, Confederate Private Sam Watkins probably summed it up about as well as any man on either side when he said, "The tale is told. The sun shines as brightly as before, the sky sparkles with the trembling stars that make night beautiful, and the scene melts and gradually disappears forever."

Bibliographical Note on Sources ★

In the writing of this book I am earnestly and deeply indebted to those dogged historians who have gone before. In focusing on a microcosm of the Civil War—those last six months of 1864 in the west between the battle of Atlanta and the battle of Nashville—much information had to be located and sifted. No writer on the Civil War can do his work in a void, and to that end I cut my teeth early on Bruce Catton's fine books *The Coming Fury*, *Never Call Retreat*, *A Stillness at Appomattox*, *Terrible Swift Sword*, and *This Hallowed Ground* as general literature. I am equally indebted to Shelby Foote's monumental three-volume narrative, *The Civil War: Fort Sumter to Perryville*, *Fredericksburg to Meridian*, and *Red River to Appomattox*. The epic works of these two authors give shape, dimension, and perspective to what is arguably the most complex subject in American history. I would have been lost without them.

As an outline for the overall Atlanta-to-Nashville campaign, one must inevitably begin as I did with the greatest single source for anyone seriously interested in the Civil War, which is *War of the Rebellion: A Compilation of the Official Records of the Union and Confederate Armies*. This huge undertaking, gathered, organized, and published by the U.S. government between 1880 and 1902, is composed of 128 volumes containing over 100,000 pages of official battle and campaign reports, correspondence, telegraphic messages, orders, letters, tables of organization, statistics—every scrap of paper generated by the Union and Confederate armies that could be located. It provides the blueprint for any historical study of the various aspects of the war.

Also immensely useful as a guide through the hundreds of battles and major skirmishes is the four-volume series *Battles and Leaders of the Civil War.* In this 1887 collection, published by the Century Company, are the voices of the men, mostly officers, recounting firsthand experiences of the great battles of the war.

On the particular subject of the 1864 Tennessee campaign, there are a number of fine works published over a hundred-year span that deal with the subject in greater or lesser depth, and I have learned much, and appreciate much, from these. Among them are T. B. Van Horne's *Army of the Cumberland*; Thomas Hay's *Hood's Tennessee Campaign*; Stanley Horne's *The Decisive Battle of Nashville* and *The Army of Tennessee*; James McDonough and Thomas Connelly's *Five Tragic Hours,* as well as Connelly's *Autumn of Glory*; General J. D. Cox's *The Battle of Franklin*; Richard McMurry's *Two Great Rebel Armies*; Sims Crownover's *The Battle of Franklin*; Page Smith's *Trial by Fire*; James McPherson's *Battle Cry of Freedom*; Herman Hattaway and Archer Jones's *How the North Won: A Military History of the Civil War*; Allen Nevins's *The War for the Union: The Organized War*; Francis Miller's (ed.) *The Photographic History of the Civil War*; J. T. Headley's *The Great Rebellion*; and Clifford Dowdey's *The Land They Fought For.*

Of the lives and backgrounds of the major players there are some excellent accounts, and I owe them deeply for their insights and information: Lloyd Lewis's *Sherman*; John F. Marzalek's biography *Sherman: A Passion for Order*; Richard McMurry's *John Bell Hood and the War for Southern Independence*; Richard Dyer's *The Gallant Hood*; Irving Buck's *Cleburne and His Command*; Howell and Elizabeth Purdue's *Pat Cleburne, Confederate General*; T. B. Van Horne's *The Life of Major-General George H. Thomas*; Freeman Cleaves's *The Rock of Chickamauga*; Christopher Losson's *Tennessee's Forgotten Warrior: Frank Cheatham and His Confederate Division*; Brian S. Will's *A Battle from the Start: The Life of Nathan Bedford Forrest*; and Horace Porter's *Campaigning with Grant.*

For political overview and specifics about the government officials and the various doings in Washington and Richmond, there was Carl Sandburg's two-volume opus *Abraham Lincoln*; Stephen Oates's *With Malice Toward None: The Life of Abraham Lincoln*; Steven Woodsworth's *Jefferson Davis and His Generals: The Failure of Confederate Command in the West*; William C. Davis's *Jefferson Davis: The Man and His Hour*; as well as my old college professor Hudson Strode's *Jefferson Davis: Tragic Hero*.

And then there are the autobiographies by the players themselves. For the personal recollections and documentation of Sherman's movements before, during, and after Atlanta, as well as his biographical history, *The Memoirs of General W. T. Sherman* is a prime source of information, as is the *Personal Memoirs of U. S. Grant*. John Bell Hood's *Advance and Retreat* contains a wealth of similar material. Likewise, General John Schofield's *Forty-six Years in the Army*, General James Wilson's *Under the Old Flag*, General David Stanley's *Personal Memoirs of Major General D. S. Stanley*, and Jefferson Davis's *The Rise and Fall of the Confederate Government* were extremely useful, although like most memoirs, they are self serving to a greater or lesser extent.

For biographical information on the various subordinate generals in this contest, Ezra Warner's indispensable two-volume work *Generals in Gray* and *Generals in Blue* is one of the most commendable examples of historical research extant. Over a period of years, Warner researched, compiled for the record, and published the biographies and photographs of every Confederate and Union general officer who served in the Civil War, of which there were more than a thousand. These books represent nothing less than a historical labor of love.

Regarding the various accounts of this campaign by soldiers in the ranks, I have relied on an abundance of information from books, diaries, letters, newspaper stories, and other commentary published by the participants. A chief source of many firsthand accounts I found is *The Confederate Veteran*, a monthly magazine published in Nashville from 1893 to 1933, when the last of the old soldiers were dying away. The magazine was founded and edited by Sergeant-major S. A. Cunningham, one of the participants in the Tennessee campaign. This invaluable tool, now bound in forty volumes with an index, contains letters written not only by thousands of Confederate participants in the contest but by Union soldiers as well, making for some lively exchanges. Also contained therein are such gems as the accounts of the battle of Franklin by the schoolchildren Harding Figures and Frances McEwen, who, in their golden years, at last found a place to contribute their recollections. Likewise, the *Southern Historical Society Papers,* as well as the historical society papers of various states, especially Tennessee, provided good— if difficult to ferret out—firsthand accounts, such as the diary of Captain E. T. Eggleston, who recorded in the *Tennessee Historical Society Quarterly* the hardships of Hood's march in the cold from the Tennessee River to Columbia.

There are also some very useful general books that include contemporary accounts of the campaign, most of them published about the turn of the century. Among them are William Murray's *History of the Twentieth Tennessee Regiment,* Bromfield Ridley's *Battles and Sketches of the Army of Tennessee,* and Stanley Horne's *Tennessee's War,* which appeared during the Civil War Centennial in 1965. Also, David Logsdon's well-done *Eyewitnesses at the Battle of Franklin* and Larry Daniel's fine book *Soldiering in the Army of Tennessee* were both very helpful.

The Reverend W. A. Keesy's *War as Viewed from the Ranks* is a solid diary by a Union soldier who served during the entire campaign. Sam Watkins's *Company "Aytch": A Sideshow of the Big Show* is a similarly colorful account from the Confederate side. Captain Levi Scofield's *The Retreat from Pulaski to Nashville Tenn.* is a remarkable document by a federal officer who served on the staff of General Jacob Cox. I was both astounded and elated to receive by interlibrary loan from North Carolina State University an original 1909 copy of this beautifully bound book, signed in ink by the author! The Reverend Charles T. Quintard's *Doctor Quintard, Being His Story of the War (1861–1865)* is a lucid account, especially his exchanges with Hood at Columbia, Spring Hill, and Nashville. Confederate Captain Samuel T. Foster's *One of Cleburne's Command* contains a solid and spellbinding diary of his experiences during the campaign. Union Captain John K. Shellenberger's writings in *The Confederate Veteran* and elsewhere contains his bitter 1916 recollection of being left out in the front with Wagner's two brigades during the fight at Franklin. Wirt Cate's *Two Soldiers* is also useful.

The Tennessee State Archives at Nashville has on file hundreds, if not thousands, of personal accounts of the period, some of them priceless, like old Nimrod Porter's "River of Fire" declaration and William Pollard's recollections of General Walthall appraising his aide's horse in the midst of battle. Many of these are not classified and simply must be scrounged out by hours at the microfilm projector. Other state archives contain similar jewels, such as Uncle Wiley Howard's pathetic account of the death and burial of his owner, General States Rights Gist, at Franklin, which is available in the Marjorie Adams Gist Papers at the South Carolina Library at the University in Columbia.

For information on technical, tactical, strategic, and other such material respecting the campaign, I relied on a wealth of sources, many already mentioned. Particularly insightful were Archer Jones's *Civil War Command and Strategy: The Process of Victory and Defeat* and Richard McMurry's *Two Great Rebel Armies*. Grady McWhiney and Perry Jamison's *Attack and Die: Civil War Military Tactics and the Southern Heritage* is an extraordinary and professional look at why men did what they did. As well, Larry Daniel's *Cannoneers in Gray: The Field Artillery of the Army of Tennessee* is unparalleled in its comprehension of the "long arm" of the service. Alan Axelrod's *The War Between the Spies: A History of Espionage During the American Civil War* was useful for the light it shed on that dark subject. For insight into the history of the U.S. Colored Troops, Joseph Glatthaar's *Forged in Battle: The Civil War Alliance of Black Soldiers and White Officers* is a monument of its type.

For background on the city of Nashville and the civilian and political conditions in Tennessee during the period, an excellent book by Peter Maslowski, *Treason Must Be Made Odious: Military Occupation and Wartime Reconstruction in Nashville, Tennessee, 1862–1865*, is a must. Likewise, Jim Hoobler's *Cities Under the Gun* and Steven Ashe's *Middle Tennessee Transformed: War and Peace in the Upper South* were both very useful. For contemporary newspaper accounts I relied in part on I. William Hill and John Stepped's *Mirror of War: The Washington Star Reports the Civil War*, *The American Civil War: Extracts of the Times* (London *Times*), and J. Cutler Andrews's *The North Reports the Civil War*.

Respecting the Spring Hill affair, probably the best summarization was developed by Judge J. P. Young, who studied events surrounding the episode for years, then published his findings in the Memphis *Scimitar* in 1892; they were also later published in *The Confederate Veteran*. But Judge Young never quite solved the mystery.

With the exception of a few offhand mentions in Mrs. Burton Harrison's *Recollections, Grave and Gray,* the only source of information on Hood's romance with Sally Buck Preston is gleaned from the diaries of Mary Chesnut, of which there are several versions: Isabella Martin and Myrta Avary's *A Diary from Dixie,* C. Van Woodward and Elisabeth Muhlenfeld's *The Private Mary Chesnut,* and finally Woodward's prize-winning *Mary Chesnut's Civil War.* This last is unquestionably the most comprehensive and thorough. Mary Chesnut kept these remarkable diaries between 1861 and 1865, but the only *originals* that survived were from the individual years 1861 and 1865. However, Woodward is convinced that Mrs. Chesnut's entries for the missing years—which include the period of Hood's romance with Buck—were reconstructed by Mrs. Chesnut from the originals and are therefore pretty accurate accounts.

To all of the above I owe a profound debt of gratitude.

Index ★